THE
CATHOLIC CHURCH
in
CONTEMPORARY EUROPE
1919-1931

Vol. II
Papers of the
American Catholic Historical Association

EDITED BY

PETER GUILDAY

WITH AN INTRODUCTION BY

CARLTON J. H. HAYES, PH.D.
PAST PRESIDENT OF THE ASSOCIATION

NEW YORK
P. J. KENEDY & SONS
Publishers to the Holy Apostolic See
1932

NIHIL OBSTAT:

ARTHUR J. SCANLAN, S.T.D.
Censor Librorum

IMPRIMATUR:

✠ PATRICK CARDINAL HAYES
Archbishop, New York

New York, October 25, 1932

Printed in the United States of America

CONTENTS

iii

/2 15/

CONTENTS

FOREWORD

THROUGH the generous coöperation of the century-old firm of Messrs. P. J. Kenedy and Sons, the American Catholic Historical Association was enabled to publish in 1926 as Volume One of its *Papers* the fourteen scholarly essays read at the meeting in Ann Arbor (December 29-31, 1925) under the general title: *Church Historians*. A second time, due to the good offices of the same firm, we present as Volume Two of our *Papers* the nine conferences given at the twelfth annual meeting in Minneapolis (December 28-30, 1931) under the title: *The Catholic Church in Contemporary Europe: 1919-1931.* To the nine writers who prepared these valuable historical essays, to the publishers and their capable staff of assistants, and to Professor Hayes for his scholarly Introduction, the American Catholic Historical Association offers its profound gratitude and appreciation.

PETER GUILDAY, *Secretary.*

INTRODUCTION

It was not unusual during the World War for a certain type of publicist to represent the Catholic Church as tied to the fortunes of the Central Powers and to predict its rapid and irretrievable ruin, along with its chief patrons, the Habsburgs of Austria, from the combined attack of "Protestant England," "anti-clerical France," and "liberal Italy." The Central Powers, it is true, suffered military defeat and political and economic debacle; the Catholic Habsburgs, as well as the Protestant Hohenzollerns, ceased to reign. But the rest of the prediction is now amply disproved. For there can be no doubt that the Catholic Church is more influential in Europe—and the world at large—in 1933 than it was in 1913.

Italy, ceasing to be "liberal," has accorded real liberty to the Sovereign Pontiff and an honored position to the Church throughout the peninsula. France, softening her "anti-clericalism," and England, departing from a centuries-old tradition of militant Protestantism, have both entered into regular diplomatic relations with the Vatican. Moreover, England has formally repealed almost the last of her anti-Catholic legislation, and France has allowed much of her "anti-clerical" legislation to become obsolescent. In Germany, too, though the number of Catholics has been lessened by the cession of territory, the growth of their influence has been clearly demonstrated by the final removal of all Catholic disabilities and by the decisive rôle of the Centre Party during the last fourteen years. Furthermore, from the World War the traditionally Catholic state of Belgium has reëmerged with new lustre, and the traditionally Catholic nations of Poland and Ireland have come forth in new habiliments of sovereign independence. Simultaneously in the so-called "succession states" of the old Austrian Empire—Austria, Hungary, Czechoslovakia, the new Yugoslavia, and the new Rumania—the status of the Catholic Church has been perceptibly bettered. If latterly the Church has been assailed in republican Spain, it has won an unwonted peace in republican Portugal. Only in Russia, which is not a traditionally Catholic country, has the Church been a victim of the cruel warfare which a Communist régime has waged against all supernatural religions.

The general improvement in the public position of the Catholic Church throughout the greater part of Europe has been such an obvious and outstanding feature of the years since the conclusion of the World War that it naturally arrests the attention and arouses the interest of a very large number of thoughtful persons—both those who are inimical and those who are friendly to the claims of the Church. It is in response to this interest that the present volume has been prepared. It consists of a series of papers written by scholarly members of the Ameri-

can Catholic Historical Association and presented at
the annual meeting of the Association in Minneapolis
in December, 1931. Each of the papers is in the
nature of a survey of the recent developments of
Catholic life and action within some particular European country, with just enough historical background
to bring out the significance of such recent developments. The authors are all specialists in their several fields; they write now for the general public;
and there is no other work, in any language, which
attempts to do what they do here by way of supplying substantial information for persons curious about
contemporary religion and world affairs.

The utility of the present volume is, indeed, far
beyond the service which it may render in describing
the present public position of the Catholic Church in
various European countries. It suggests, in every
paper and on almost every page, what I would call
the private (that is, the individual) appeal of Catholic Christianity to disillusioned and suffering humanity of the present day. In the economic chaos of the
post-war world, in the welter of its conflicting and
shifting philosophies, in the midst of its huge arma-
ments and even more portentous nationalism, Catholic Christianity stands forth as the greatest and most
unyielding of international teachers. In all countries it preaches certitude instead of doubt, faith in
God as well as in man, in the supernatural as well as
in the natural, peace and amity among nations, justice and coöperation among individuals.

This *positive mission* of the Catholic Church is the

real secret of its enhanced position and appeal in the contemporary world. The following papers indicate, some in so many words and others between the lines, just how the Church and its faithful have sought since the World War to give effect to that mission— to promote international peace, social justice, human dignity, and the recognition of divine authority. It will be noted that nowhere does the reality quite square with the ideal; that everywhere some very serious practical problems confront the Church. Yet from almost all the papers may be gathered a similar story of the redoubling efforts of Catholic Christianity to apply its cure to the maladies of the contemporary world. In such efforts, let me add, the martyrs of Russia merit even more consideration than the confessors of traditionally Catholic lands. As the paper on Russia shows, organized Catholicism has all but disappeared from Russia, but even here, in the midst of most novel developments, Catholics can still die for the undying faith which is within them. The blood of martyrs, in the twentieth as in the second century, may well be the most fruitful seed of the Church.

To all the following papers, then, I would invite attention. They help to expound and to explain the present position of Catholicism—its chief problems and its partial failures, as well as its undoubted successes—in the major countries of that Europe from which all our modern "Western" civilization is derived.

CARLTON J. H. HAYES.

CONTRIBUTORS

CARLTON JOSEPH HUNTLEY HAYES, PH.D., President of the Association during the year 1931, is professor of history in Columbia University, and the author of many volumes, among which are: *An Introduction to the Sources relating to the Germanic Invasions*, 1909; *British Social Politics*, 1913; *A Political and Social History of Modern Europe* (2 vols.), 1924; *Brief History of the Great War*, 1920; *Modern History*, 1923; *Essays on Nationalism*, 1926; *Ancient and Medieval History*, 1929; and *National Psychology in Post-War France*, 1929. He has also contributed to the following works: *League of Nations*, 1919; *History and Nature of International Relations*, 1923; *These Eventful Years* (Encl. Britannica), 1924; *Political Theories in Recent Times*, 1925; and *A Quarter Century of Learning*, 1931.

REV. FRANCIS S. BETTEN, S.J., professor of history in Marquette University, Milwaukee, Wisconsin, has spent a half-century in historical study, research and authorship. He has taught principally since 1898 at Canisius College, Buffalo, John Carroll University, Cleveland, Ohio, and in Marquette University, Milwaukee, where he is now professor of history. He has contributed to leading Catholic periodicals here and abroad, and is the author of several historical works, the best known of which is *Historical Terms and Facts*. Father Betten has read papers at the meetings of the Association in 1920, 1922 and 1925, and is among the best loved members of the Association.

Right Reverend Monsignor VICTOR DAY, D.D., V.G., Diocese of Helena, Montana, has had a life-long interest in historical study and research, and is the author of various important translations: Kurth's *What is the Middle Ages?*; Kurth's *The Church at the Turning Points of History;* and Bossuet's *Continuity of History* from the celebrated *Discourse on Universal History.* Monsignor Day is at present engaged upon a complete translation of this last work.

DR. JAMES F. KENNEY, Director of Publicity and Historical Research, Public Archives of Canada, Ottawa, Canada, President of the American Catholic Historical Association for the year 1932, is a graduate of the Universities of Toronto and Columbia. Among his writings are: *Catalogue of Pictures in the Public Archives of Canada with an introduction and notes.* Part I, 1925; and *The Sources for the Early History of Ireland,* Vol. I, 1929.

MARIE MADDEN, PH.D., professor of Spanish history at Fordham University, and of Spanish-American history and Sociology, Maxwell Training School for Teachers, New York City, has written considerably on Spain in our leading Catholic periodicals.

Rev. WILFRID PARSONS, S.J., studied at Woodstock College, Louvain University and the Gregorian University, Rome. He was ordained in 1918, and has been editor-in-chief of *America* since 1925; he is President of The America Press, Fellow of the American Geographical Society, and the author of *Italy and the Pope.*

DANIEL SARGENT, instructor in history in Harvard University, was graduated from that University in 1913, having devoted himself particularly to the study of philosophy. For one year after that he assisted Barrett Wendell in teaching comparative literature, and took an A.M. in English in 1914. For the next four years his academic life was interrupted; he served as an ambulance-driver with the French army, and then in the American artillery. Since the war, with the exception of three years spent studying in Europe, mostly in France, he has been engaged at Harvard University as a tutor in the Department of History and Literature, and has written a great deal of verse. He was received into the Catholic Church in 1919.

Very Rev. Charles L. Souvay, C.M., D.D., former Rector of Kenrick Seminary, Webster Groves, Missouri, is one of the founders of the Association. Dr. Souvay helped also to found the St. Louis Catholic Historical Society and was editor of its quarterly *Review*. He is one of the promoters of the Cause of Mother Seton and of Father Felix de Andreis, the celebrated St. Louis missionary, and is now living in Paris as *Socius* of the Superior-General of the Vincentians.

Leonid Strahkovsky, Docteur en Histoire (Louvain), is professor of history in Georgetown University. He is the author of several important works on the history of Poland and Russia, and has contributed to various Catholic periodicals, particularly the *Commonweal, Catholic Historical Review,* and others.

Very Reverend Edmund J. Walsh, S.J., Vice-President of Georgetown University, Washington, D. C., founder and regent of the Foreign Service School of that University, has for years been the accredited representative of the Holy See to treat with the Soviet Government in Russia on Catholic interests; he is the director of the papal relief commission for Russia and Mexico, and past-President of the Near East Relief Association. Among his published works are: *The Fall of the Russian Empire* and *The Last Stand*. Dr. Walsh is now preparing further studies on Soviet Russia. His *Reply to George Bernard Shaw*, which was recently broadcasted, is now printed in pamphlet form.

I

THE CATHOLIC CHURCH IN BELGIUM

Victor Day

Geography and History. Belgium is the little
buffer state between France and Germany.[1] It proclaimed its independence from Holland in 1830,
adopted a constitution in 1831, was recognized as a
neutral country in 1839, in the treaty of London,
by Austria, France, Great Britain, Holland, Prussia,
and Russia. By its fundamental charter, Belgium is
a constitutional, representative, and hereditary monarchy. The treaty of Versailles abrogated the
treaties guaranteeing Belgium's neutrality, and established it as a sovereign State. In 1920, a military
alliance was concluded with France. In 1921, an
economic union was established between Belgium and
the Grand Duchy of Luxemburg, doing away with
customs between the two countries.

Belgium negotiated a treaty with Holland concerning the navigation of the Scheldt, April 3, 1925.
The agreement provides that the Scheldt is to be
closed to war vessels in time of war, but open to

---

[1] Though smaller than Maryland, Belgium has almost five times
its population, having 7,995,558 inhabitants, or an average density
of population of 680 inhabitants per square mile. With the suburbs
Brussels, the capital, has a population of 815,198; Antwerp,
421,908; Liége, 250,187; Ghent, 204,105; Bruges, 78,000; Louvain,
40,371; Courtrai, 40,000.

all others of every country, in war and peace.

History. The constitution of Belgium, modeled after that of the United States, proclaimed the freedom of worship, of the press, of education, and of association. The civil marriage became obligatory. This was deemed necessary at the time so that the people who were convinced of the exclusive importance of the religious ceremony, might become accustomed to the performance of the legal formalities.

Albert I is the present King of Belgium. He is the son of the Count of Flanders, who was a brother of King Leopold II. Born April 8, 1875, Albert married Princess Elizabeth of Bavaria, at Munich, October 2, 1900. In 1925, on the occasion of their silver wedding, the bishops of Belgium, in a joint pastoral, paid an eloquent and touching tribute to the watchful, knightly, soldier-King who had endeared himself to his people by his simple life, his uprightness, and unfeigned kindness. They praised Queen Elizabeth, the nurse and mother of the soldiers during the dreadful days of the war, and spoke in glowing terms of the happy home life of the royal family.

Government. The executive branch of the government is in the hands of the King and a responsible ministry. The latter consists of the heads of ten departments who are named by the prime minister, on his appointment by the King. The legislative department consists of two branches, the Senate and the Chamber of Representatives. Senators are elected in part by the people, in part by the provincial councils. Representatives are chosen by the direct vote of the people. The principle of proportional representation of parties, introduced in 1899, is applied in the election of both senators and representatives. After the World War, the King granted suffrage without restriction, acceding to the Socialist plan of one man, one vote. Voting is compulsory. The question of woman suffrage has not been completely solved. In 1921, women were granted the vote in municipal elections and given the right to sit in elective bodies, but the bill to grant them full suffrage, brought forward in 1925 by the Catholics, was rejected by the Senate with a vote of 71 to 56.

Language Question. A line drawn across the center of Belgium from Mouscron, West Flanders, to Maastricht in Belgian Limburg, divides Belgium into two sections: namely, the northern section inhabited by the Flemings, a Teutonic race, who speak Flemish, and the southern section occupied by the Walloons, of Gallic or Celtic origin, who speak French. The most burning of internal problems is the language question between the Flemish provinces and the Walloon or French provinces. In 1830, the French language had been established as the official language of the new kingdom. By 1898, the Flamingants, or promoters of the Flemish movement, had obtained equal legal and official rights for the two languages.[2] In 1911, it was suggested to Flemi-

[2] The Flemish language spoken by the Flemings in Belgium is the continuation of the language of the Franks. It is the same language as the Dutch; it is very similar to Low German. A thou-

cize the State University of Ghent in East Flanders, as an offset to the French State University of Liége, and the two French Universities of Brussels and Louvain. After prolonged, rancorous discussions and two Cabinet crises, the University of Ghent was made a Flemish university towards the end of 1930. In the same spirit, the Catholic University of Louvain chose to become a bi-lingual university and, in all the Church and State colleges in the Flemish part of Belgium, French gave way to Flemish as the official language of the college.

This tardy recognition, however, has not satisfied some ultra-Flamingants. Some of them, known as "activists," do not hesitate to demand autonomy for the Flemish provinces under a federal régime. The majority of the Flemings, however, are unalterably opposed to such a division of the little country. The loyalty to undivided Belgium was one of the striking features of the centennial celebration of the independence of Belgium in 1930.

Finances. Prior to the World War, Belgium enjoyed a sound financial condition. The war added $8,000,000,000 to the public debt of $1,000,000,000. The coalition Cabinet, under Henry Jaspar, increased the taxes, established a sinking fund to wipe out the public debt, sought the renewal of foreign

sand years ago, English, Flemish, and German were practically the same language. The Flemings outnumber the Walloons in the proportion of 8 to 7. The Flemish birth rate is about three times that of the Walloons. The educated Flemings talk French as well as Flemish. The Walloons, as a rule, besides their Walloon dialect, know but the French language. Thirty thousand Belgians speak the German language.

credit, stabilized the franc at 35.96 to the dollar, and created a new monetary unit, the "belga," equal to five Belgian francs, for foreign trade. This strong, unselfish policy restored confidence, attracted foreign capital to Belgian industries, and brought about a surprising industrial revival. On September 30, 1929, the public debt had been reduced by 1,349,-896,000 francs.[3]

Political Parties. The three leading political parties are the Catholic Party, the Socialist Party, and the Liberal Party. The Catholic Party and the Liberal Party date back to the French domination in Belgium, about the time of the Revolution. Both were anti-French. The Catholic Party was and is devoted to the Church and the older national institutions. The Liberal Party was and is for "liberty" in religion and politics; it is against the Church in many matters, for instance in questions of Christian education. The Socialist Party became a factor in politics with the revolutionary outburst of 1886. It had been gaining recruits for ten years before an organized effort was made to combat it.[4]

[3] Belgium's war debt to Great Britain and France was waived by these governments and charged to German account. The Belgian debt to the United States was funded at Washington by the agreement of August 18, 1926.

[4] The party strength of the lawmakers in Belgium resulting from the elections of 1921, 1925 and 1929 is as follows:

	Senators			Representatives		
	1921	1925	1929	1921	1925	1929
Catholics	73	71	70	80	78	76
Socialists	52	59	55	67	79	70
Liberals	28	23	23	33	22	28
Others	..	..	5	6	8	12

Reconstruction. At the conclusion of the war, Belgium, ruined in a vast number of its public and private buildings, stripped of the machinery of its factories, robbed of its domestic animals, faced the problem of rebuilding its homes, its public buildings, its factories, its livestock business, its agriculture, and its industries. Under the mighty impulse of reparation money granted to the rebuilders, Belgium, under George Theunis (1921-25) as prime minister, arose from its ashes, more substantial, more modern, more beautiful, more efficient than ever. By 1922, the iron, steel, chemical, and textile industries had almost gone back to the pre-war level. By June 30, 1924, reconstruction of the devastated areas was almost complete. By the end of the same year, in West Flanders, 290,000 persons out of 315,-000 driven out by the war, had come home again. At the end of March, 1928, the general average of stocks on the exchange had increased 88.5% since the stabilization of the franc. Ten years after the Armistice, 215,000 acres of ravaged fields were again under cultivation. The paved highways and railroads had been rebuilt. It may be mentioned here that Belgium has more miles of railroad to the square mile than any other country in the world. It has also more miles of navigable waterways to the square mile than any other country in Europe.

The new fireproof library of the University of Louvain, designed by Whitney Warren of New York, in the purest Flemish Renaissance, was dedicated on July 4, 1928. It replaces the one burned in the

World War. In 1929, it already housed 750,000 books, 300,000 of which were sent from Germany. The cost of $2,000,000, including the endowment, was raised entirely in the United States, and the $80,000 chimes were a gift of the engineers of America.[5]

Louvain is putting up another set of chimes, cast partly from the bronze of the bells destroyed in 1914. It will have forty-two bells and weigh nineteen tons. Placed in the central tower of the Church of St. Peter, which was destroyed during the war, these bells will ring the hour, the half-hour, and the quarter.

On July 29, 1919, in the presence of the bishops of Belgium, of the King and Queen, the speakers of the Senate and the House, and of all the Catholic ministers with portfolio or of State, in presence of the senators, representatives, and a crowd of 200,000 people, on the site of the National Basilica of the Sacred Heart, Cardinal Mercier celebrated a Mass of Thanksgiving for the restoration of Belgium. He delivered a brilliant oration, at the conclusion of which he personally read, both in French and Flemish, an Act of Consecration of Belgium to the Sacred Heart, repeated by the whole assembly.

Industry. Belgian agriculture boasts the highest yield per acre in Europe. From the days of Philip II, in 1555, "the whole countryside has been

---

[5] According to the plans of Whitney Warren, one of the balustrades of the Library building was to carry a Latin inscription to this effect: "Destroyed by Teutonic fury, rebuilt by American generosity."

kept with the neatness of a garden." The flax,
linen, and lace industries, with damask linen of
Courtrai, Bruges lace and Mechlin (Malines) lace,
are world renowned. The cotton industry has ex-
panded from a production of 45,000 metric tons of
yarn in 1913 to 74,000 metric tons in 1929. The
coal mining industry which, before the war, employed 145,350 miners, gave work in 1929, to
157,000 men. The production of pig iron and steel
exceeded that of 1913 by about 50%. Zinc production surpassed the record year of 1913. Glass
manufacture of the highest quality continues to be
a leading industry. The National Society of Belgian
Railways reports satisfactory earnings. Antwerp
has become the greatest port of Europe. It is surpassed by only two ports in the world, New York and
Hongkong.[6] Belgium, poorer than its neighbors in
1830, had, on the eve of the war, become as rich
per capita as France and Germany, and richer than
Holland and Italy and many other countries.

Ecclesiastical Situation. Renouncing the privileges of the ancien régime, the Catholics of Belgium
with their fellow-citizens of the Liberal Party demanded in 1831, the mutual independence of Church
and State, requested full liberty for themselves, and
granted the same liberty to the members of the Liberal Party. In virtue of this mutual independence,
the State gave up the prerogative of intervening in
the appointment of bishops and pastors conceded

[6] The national budgets have recently been balanced. Statistics
show that the estimated receipts for 1930 were 11,561,508,000
francs; the proposed expenditures, 11,513,669,000 francs.

by the Concordat of 1801. In virtue of the same independence of the two powers, the State may not forbid the ministers of worship, bishops and priests, to correspond with their superiors or to publish their official messages. The sole restriction to the complete independence of the Church in Belgium is contained in Article 16 of the Constitution: "The civil marriage must always precede the nuptial blessing, save in cases to be determined by law, if need be." The Catholic members of the Constituent Assembly of 1830 consented to this restriction to assure the performance of the civil formalities of marriage. The law of August 3, 1919, specifies deathbed marriages as an exception to the above provision and authorizes the minister of religion to proceed with the marriage ceremony if danger of death to one of the contracting parties does not permit them to wait for the celebration of the civil marriage.

Article 117 of the Constitution guarantees the salaries and pensions of the ministers of religion, a sacred obligation contracted by the French Government when it nationalized (*i.e.*, confiscated and sold) Church properties. On the other hand, the decree of December 30, 1809, completed by the law of March 4, 1870, continues to govern the "fabriques d'Église" (Church trustees), of whom the pastor is an ex-officio member, and who, as civil persons, take care of the upkeep of church buildings, administer the funds destined for the maintenance of public worship, regulate its expenses, and raise the money required for the purpose. Thus, the Catholic religion enjoys the fullest liberty; but it enjoys this privilege as any other religion which is not opposed to public peace and order. The Catholic religion is recognized; but it shares this title with the Protestant and Jewish forms of worship, which existed in 1831, and whose ministers also receive their yearly salaries. The vast majority of the Belgian people are Catholic. There are 30,000 Protestants in Belgium and 3,000 Jews.

Diocesan Clergy; Religious. At the head of the Catholic organization of Belgium is the nunciature, the connecting link between the Vatican and the Belgian government. The present incumbent is His Excellency, Clement Micara, titular Archbishop of Apamea. In Belgium there are the archdiocesan and primatial See of Mechlin (Malines), immortalized by Cardinal Mercier, and the dioceses of Bruges, Ghent, Liége, Tournai, and Namur, of which last named See His Excellency, Bishop Heylen, the president of the International Eucharistic Congress, is the bishop.

In 1922, the Catholic clergy subsidized by the State numbered 6,030 priests, or one diocesan priest per 1,210 inhabitants. However, to the clergy whose salary is paid by the State must be added hundreds of priests in diocesan colleges, hundreds of chaplains of convents, hospitals, and various other charitable institutions, who are not remunerated by the State. Each diocese in Belgium has its own diocesan theological seminary, its own philosophical college or preparatory seminary for candidates for the diocesan priesthood. All these seminaries have a standard course. They are conducted by members of the diocesan clergy, under the supervision of their respective bishops. However, the number of new priests has not kept pace with the growth of population, nor with the need for priests arising especially from the establishment of various social works. But if, of late years, the Belgian clergy has, proportionately speaking, gone down in numbers, they have grown in priestly zeal, in proportion to the difficulties of all kinds which they have met. This spiritual growth may be attributed to the intensive spiritual training received in the seminaries and to such stimuli to priestly piety as annual retreats, theological conferences, and monthly days of recollection for priests in the ministry.[7]

At the census of December 31, 1920, there were 1,763 Religious houses and 54,511 Religious persons, of whom 9,858 were men and 44,653 were women. In 1910 there was a total of 58,351 Religious. This decrease in numbers is accounted for by the return to France of thousands of Religious after the war. A decrease of religious vocations since the war has closed schools in several places. To make up for the lack of hospital Sisters, large training schools for nurses have been established in different parts of the country.

[7] In accordance with Article 20 of the Belgian Constitution, the right of association may not be curtailed by law. Belgian religious corporations used this liberty extensively. Nay more, at different times, foreign Religious Congregations, mostly French, when proscribed by their own governments, established themselves and continued their work across the French line, on Belgian soil.

Religious Societies. First and foremost among these societies come the Catholic Action organizations, whose members coöperate with the clergy in promoting objects directly connected with the mission of the Church, by placing themselves under the immediate direction of the bishops and their representatives. Among such organizations must be mentioned the Catholic Associations of Belgian Youth, established at the suggestion of the late Cardinal Mercier in 1919, among the French-speaking young men. This organization aims to unite in a Parochial Association of Youth the various homogeneous sections of Young Catholic Laborers, Young Catholic Students, Young Catholic University Students, and Young Catholic Farmers. The Parochial Associations of Youth are grouped by deaneries. Each one of these organizations publishes two bulletins, one for the ordinary members, and a technical bulletin for the leaders.[8]

The best developed, the most interesting, the most promising, the most needed of these various Catholic Action organizations is that of the Young Catholic Laborers. This society assists the young laborers by the formation of study clubs, retreats, recollections, by taking an interest in special temporal needs, such, for instance, as the selection of a trade. Working along the same lines, there is a Young Catholic Laborers Association of French-speaking girls, as well as one for Flemish-speaking girls. In 1926, the

[8] General Conventions of the Catholic Association of the Belgian Youth took place in 1911, 1922, 1924, and 1927. Sixty thousand members attended the Congress held in Liége in 1927.

first had 4,000 members; the second, 4,500.
Finally, there is an organization for Flemish-speaking Young Catholic Laborers. At their first convention there were 400 delegates; in March, 1927, there were 5,000 associates. The study week held in Antwerp, in August, 1927, was attended by 250 directors. This is a movement in the right direction, but only a beginning, since all the associations for Young Catholic Laborers together have not reached one-tenth of the 500,000 laborers between 12 and 21. Yet, all of these need protection against the dechristianizing influences of industrial communities. Next comes the Federation of the Catholic Women of Belgium, and the Catholic Association of Young Women, with 70,000 members. Here also may be mentioned the Archconfraternity of the Holy Family established by the Redemptorist Fathers in Belgium for the preservation of the Faith among the people, and the Archconfraternity of Xaverians, organized by the Jesuits, also among the laborers. Besides these organizations, there are important publications in Belgium, among which may be mentioned French and Flemish religious weeklies published at the Norbertine Abbey of Averbode for the Christian Family, for the Eucharistic Crusade among the children, for the Eucharistic Crusade among adults, and the Archconfraternity of Our Lady of the Sacred Heart. Then come the doctrinal, historical, apologetical publications of the Dominican Fathers of Liége and Ant-

werp, for laborers, the educated people, and for priests.

Is Belgium doing anything in the line of closed retreats for men and women? During the last fifty years, this movement has developed in a wonderful way in Belgium. Scores of houses have been opened by the Religious of both sexes for this exclusive purpose in all sections of the land: namely, by the Benedictines, the Redemptorists, the Jesuits and the Trappists, for men; and by various Sisterhoods for women.[9]

Since the days of Pope Pius X, the movement for frequent and daily Communion has grown apace, especially among the children. The Norbertines of Averbode lead in the Eucharistic Crusade Movement. Under the impulse given by the League of the Sacred Heart throughout the land, families have consecrated themselves to the Sacred Heart; nay more, numerous cities have consecrated themselves to the Sacred Heart officially, with public solemnity, and amidst general rejoicing.

After the war, the conferences of St. Vincent de Paul also resumed their charitable work of visiting the poor. A Third Order is maintained by the Sons of St. Francis, whilst the Dominican Fathers have numerous tertiaries. As explained in recent issues of the *Orate Frates*, Flanders occupied a place of

[9] From 1910 to 1914, within seven retreat houses, the Jesuits preached respectively 258, 239, 235, 225 retreats to 10,170, 9,387, 8,733, and 9,075 men. After the war, from 1919 to 1926 the same work was taken up again with 3,950, 5,042, 5,120, 4,722, 5,700, and 6,317 participants.

honor in the First International Liturgical Congress
held in Antwerp, July 22-27, 1930. It was there
that the initiative was taken from which originated
the now flourishing liturgical movement.[10] Monsignor Callewaert, president of the Grand Seminary
of Bruges, was the soul and inspiration of the movement. This movement blossomed forth in a great
variety of liturgical books, in liturgical missals and
rituals, liturgical days, the annual liturgical week,
liturgical exhibitions, liturgical plays, liturgical illustrated lectures, etc., etc. To give an instance,
Kerklyk Leven (Church Life) within a few months
reached more than eighty thousand subscriptions.
Then there were special schools for sacristans,
sacristan societies, sacristan conferences, sacristan
retreats. The movement begins to be felt in sacred
music, in the liturgical construction and furnishing
of the churches.

In the Walloon part of Belgium, a revival of the
liturgical life is attributed to the influence of Dom
Guéranger. It has the same general features as the
movement in the Flemish part of Belgium. Its *Vie
Liturgique* has seventy thousand subscribers.

Fourth Provincial Council. A religious event of
the first magnitude was the holding of the Fourth
Provincial Council of Mechlin in 1920, under the
presidency of the late Cardinal Mercier, in the pres-

---

[10] In 1930, as a part of the celebration of the Centenary of the
Belgian Independence, a National Eucharistic Congress was held
at Mechlin. Under the leadership of the bishops of Belgium, it
was attended by immense throngs of priests and people from all
parts of the country.

ence of the Apostolic Nuncio, Archbishop Nicotra, the bishops, coadjutor and auxiliary bishops of Belgium, the abbots of monasteries, the delegates of the cathedral chapters, the delegates of the diocesan clergy, and the superiors general of religious Orders. Preceded by months of intense preparation, two sessions were held, one April 12-14, the other October 26-28. The *Acta et Decreta* of the Council in 174 pages, prepared by a galaxy of ecclesiastical scholars and leaders, contain four distinct sections, dogmatic, moral, disciplinary, pastoral and liturgical. With very few exceptions, the decrees of the Council were approved on November 16, 1922, by the Sacred Congregation of the Council "with the confident hope that they would greatly promote religion and the salvation of souls." On the same date, the decree of the Sacred Congregation of the Council was approved by Pope Pius XI.

Social Legislation. The agricultural and industrial depressions of the early '80's led to revolutionary strikes in Liége and in the province of Hainaut (both in the Walloon part of Belgium) in March, 1886. The following month, the Minister of Agriculture and Labor of the Catholic Party appointed a labor commission of thirty-five members to investigate agricultural and industrial conditions and recommend remedies for them. Under the direction of the Catholic Premier Beerneart, the commission was fruitful of immediate results. In November of the same year, the speech from the throne, read at the opening of parliament, definitely renounced the policy of abstention adhered to for fifty years and set on foot a Christian social policy. This social policy is the chief characteristic of Catholicity in Belgium since 1886.

The keynote of the new policy was struck in these words of the discourse:

The condition of the laboring classes is worthy of the highest interest, and it will be the duty of the legislature with increased solicitude to strive to improve it. It is just that the law should surround the weak and the unfortunate with special protection. In particular, it is proper to favor labor unions, to establish between the captains of industry and the working men new bonds in the form of arbitration and reconciliation councils, to regulate the work of women and children, to stop the abuses found in the payment of salaries, to facilitate the construction of suitable dwellings for laborers, to foster the development of societies of foresight, of aid, of insurance and pensions, and to strive to fight the ravages of drunkenness and of immorality.

A vast, a wonderful program this was, and all the more wonderful because it was proposed five years before the publication of the epoch-making encyclical *Rerum Novarum.*

An evolution of the policy of Bishop von Ketteler (1811-1877) of Mainz, of Bishop Mermillod (1824-1892) of Switzerland, of Bishop Doutreloux (1837-1901) of Liége and the other bishops of Belgium, this policy was carried out, nay, surpassed. As early as 1887, Minister Charles Woeste proposed a bill including the principal planks of the above platform.

In 1891, the year of *Rerum Novarum,* the Catholic
Congress of Malines, Bishop Doutreloux of Liége in
a pastoral of 1894, and the bishops of Belgium in
their joint pastoral letter of 1895 sounded the clarion
call, inviting all Catholics to unite their efforts to
improve the lot of the laboring man. The Belgian
Democratic League took charge of the movement,
opposed on the one hand by the Socialist syndicates,
already ten years in the field, and on the other hand
by the employers. Under the skillful guidance of
G. Helleputte and Arthur Verhaegen, its first two
presidents, with the assistance of the popular orator
Léon Mabille, the eloquent historian Godfrey Kurth,
and the learned theologian Dr. Pottier, the Democratic League gradually overcame all opposition.[11]

The World War accelerated the syndical movement in Belgium. From 250,000 before the war,
the syndical membership rose to 800,000, of which
only 200,000 belong to the Christian groups. In
the great industrial centers, the Socialists control the
labor movement. On the other hand, the pre-
ponderance of the Christian organizations is seen in
the country districts. The organization of these
rural Christian forces is due to G. Helleputte. With

[11] In 1901, the Belgian Democratic League had 16,000 adherents,
whilst the Socialist syndicates, euphemistically called the Belgian
Labor Party, had seven or eight times that many members. In
1913, the Belgian Democratic League had 102,000 as against
130,000 in Socialist syndicates and from 20,000 to 30,000 in the
independent syndicates. The Socialist syndicates are recruited
principally in the Walloon part of Belgium, namely, in the provinces of Hainaut and Liége, the mining, quarrying, and smelting
and steel manufacturing sections of Belgium; whilst the Christian
syndicates of the Belgian Democratic League flourish chiefly in the
Flemish section of Belgium, and particularly in the two Flanders.

the assistance of F. Schollaert (1851-1917) and Father Mellaerts (1845-1925), on August 1, 1890, he founded the Boerenbond (Farmers' League) of which he remained the president and inspiration until his death. This League, in 1929, had a membership of half a million members among the farm laborers and small farmers. In 1913, the Boerenbond had 762 savings banks; in 1926, 1,200. In 1913, it had deposits to the amount of 16,000,000 francs; in 1925, of 800,000,000; in 1930, of 1,481,-300,000 francs. In 1930 it built the first skyscraper in Belgium, at Antwerp.

The Boerenbond organizes coöperative societies in all the domains of rural life, in buying agricultural implements, livestock, feed, fertilizers; in issuing insurance against fire, accident, burglary, hail, and mortality of livestock; in selling in foreign markets butter, eggs, and vegetables, produced by its members. It conducts a seed-selection station, laboratories, mills, agricultural schools; it organizes lecture tours, study days, and courses on agriculture throughout the country. It has its technical advisers and inspectors, its newspapers and its reviews. Whenever it wishes, it can mobilize 100,000 men, and could loan 50,000,000 francs to the government. The Boerenbond has helped the small farmer so successfully that larger farms give place to smaller farms. The Boerenbond is active principally in the Flemish part of Belgium. It also more or less supports farmers' unions existing in the Walloon part of Belgium. The success of the rural Christian organization has helped industrial sections to develop hundreds of coöperative food and clothing stores which promise soon to rival the Socialist coöperative stores.[12]

When the conservative Catholics and the Catholic members of the Belgian Democratic League unite with the Socialists, they can pass any bill they please, against the Liberal Party. But the conservative Catholics are cautious. They fear changes which have not been given long and serious study. The social legislation of Belgium from 1886 to 1914 is admitted to be one of the best and most progressive in Europe.

The Ministry of Agriculture, created on June 16, 1884, has rendered yeoman service to agriculture by imparting scientific rural information through lectures, short courses, by the establishing of experimental stations, bureaus of consultation and various rural associations for the farmers, and by providing or subsidizing schools and colleges for the teaching of the science of agriculture to the farmers' sons. But the science of farming without the necessary capital would remain inoperative. The law of 1894, completing that of April 15, 1884, provided the necessary funds through the erection of rural banks. Thus, farming in Belgium has become more intensive and productive than in any other country in Europe.

[12] By adding to the 200,000 members of the Christian syndicates, the 500,000 members of the Farmers' League, hundreds of coöperative stores and 700,000 mutualists, one has an idea of the social works born of the Catholic social policy in Belgium.

The Ministry of Industry and Labor, erected in 1895, maintains a Labor Bureau created to study labor problems, pursue investigations, collect statistics, and draft bills for the improvement of the condition of the wage-earner. This Labor Bureau is assisted in its work by a Superior Council of Labor composed of experts in sociology, of employers and employees whose duty it is to subject to a searching examination all projects of laws or proposed ministerial decrees for the protection of labor. This Superior Council of Labor, in turn, is guided in its work by a Council of Industry and Labor, composed equally of employers and employees. This Council of Industry and Labor was also entrusted by law with a mission of conciliation and arbitration in labor troubles. The same Ministry of Industry and Labor fosters technical education by establishing or subsidizing schools which impart technical knowledge. A Superior Council of Technical Education established June 25, 1905, coördinates, unifies, and guides all technical teaching.

Already in 1887, by the laws of August 16 and 18, wages were protected by the repression of the "truck-system" (payment of wages in goods instead of money), by freeing four-fifths of the wages from seizure, and making three-fifths of them inalienable. A royal decree of July 2, 1896, prescribes a schedule of minimum wages to be paid in all contracts for public works. Laws of December 14, 1889, and of 1892, 1905, 1906 and 1911 regulate the labor of women and children. Since 1919, the law forbids all night work to women in firms employing more than ten persons, men or women. A law of June 15, 1896, prescribes that all industrial and commercial enterprises employing at least ten laborers must have "Regulations for the Workshop." In 1899, the law was extended to any industrial or commercial business employing at least five laborers. A law of March 31, 1898, grants legal personality to labor unions formed for the study, the defense, and the development of the interests of the labor union. A law enacted in 1905 forbids work on Sundays. The law respects the individual liberty proclaimed in the Constitution; it merely forbids employers to make others work on Sunday. On December 31, 1909, the House of Representatives voted a nine-hour day for miners with only five dissenting votes. The Senate ratified its work by sixty-four votes against ten and two abstentions. A law of July 2, 1899, authorizes the government to prescribe measures to insure the wholesomeness of the workshops or of the work, and the security of the laborers in all industrial and commercial enterprises without exception, whenever the work entails danger. Making use of these powers, governmental decrees have established for each industry a code of hygiene and safety. Free public employment offices are subsidized by the government since 1904.

Insurance against sickness, disability, old age, and involuntary unemployment has early held the attention of the government, which encourages all such insurance. The laborer remains free to affiliate with a fraternal organization, to pay dues to an unemployment fund, but, when he takes out a policy with such organizations, he receives a government premium. The present laws concerning sickness and disability were enacted on June 23, 1894, March 19, 1898, and May 5, 1912. These laws ordain that only recognized societies and federations will be entitled to public subsidies. The local societies contribute a small fraction of their income to regional societies. The regional societies then become enabled, in return, to pay sick benefits to persons of a local society after six months of sickness, when the local society discontinues its assistance. In general, the regional society organizes all medical, surgical, and hospital assistance which is beyond the power of local societies. The government subsidizes new local and regional societies, grants cash donations for statistical information sent in, to help the new societies to get on their feet. To the subsidies granted by the central government must be added those of the province and of the municipality. These three agencies unite thus to encourage foresight. A law enacted in 1894 makes it possible to assure an indemnity to members of these societies in case of loss or sickness of livestock, or of damages caused to crops by fortuitous circumstances. As in the previous case, the government grants cash donations in cases and for reasons mentioned in the preceding law. A law of May 10, 1900, establishes a pension system for the laborer. By this law a workman who annually pays fifteen francs to a pension fund, guaranteed by the central government, receives a yearly government premium of from nine to eleven francs and is entitled to a pension of 360 francs at the age of sixty-five. Here again the provincial and communal governments add to the pension of the central government. This beneficent law enables old workmen to take care of themselves in their own homes instead of going to old people's homes or the poorhouse. Whilst the ordinary workman is free to pay into the pension fund, the miners are bound to do so by law. Miners receive their pension at sixty and, eventually will get it at fifty-five years of age.[13]

Since the war, a law compelling the laborer to insure against sickness, disability, and old age, was voted by the federal legislature. A compulsory old-age insurance for workers of both sexes earning less than 12,000 francs a year, was voted on December 10, 1924. For old age and premature decease it implies a threefold contribution to the insurance policy by the employer, the employee and the State. A compensation act for industrial labor accidents was voted unanimously by the Catholic Party and opposed unanimously by the Liberals and Socialists; by the Liberals, on the pretext that it was placing too heavy a burden on industry; by the Socialists, on the ground of alleged insufficiency of the compensation.

[13] The popularity of this pension law may be gauged by the growth of local mutual societies recognized by the State, from 579 in 1894 to 9,837 in 1914, with 1,500,000 members. In 1912, the Ministry of Industry and Labor, with an ordinary budget of 27,000,000 francs, spent 19,000,000 for social foresight. Of 450,000 persons who reached the age of sixty-five, 220,000 received the pension of 360 francs a year.

The granting of labor railway rates has tended to raise the laborers' wages. Since 1910, the laborer may travel sixty miles, in both directions, six times a week for the sum of 3.15 francs (60 cents). This has made the whole of Belgium one labor market, and the Belgian laborer the most mobile man in Europe. In 1910, 325,000 laborers, or one-fifth of the total number, availed themselves of these facilities, to the benefit of all concerned. This system raised the wages of the rural laborer without lowering those of the industrial centers, taught the farmer to use farm machinery more extensively, and prevents unwholesome congestion of industrial centers.

To protect the work and the wages of the laborer, to prevent accidents, and to insure the laborer against their burdensome consequences, is a good thing. What is better still is to increase the wages of the laborer and to raise the laborers to the level of property owners.

One of the beneficent laws in Belgium is that on Workmen's Dwellings. It authorizes the savings banks under the guarantee of the government to advance funds for the building of their homes through the intermediary of a local savings bank. These local savings banks are of two kinds: the constructing societies, which build the homes and sell or rent them to the laborers; and the loaning societies which lend the laborer money with which he may build. The latter are the more popular. Before the World War, there were 151 local loaning societies as against sixty-four building societies. To obtain a loan the laborer must put down one-tenth of the cost of construction, which may not exceed 10,-000 francs. The loan is paid by annuities, in 10, 20 or 30 installments, so arranged that the debt is paid by the time the laborer reaches the age of sixty-five. Under this law, by a payment of twenty francs a month, a laborer may, within twenty-five years, become the owner of a larger, more comfortable, more sanitary house than he could have rented at a scarcely lower price. From 1889 to 1913, 60,000 laborers' homes were constructed under this law.[14]

These laws taken as a whole have given the Belgian laborer more comfort, longer hours of leisure and greater security because he is more effectively insured, and have inspired him with a spirit of greater thrift. In 1870, there were 51,000 savings deposit books with aggregate savings amounting to 10,000,000 francs; in 1913, there were 3,109,000 accounts with deposits amounting to a billion francs, an average of 2,000 francs per hearth.

Belgium, poorer than its neighbors in 1830, had, on the eve of the war, become as rich as France and Germany, and richer than Holland and Italy and many other countries. The general rise of material conditions in Belgium is due to the organization of labor unions, the enactment of laws favoring labor as explained above, and the coöperation of the employers. The Catholic Party prides itself on having

[14] As early as 1913, a bill proposed to extend the benefits of this law to employees and farmers under an organization known as the National Society of Inexpensive Dwellings. The war prevented the enacting of the bill.

enacted these beneficent social laws; the democracy of labor made up of the Christian Democrats and the Socialists, glories in having compelled the party in power to enact these laws. The coöperation of the employers may be credited in great part to their Christian spirit, stimulated by the immortal encyclical *Rerum Novarum* of Leo XIII.

A second characteristic of Belgian Catholicism in the last fifty years is the holding of Catholic Congresses for the purpose of formulating a platform, of perfecting Church organization, and of fostering the Catholic press. Chief among these congresses was that held at Malines, the primatial See city of Belgium, September 23-26, 1909. Three thousand priests and laymen assembled there, discussed Belgium's religious, moral, and social welfare, and formulated a program of Catholic action, which has been fruitful of results up to the present day.

Education. Higher Catholic education in Belgium is represented by the University of Louvain, established as a "Studium generale" by Pope Martin V, in 1425. Its administration, teaching, and budget are independent of the State. The Belgian episcopate controls the institution, and appoints its head, the rector magnificus, who governs with the assistance of a rectoral council composed of the deans of the five faculties: theology, law, medicine, philosophy, and letters. The professors are appointed by the bishops on presentation by the rector. The University has a large number of affiliated institutions, among them the higher philosophic Institute estab-

lished by Pope Leo XIII and organized by the late
Professor Mercier. There are also additional courses
on social, consular, and colonial sciences; special institutes for bacteriology, biology, neurology, pathol-
ogy, chemistry; schools of art, manufacturing, civil
engineering, mining, architecture, agriculture, and, of
late, a school of brewing.[15] Besides the free Catholic
University of Louvain supported by the Church,
there is a free University of Brussels with 1,945
students, the Flemish State University of Ghent
with 1,551 students, and the State University of
Liége with 2,278 students.

Schools are supported partly by local taxation,
and each commune must have at least one primary
school. A law passed in 1914 made education compulsory for children between the ages of six and fourteen. The percentage of illiteracy has been decreas-
ing rapidly. The percentage of illiterates was 9.3 in
1920; 13.1 in 1910; 19.1 in 1900; 25.0 in 1890;
30.26 in 1880. Religious education was made compulsory by law in 1895. Children whose parents
object are dispensed from attendance. In some of
the larger communities, the law is evaded by substi-
tuting civil ethics. In free (religious) schools the
salaries of teachers are partly paid by the government, and diplomas of private normal schools and
colleges have the same authority as those of the
State schools.

The Catholic colleges in Belgium have generally a

[15] During the scholastic year 1930-1931, the University had an
attendance of 3,551 students; its faculty numbered 163 professors.

full six years classical course, a preparatory course, as well as a business or commercial department. These colleges are strictly diocesan colleges, conducted by secular priests under the supervision of the bishop of each diocese. Before the war, the Archbishop of Malines had twenty such colleges; the Diocese of Bruges had seventeen, thirteen of which have a classical course; the Diocese of Ghent, eight; the Diocese of Liége, thirteen; the Diocese of Namur, four; and the Diocese of Tournai, seven. In the diocesan colleges in Belgium, the students aspiring to the priesthood go on with students who propose to pursue secular studies in the universities. In other words, Belgium has no minor seminaries, like Nazareth Hall in St. Paul, or St. Edward's Seminary in Seattle. The Jesuits have thirteen classical colleges scattered throughout Belgium. The Josephites, the Benedictines, the Crosier Fathers, and the Brothers of the Christian Schools conduct several well-known institutions.

As a rule the junior and senior courses of our American colleges are given in the universities in Belgium. The St. Louis College conducted by diocesan priests in Brussels and the College of Notre Dame of Peace at Namur, conducted by the Jesuit Fathers, have the four years college course of our American colleges. There are 134 State high schools, 44 of which are for girls. There are seven higher schools of commerce, a polytechnic school at Mons, a State agricultural college at Gembloux, a State veterinary school at Cureghem, four royal conserva-

tories at Brussels, Liége, Ghent, and Antwerp, a
Royal Academy of Fine Arts at Antwerp, and sixty-
eight schools of drawing. In 1923, the new Colonial
University was organized by combining the Colonial
School of Antwerp and the School of Tropical Medicine. In 1928, it had about 228 students. Formerly,
all the courses in the Belgian Catholic colleges, with
the exception of those in Christian doctrine in the
lower grades, and of those in Flemish, English, and
German, were given in French; French was the official language of the college; the prospectuses, pro-
grams, year books, were all in French; now all the
courses but those in French are given in Flemish,
and Flemish is the official language of the Catholic
colleges in the Flemish part of Belgium.

Belgian Writers. Belgium has writers in both the
French and Flemish languages. Among those who
write in French are not only Walloons but also Flemings. The literature of Belgium is distinctive, and
a faithful mirror of Belgian life. Among the Belgian
writers in the French language in the last decade, we
must mention George Eekhoud (1854-1927), writer
of a powerful satire on modern Antwerp, *La Nouvelle Carthage,* and novelist of Flemish peasant life,
whose style is often marked by blunt realism; George
Virres (1869-——), who pictures with more idealism
the joys and sorrows of the humble dwellers in the
Campine; the popular writer of prose tales, Eugène
Demolder (1862-1919); the poets Iwan Gilkin
(1858-1924) and Albert Giraud (1860-——), one of
the "Parnassians," who wishes to revive classic

models; Max Elskamp (1862-—), the religious poet; and Maurice Maeterlinck, dramatist and philosopher, who is known internationally (1862-—). Mention should also be made of the novelists, Horace Van Offel and Frans Hellens; the poets, Emile Cammaerts, Victor Kinon, and Pierre Nothomb; the Franciscan, Martial Lekeux, who published his war memories; and the dramatist, Paul Spaak; Fernand Crommelynck, the mystic; and Gustave van Zype, the realist.

Among recent Flemish writers, Father Guido Gezelle is universally admitted to be foremost. He is the greatest Flemish poet of modern times. Much of what he wrote towards the end of his life is unsurpassed in Flemish literature. He is considered as one of the most original religious poets of the world. His rich, marvelously supple and musical language expresses to perfection the genuine emotions of his poetic soul and begets in the reader identical feelings. He is a lover and interpreter of nature. He has written poetry which is enjoyed in Holland no less than in Flanders; nay more, poetry which, done into French, is treasured by the Walloons. His poetry will live as long as the Flemish language is spoken. He translated Longfellow's *Hiawatha* into easy, natural, fluent Flemish verse, as musical as the American original. Both Courtrai and Bruges have recently erected statues to his memory. With the name of Guido Gezelle must be linked that of his friend, Pastor Hugo Verriest, literary critic and popular lecturer. A statue erected to him in his former parish by the legion of his admirers bears testimony to the esteem in which his literary works are held. A new generation of young West Flemish poets continues the work of Guido Gezelle. Among them should be mentioned D. Van Houtte, Om. K. De Laey, César Gezelle, Alois Walgraeve, René De Clercq, and above all Father Cyrille Verschaeve, eminent as dramatist, lyrist, and essayist. The school of Guido Gezelle spread into the other Flemish provinces and gave Belgium Henry Claeys and Alphonse Janssens in East Flanders; and J. Lenaerts and August Cuppens in Limburg; Prosper Van Langendonck (1863-1921), Karel Van de Woestyne (1878-1929), a poet of merit, eminent also as a prose writer; August Vermeylen, the theorist of the new literary movement; Herman Teirlinck, its novelist; Styn Streuvels, nephew of the late Guido Gezelle, who from a baker became one of the leading and most prolific novelists, a true exponent of humble life, whose works have been translated into almost every language of Europe. "The Flemish literature of the last forty years boasts some thirty names whose books are read as soon as they come off the press, whose writings keep abreast with world literature, and which for perfection of style and beauty of form are not surpassed by any literature in the world today."

Scientists. The limits of this paper do not permit us to detail the scientific activities of Belgium. Suffice it to say that, under the leadership of its four flourishing universities, little Belgium contributes a generous share towards the progress of knowledge. In the field of mathematics and astronomy may be mentioned Ch. de la Vallée-Poussin, the first president of the international mathematical union; Alphonse Dumoulin, in geometry; Giuseppi Cesaro, in mathematical crystallography; Charles Lagrange, in celestial mechanics; Théophile De Donder, in relativity; Paul Stroobant, in astronomy; and Marcel Dehalu, in geodesy. In physics, Belgium glories in the name of Z. Gramme, the inventor of the electric motor; in the names of Van der Mensbrugghe, who first explained the calming influence of oil on the waves; of Walter Spring, specialist in physical chemistry, and of a host of present-day physicists who have obtained wonderful results in the after-war period. In chemistry, Paul Henry, Maurice Delacre, and Pierre Bruylants recall the name of their master, Louis Henry, the distinguished organic chemist of the second half of the nineteenth century and the discoverer of several new substances. F. Swarts, too, has acquired a renown which succeeding years will not dim. Edward Van Beneden, son of the eminent zoölogist, J. B. Van Beneden, close friend of Louis Pasteur, and Canon J. B. Carnoy have achieved an international reputation in cytology. Belgian botanists have contributed their share in the international coöperation towards progress in botany. In all branches of zoölogy Belgian scientists have done honorable work. Nor did the Belgian scientists lag behind in geology. Omalius d'Halloy, Dumont, and De Walque published geological maps for Belgium and neighboring countries. Omalius d'Halloy prepared the first geological map of France under the first Empire, when French territory stretched from the North Sea to Italy. Dumont composed the first geological map of Europe. The research work of these men is continued by present-day Belgian scientists. Belgium is well represented by its school of scientific historians founded by Godfrey Kurth (1847-1916), whom Belgium honored with a national funeral on the occasion of the transfer of his remains to their last resting place at Arlon, his native city, after the war. Among the principal Belgian followers of Kurth in the scientific teaching of history may be mentioned Vanderkindere, Lonchay, Desmarez, at Brussels; P. Frederick, H. Pirenne, at Ghent; Ch. Moeller, Canon Cauchie, L. Van der Essen, at Louvain; E. Hubert, K. Hanquet and J. M. Closon, at Liége.

Belgium has a host of eminent ecclesiastical writers. Among the most noted scriptural scholars are Doctor Caemerlynck, Doctor Van der Heeren, Doctor Albin A. Van Hoonacker, professor of the critical history of the Old Testament and of Hebrew in the University of Louvain. Among the canonists, Doctors De Becker and Creusens are eminent. Among the most prolific theological writers come Doctor Oscar Dignant, former professor of moral theology at the University of Louvain, Canon A. De Smet, former professor of sacramental theology in the seminary of Bruges, and his Excellency, Msgr. Waffelaert, the late Bishop of Bruges, and former professor of moral theology in the major seminary of the same city. To these names must be added those of Rev. Drs. J. Bittremieux, J. Forget, A. Janssens, C. Van Crombrugghe and A. Van Hove, the editors of the internationally known *Ephemerides Theologicæ Lovanienses*. Among ascetical writers Rt. Rev. Henry Van Den Berghe, V.G., of Bruges, must be mentioned. At the head of the Belgian liturgists stands the name of Monsignor C. Callewaert.

The outstanding ecclesiastical writer and teacher of recent years in Belgium is Cardinal Mercier. Called by Pope Leo XIII to fill the chair of Thomistic philosophy at Louvain for the purpose of constructing the presentation of scholastic philosophy to meet the requirements of modern science, he acquitted himself of his task so masterfully that the great Leo expressed his approbation of Professor Mercier's work by making him a prelate. In his special field, Professor Mercier published successively *General Criteriology, Logic, Psychology,* and *Origins of Contemporary Psychology*. These works have been translated into various languages and are known to students of philosophy all over the world. Professor Mercier entered one of the above works in a national contest for the most scientific work produced by a Belgian author, and was awarded the first prize by a jury composed of professors of the four Belgian universities.

To the world Cardinal Mercier is known as a heroic patriot because of the fearless stand taken by him against the invaders of Belgium in his pastorals

—*Voice of Belgium* and *The Voice of God*. Referring to these utterances, Elihu Root said of Cardinal Mercier: "He was the embodiment of moral power standing alone and undefended." William D. Guthrie, President of the New York Bar Association, at the unveiling of a bust of Cardinal Mercier at the Library Hall of the New York University, called him the noblest and most heroic teacher of moral philosophy that the world had yet known.

Architecture, Painting, Music. What is Belgium doing in architecture? Though Belgium is studded with splendid monuments in all the historic European styles of architecture, Belgian architects of the present day have evolved a modernist style in which the glorious traditions of the past are blended with present-day principles of construction and decoration. The style is called cubism. It has been exemplified in a dozen or more monumental buildings. The buildings of the expositions of Antwerp and Liége in 1930 were the beginning of this style. The new style has attracted international attention. Like their illustrious predecessors, Belgian painters distinguish themselves by the power of their colors and their love for truth and life. The outstanding names of the past decade are Bartsoen with his canvases on Ghent, its canals, its bridges, and its Flemish gables; Emile Claus, the painter of the Lys country, which he floods with light; Van Rysselberghe, the interpreter of Mediterranean scenes; De Gouve of Nuncques, the painter of the Ardennes; Alfred Venhaeren, a leading colorist of the school; Amédée Lynen, authentic heir of the masters of the seventeenth century; and Jakob Smits, the mystical painter of the Campine. Among recent Flemish musical celebrities are Pierre Benoit (1832-1901), founder of the School of Flemish Music in Antwerp in 1867, which became the Royal Flemish Conservatory in 1898; Edgard Tinel (1854-1912), director of the Royal Conservatory of Brussels, whose oratorios *Sinte Godelieve* and *Franciscus* are reputed the best written since the *Elie* and *Paulus* of Mendelssohn; Canon Van Nuffel, the organizer of the marvelous mixed choir of the Metropolitan Cathedral of Malines, which some musical critics compare or even prefer to the Sistine Choir. Among Walloon musicians of Belgium must be cited Adolphe Samuel, composer and writer (1824-1898); Aug. Dupont, composer; G. Huberti, professor of musical composition; and César Franck (1822-1890), who, according to eminent critics, surpasses Richard Wagner in the boldness of harmony and modulation, and who founded the Young French School. It is claimed that he introduced into French music a certain German element, accounted for by his descent from a Flemish father and a German mother. Among the writers on music of recent years are Victor Mabillon (1841-1924), founder and first director of the museum of the Conservatory of Brussels; H. Van Duyse, M. Kuffenrath, G. Van Doorslaer; P. Bergmans, Charles Van den Boven, R. Van Aerde and Fl. Van der Meuren. Eugene Isaye led all Belgian artists on the violin. Belgium has also its noted grand opera singers, among whom are Marie Sass, Marie Cabel, Ernest Van Dyck, Blauwaert, and Anseau.

Catholic Press. According to the *Annuaire Statistique de Belgique* (1924-25) there were sixty-seven political daily newspapers published in Belgium. Among the leading papers, six were Socialist; fifteen, Liberal; twenty-nine, Catholic. Seventeen of these are in French; twelve, in Flemish. Of the six daily papers which had the largest circulation, three were Catholic; two were liberal; one was non-partisan. Besides the Catholic dailies, there exist a large number of Catholic weeklies, bi-weeklies, and monthlies. The Catholic University of Louvain publishes five major theological and scientific reviews. Each diocese in Belgium has its own theological monthly review. Recently, some professors of theology have written popular textbooks of dogma, manuals of asceticism and mysticism. Among the Jesuits, the Bollandists pursue their gigantic work, the *Acta Sanctorum*. In 1926, this work published its sixty-fifth volume in folio. Besides the *Acta Sanctorum*, the Jesuits publish *La Nouvelle Revue Théologique, Revue de Communautés religieuses,* and the *Museum Lessianum*. The Benedictine Abbey of Maredsous publishes the *Revue Bénédictine, Revue Liturgique et Monastique,* and *Pax*. At the Abbeys of Mont-César, near Louvain, of Afflighem, St. André and Steenbrugghe are published several parochial liturgical reviews in either French or Flemish. There is also the *Revue Générale,* and finally two reviews launched in recent years by the diocesan clergy:

La Revue Catholique des Idées et des Faits and *La Cité Chrétienne*.

Foreign Missions. What is Belgium doing for the foreign missions? According to the 1925 edition of the *Manuel des Missions Catholiques* of Rev. B. Arens, S. J., Belgian missionaries are at work in Brazil, in China, in Chile, in Ceylon, in English East Africa, in Colombia, in New Guinea, in the Hawaiian Islands, but above all in India and the Belgian Congo. The Belgian Congo offers a unique example of what a Catholic colonizing nation may accomplish for the conversion of the heathen. In 1928, the Belgian Congo comprised twenty-one prefectures and vicariates-apostolic. These are in charge of the White Fathers, the Fathers of Scheut, the Priests of the Sacred Heart, the Norbertines, the Redemptorists, the Mill-Hill Fathers, the Fathers of the Holy Ghost, the Benedictines, the Capuchins, the Salesians, the Dominicans, the Franciscans, the Crosier Fathers, the Missionaries of the Sacred Heart, and the Lazarists. With few exceptions, all these missionaries are Belgians.[16]

In his report to the Governor General of the Belgian Congo, Governor Engels, a provincial governor, had this to say about the social benefits resulting from the activities of the missionaries:

[16] In 1928, the European missionary personnel in the Congo was made up as follows: 563 priests, 11 scholastics, 287 brothers, and 388 sisters. The natives had 11 priests, 24 sisters, and over 9,000 catechists. At the end of 1926, 482,684 Congolese had been baptized in the Catholic Church, and there were 342,743 catechumens and postulants. Within a short time, one tenth of the population of the Congo will have been reached by the Belgian missionaries.

It is necessary to bear in mind that the mission is the foremost and practically the only force in the regeneration of the region in which it carries on its activities. To read an account of the results obtained leaves the reader incredulous. One must see to believe. The physical health of the people has been the object of as much solicitude as the moral well-being. An idea of this may be had from the number of children in the Catholic families. Homes with six, seven, eight, and nine children are found in the villages, and the moral discipline is such that among several thousands of families, although there are some cases of divorce, the number of those who have remained united, is relatively incalculable.

Over seven hundred Protestant missionaries, belonging to twenty-five different missionary organizations, compete vigorously with these missionaries in various places.

The missionary Congregation of the Immaculate Heart of Mary founded at Scheut near Brussels, in 1863, has sent out over six hundred missionaries to China, to the Philippine Islands, and the Belgian Congo.

The American College of the Immaculate Conception of the Blessed Virgin Mary of Louvain, founded at the request of the American Hierarchy in 1857, had by 1919 sent out 773 priests to the United States. Nineteen of these had been raised to the episcopate. Eighteen had been made prelates, and one, Dr. Peter Guilday, is professor of Church history at the Catholic University of America.

Birth Prevention. Has Belgium escaped the blight

of birth prevention? It has not. The birth rate per one thousand inhabitants in 1880 was 31.13; in 1900, 28.95; in 1913, 22.40. We shall not consider the abnormal years of the World War, during which the birth rate decreased considerably, nor the 1919-20 post-war period, during which a strong increase in births was noted. Since 1921, the birth rate has decreased steadily, as shown by the following figures:

21.83 per thousand inhabitants, in 1921
20.37 "   "   "   " 1922
20.44 "   "   "   " 1923
19.93 "   "   "   " 1924
19.60 "   "   "   " 1925
18.90 "   "   "   " 1926

The Reverend Ed. De Moreau, S. J., in *Le Catholicisme en Belgique,* writes: "If the figures given for Belgium are unfavorable, that is the fault of the Walloons and of some large cities, even of the Flemish section." The Belgian birth rate as given surpasses the birth rates of Sweden, Switzerland, England, and France, but is inferior to the birth rate of Holland, Spain, Irish Free State, Austria, Portugal, as well as to the birth rate in the United States. An association has been formed to counteract the evils of birth prevention, namely: The League for Large Families. This League holds that large families—that is, families of four or more children—should be provided with resources in proportion to the services they render to society. The League for Large Families has secured a substantial grant of

benefits given by the State in the form of a wage
bonus for each child under eighteen years of age, and
of a notable reduction in federal and municipal taxes.
In many towns, a monetary grant is made to a family
at the birth of a fifth child and children born after
that. The eldest boy in the family of five is now free
from compulsory military service. All members of
the League and their families travel at reduced rates
on railroads, street cars, and buses. A loan may be
extended to members for expenses entailed in special
university studies. Allowances are made to stimulate the publication of any literary work favoring the
objects of the League. The mothers of the large
families are not forgotten. It had become almost
impossible to secure domestics who would be willing
to serve in a family of many children; consequently,
the League organized a service of Hungarian servants
for that purpose. Divorces have risen from 690 in
1900 to 2,503 in 1925. Though we have no definite
statistics on the subject, we may rest assured that
divorce and remarriage after divorce are not to be
found among practical Catholics.

Christian Piety. Since the war, the reception of
the Sacraments has diminished, in varying measure,
in many of the sections of Belgium. In the absence
of accurate statistics, this seems to be especially true
of the industrial sections of the provinces of Hainaut
and of Liége, where Socialism is firmly rooted. It
is not so true of the province of Luxemburg nor of
the Flemish provinces. In these provinces, especially outside of the large cities and some Socialist

centers, the persons who neglect to attend Mass on Sundays and to perform their Easter duties are the exception. For many of these places, daily attendance at Mass and frequent Communion are on the increase. Taken all in all, Belgium is still a strong Catholic country. The Catholic religion is officially recognized by the State: it is the only religion of the Belgian people, with the exception of thirty thousand Protestants and three thousand Jews. The country is studded with beautiful churches, where the bulk of the people worship on Sundays and holy days. On the roadside in the country, it is not unusual to find a life-size Calvary group, reminding people of their Redemption. In the cities, on the corners of the streets, in open niches of private dwellings, statues of the Blessed Virgin and her Divine Son meet the eye of the wayfarer. In city and country, the Holy Viaticum is carried to the sick in the open by the priest in cassock and surplice, preceded by a sexton who carries a lighted lantern and rings a bell. When they pass, housewives open the doors of their homes, kneel down and breathe a prayer, pedestrians kneel on the sidewalks, drivers stop their cars, and detachments of infantry or cavalry present arms. On the Solemnity of Corpus Christi, processions of the Blessed Sacrament, headed by civil and military authorities in uniform, march through the main streets of village and city, amidst clouds of fragrant incense, over pavements strewn with flowers, past homes decorated with flags and displaying little altars in the windows, between rows of kneeling people, and the murmured prayers of the faithful, the singing of religious hymns, the harmonious strains of bands, and the joyous ringing of church bells.

"For the staunch Catholic and the priest," says Father De Moreau, S. J., "it is delightful to visit such regions as the two Flanders, and the provinces of Limburg and Luxemburg, and to witness how God is almost universally honored." The enemies of Catholicism in Belgium recognize its inherent strength, the prodigious development it has given to all its works, and the matchless influence it maintains on the souls of its faithful followers.

II

THE CATHOLIC CHURCH IN CONTEMPORARY ENGLAND

Daniel Sargent

"I do not fear," said the Anglican Archbishop of Canterbury in 1890, "I do not fear that the new Italian Mission will make anything of our clergy and people." This new Italian Mission, of which he spoke, was, of course, none other than the ancient and abiding Catholic Church which during the nineteenth century was reviving in England. Why he spoke of it in these terms of disparagement was obviously that he wished to quiet his own alarm, and that of his friends, at the fancied growth of that "Mission." What added to his inquietude was, no doubt, the uncertainty in which he rested as to the size of the Catholic population of England, an uncertainty which we all still share. The government, taking the census, does not ask a man's religion; and Catholics themselves are so much in the dark, that their own estimates differ sometimes by as much as a million. It is safe to say, however, that after the World War, in 1919, there were in England (including Wales) about two million Catholics; two million Catholics—that is about as many Catholics as there are in the Archdiocese of New York, about

45

one-twentieth of the entire population of England.

Of these Catholics, more than half were of Irish blood—the rest were of English blood; a few were of Cornish or Welsh blood. They were not evenly distributed over England in a thin layer like a geological stratum. Owing to the fact that the English Catholics had been able to preserve their faith only in certain parts of England, and that the Irish immigrants had been able to find work only in certain localities, the Catholics were pocketed here and pocketed there like strange minerals. There was a region in the north, and a region in the southeast, and a region running through Birmingham and connecting them like the handle of a dumb-bell, in which the Catholics were never fewer than one in twenty, and where in some places like Liverpool, they were one in five. In other places like Norfolk and Suffolk, they were but one in a hundred. The Catholics were also not evenly distributed in the various layers of society. They were thickest in the House of Lords, and in the labor unions. In the middle class, particularly the upper middle class, they were most like intruders at a board of respectability, and most scarce.

These Catholics were organized ecclesiastically into seventeen dioceses of which three were archdioceses: Westminster, Liverpool, and Cardiff. The priests in these dioceses were in proportion to the Catholics more numerous than they are in the United States, and the monasteries and convents were not only proportionately more numerous than in the

United States, but absolutely more numerous than in England before the Reformation. Yet the country still had many of the aspects of a missionary country, for there was no corner of England where Catholics and Catholic customs predominated, and the Catholic life was one-sided in that it belonged more to the cities and the suburbs than to the soil. From the intellectual intercourse with the rest of England, the Catholics were separated in theology and philosophy by a difference which corresponds to a difference in language, for the Protestants not only disagreed with Catholics in regard to the supernatural, but they had given up thinking about the supernatural at all, and the revival of an interest in the perennial philosophy had in England, in 1919, not even shown those faint signs of awakening that it does today.

Yet there was a Catholic press, with its two outstanding weeklies, the distinguished *Tablet*, and the alive *Universe*, to go no further; and there were various monthlies conducted by the Religious which had vastly more merit than circulation. Even those who had never heard of the Catholic press could not entirely escape Catholic literature. Novel readers were still bewildered by the novels of Monsignor Benson, who had recently died. Francis Thompson, dead to be sure, had suddenly after death eclipsed all contemporary poets. His poetry, magnificent with Catholic ritual and theology, became religious poetry to thousands who had no religion. Cardinal Gasquet had given some new thoughts to the writers of history, and Hilaire Belloc was beginning that Catholic truculence which insists on, and in the end always receives, a hearing. Catholic talents were in the arts and in literature conspicuous, but, apart from that, in a country no larger than Florida, two million people, even though Catholic, cannot be entirely hid.

There was one thing, however, which kept them from being regarded: the Protestant tradition, that fixed idea which was so penetratingly, and, I might say, pessimistically, diagnosed by Cardinal Newman, and which still like a headache throws a hundred blind-spots into the Englishman's eye. According to it, England is, must be, socially, legally, commercially, Protestant. Hence—so the myth went —her success. In the 1860's—tells Lord Braye— some African chieftains were brought to Windsor Castle and presented with a King James' Bible. "This," said the donor, "is the cause of England's greatness." The absurdity of such a legend cannot guarantee its extinction, and the labors of historians, even of Protestant historians, cannot dethrone it. It owes its longevity not merely to propaganda, but to the short memory of the Englishman, which is so often contrasted with the too long memory of the Irishman. Such a memory still mistakes an ephemeral aberration, Protestantism, for a permanent English characteristic. So the Protestant tradition continues. Can a Catholic become an English gentleman? No, says Dean Inge. Can an Englishman become a saint? Yes, says Santayana, by ceasing

to be an Englishman. The Protestant tradition still,
in 1919, cast a cloud of invisibility about English
Catholics.

During the last ten years events have thinned if
not dispersed this cloud. The first of these events
was a political event: the separation of Ireland from
England. In 1919 eighty-odd Irish Catholics failed
to take their seats in the House of Commons. For
several generations they had protected English Catholics, but from 1919 on they did not return to their
seats, and they could no longer protect. Before that
day an English Catholic, unless proved otherwise,
was an Irishman. After that date an English Catholic was an Englishman.

The second event which helped to tear to shreds
the Protestant tradition was the Black Death which,
after the war, fell on English industry. It was a
disease not only painful, but malignant and alarming. Its symptoms were a constant army of two
million unemployed, and a balance-sheet which
showed that England's trade was bleeding her to
death. If this had been a passing hardship, what of
it? But the malady seemed one which brought an
end to prosperity, a fate like that of Venice.

Protestantism, Prosperity, Progress—these three
—had in the last hundred years in England grown
almost synonymous. Catholic Englishmen had to
apologize for the industrial and commercial backwardness of countries which were not Protestant but
Catholic, as if it were for a spiritual failing. And
they, though Catholics, often missed the point and

tried to explain that such backwardness was due, not to Catholicism but to racial inferiority. But now for the "Nordic" Englishman set in a terrible self-examination, for his land appeared plague-stricken. He could see that the green countryside had become a desert as far as harvests were concerned; that the cities were prisons which no man could leave; that his factories even, which were his boast, were a weight to crush him. Questions came to be asked: Is our industrial civilization really the peak of civilization? Has our evolution during the last three hundred years been all progress? What of the Reformation? What of all civilization? What of Catholic England? What of agricultural countries today, which happen to be Catholic?

The answers to these questions have been various, but one answer has been particularly dominant and ironic. Calvinists, says one school, are responsible for the exaggerated capitalism of the day. Their ethic has brought about overproduction. Their thrift has killed the artisan. Their private gains have brought about public impoverishment. They, Calvinists, whom Carlyle described as the last of the world's heroes, are made culprit of all that is worst in modern civilization. And what adds irony to irony, it is not Catholics who bring this charge, but Protestants, non-conformists in revolt, guild-socialists, socialists, sociologists who care not at all for Catholic dogma. "Protestantism has never been anything but an exotic in England," says Archbishop Goodier. But a bishop's words are heard

only by those who already agree. It is the hard
times and the bitter sociologists who have brought
the news to those who will not hear. The reputation
of the Reformation has become permanently black-
ened, and the change in public opinion is reflected
in the title of C. G. Coulton's latest book, a title
which ten years ago would have been inappropriate
to its readers, namely, *The Defense of the Reformation*.

Then in the new day the Protestant churches
proved inadequate. For a long time they had appeared adequate, because they were adequate to do
all that they had to do—nothing. True, Christian
doctrines were disappearing. True, there were at
least nine million people in England who did not
know what church they belonged to. True, those
who did belong to a church were ceasing to attend
its services. True, on one Sunday before the war,
an Easter Sunday, it was found that only seven per
cent. of the population of London entered a church
door. Nevertheless, the religiosity of the average
Englishman was proof against atheism. And why
be disquieted? Said Father Ronald Knox (*Studies*,
vol. 15, 1926, p. 21): "The Englishman is rather
sorry if he is told that there is no God; it seems
to him that another of the old land-marks is disappearing, and he doesn't want it to disappear."
And the average Englishman had too much sense
of respectability to shock his neighbors by too fla-
grant breaches of private morality. A vague belief
in God, the conduct becoming an Englishman, was

all that the Protestant churches could ask for, and enough to make them content.

But after the war new issues arose. What guidance had the non-conformist churches to offer when Labor was clamoring for a new place? They had good will, their adherents were able, but they could not, as churches, lead. And for the individual, what could they teach him of mysticism, when his curiosity was awakened, when he was being advised even by psychoanalysts to read St. John of the Cross? There were Catholic mystics. Where were the Protestant? And how could these churches defend the belief in God, against the new psychological attack? How could they relate God to the intelligence, when they had reduced God to an emotion? Had they not been established, these churches, in the very "dispraise of philosophy"? And against Freud could they defend morality? They had no authority to command, no logic to defend. And there was a desire here and there among all the sects for a sacramental life, for a means of escape from their mere selves. Could they give that? And the heart of the whole world was crying for unity, a religion above nations—how could they give that? These Protestant churches had been founded for problems of a particular age. That age had vanished.

The Established Church seemed more adequate. It could combat atheism, and demoralization, by social prestige. It could attract those who liked the best in the past ages by its gentility, by its humanistic discipline, by its amenities. Moreover, it was a church which had never wholly lost sight of the sacramental life, and owing to its origin as a compromise, it had always shown a comprehensiveness that looked like unity. Now that the whole world, after the disruption of the war, was thinking of reunion, might not this comprehensiveness serve as the very basis of reuniting Christendom? The English Church was the only one in the world which claimed to be Catholic and Protestant at the same time.

It was the "Prayer-Book" episode which proved the Established Church inadequate. The story is this: During the last half-century the disturbing force in the Established Church had been that party which was enamored of a sacramental religion, which liked to think of itself as Catholic, and was generally called Anglo-Catholic. There were in the Anglican Church about sixteen thousand priests in all, of whom something like four thousand thought of themselves as Catholic, not Protestant. Thus the Anglo-Catholic group was about one-fourth of the entire Anglican Church. This group pleased its bishops for two reasons: it was a string dangled towards Rome. It kept many people who long for a sacramental religion from going to "Rome." But these Anglo-Catholics were obnoxious to their own bishops because their idea of reunion turned its back on the other Protestants, and on the Reformation, and because, what is more immediately disconcerting, they refused to follow the Book of Common Prayer which their bishops had sworn to make them follow. To end this latter difficulty the bishops decided twenty years ago to change the prayer book, and to change the prayer book Parliament's permission had to be received.

In 1927 the nature of a new proposed prayer book was disclosed. It was to be a prayer book with two alternative forms of ritual, either of which might be used. One would be to suit those who considered themselves Protestants, the other for those who considered themselves Catholic: a device quite in keeping with the Anglican concept of comprehensiveness, and also in keeping with the English political system of treating the opposition as a necessary part of the government. On December 4, 1927, the House of Lords, out of respect to the bishops, accepted this new prayer book. On December 15, the House of Commons rejected it. Said Mr. Rossyn Miller: "If the new prayer book is allowed, England will become Catholic in one generation." Mr. Miller represented the extreme Protestant party, and it was that party which killed the measure, but there was something else which helped kill it: distrust of those servants of the state, the Anglican bishops. Sir John Simon pointed out that the bishops were witnesses not to be trusted. The Bishop of London, supporting the measure, had said that the new prayer book gave the Anglo-Catholic party all that it had clamored for for forty years; and the very same Bishop of London, still supporting the measure, said that it did nothing except change some color and emphasis. After the defeat of the prayer-book measure, the Anglican Church was revealed as not comprehensive except by fraud, and not sacramental except by revolt.

Momentous days these in the history of England, days comparable to those after the Black Death, or after the pillage of the monasteries by Henry VIII! In such a time nothing can stand still. A thing must go with the old, or come with the new. The Catholic Church has shown that it is of those things which come with the new. Among the various ways in which it has responded, several are particularly interesting, because peculiarly English. It has protected itself politically without the aid of a Catholic party. It has disseminated the social teaching of Leo XIII and of Pius XI, without causing a breach between reactionaries and reformers; it has, against the spirit of the times, affirmed, taught.

There is no Catholic political party in England. Cardinal Bourne does not want one, and any prophet could see that it would fail. Yet Catholics have at times to act politically, through other parties. For instance, up till 1926, Catholics still suffered from various disabilities. There were laws, unrepealed, though not enforced, which made Catholic charities illegal, and could well have rendered forfeit the property of the Religious Orders. Furthermore, Catholic churches could not have belfries and bells, and Catholic priests could not, legally, appear in public view—even in a cemetery—in their priestly vestments. Through the Conservative Party, through the good offices of an Anglican who introduced a private bill for Catholic relief, these bothersome restrictions were removed. From 1926 on, the Catholics are equal with the Protestants before the law, except that one of them can never be King, or keeper of the King's conscience, Lord Chancellor.

The Catholics have also kept on good terms with the only other party which has ruled since the war, the Labor Party. There have been many Catholic working-men who have voted for the Labor candidates. Some of the Labor candidates have themselves been Catholics. There were of Catholic Laborites seventeen members in the House of Commons during the last Labor Government, and the first Labor Government had a Catholic in its Cabinet. When it came to the bill for Catholic Relief in 1926, several Laborites spoke in favor of it. That Catholics have been able to coöperate with the good intentions, and, more important, with what schemes of the Labor Party are wisest, is a matter of congratulation. It is so much less pernicious than the situation in some countries where the *"right"* means Catholic, the *"left"* means atheist.

But Catholics, however, have not been willing to sell their souls to any political party. Those in the Labor Party have never hidden their opposition to the principles of what few intellectuals there are in that party, who are Marxists or atheists. Fortunately, most of the Labor Party are conservative in matters of religion. Their speeches take on the religiosity of sermons, and Ramsay MacDonald, while he may not compliment Catholics by writing a life of John Knox, which he never finished, yet shows thereby that he is far from being a Combes or a Viviani. There is only one matter in which Catholic Laborites have had to break with their Labor Party. Last year the Labor Party put forth a measure which, while not aimed against Catholic schools, would seriously hurt them, by deflecting a horde of pupils into non-religious schools. The Catholic members of the Labor Party, led by a Mr. Scurr, joined with other Catholics in other parties, and with the Conservative opposition, and by skilfully adding to the measure the so-called "Scurr amendment," brought about its defeat. Two things are important in this episode. Catholics could unite in a common cause even when that cause appeared unpopular. And it turned out that the Labor members who seemed to be jeopardizing their career, won increased respect from the party from which they had bolted.

The economic calamities of England found the Catholics in a favored position, not in their pocketbooks but in their minds, for some of them, like Hilaire Belloc, and the Dominican, Father Vincent McNabb, had prophesied since before the war those very calamities. And Catholic bishops and Catholic clergy, with long Catholic memories, were not at all blind to faults of the days that had gone by, and to which most Protestants wished to return. Said Cardinal Bourne immediately after the Armistice:

The problem to be solved is to find a way of distributing the surplus wealth so that the poor man, manual laborer, or inferior clerk, may have the additional remuneration that he rightly needs; and the rich man no longer receive the heaped-up increment which he in no sense requires and cannot efficiently control. The problem is international, as is the problem of obtaining a just peace. There are in the world two forces: Christianity and Labor, to which will fall in large measure the task of solving these problems. Let these two forces come to a complete understanding and they will be invincible. (Quoted in the *Tablet*, p. 548, vol. 132.)

Said the Jesuit editor of *The Month* a year later: "It follows that all schemes of settlement which contemplate the continuance of the old order with its governing class, bourgeoisie, its proletariat, and only aim of improving the material condition of the worker, are bound to prove wholly inadequate." It was not surprising, then, that those who are not Catholic have not found it strange or inappropriate to follow those who are Catholic, as they have done in taking, for instance, the leadership of G. K. Chesterton in the Distributist League, or that those who are perplexed and discouraged about the destiny of civilization have turned to the eminently sane writings of the Catholic sociologist, Christopher Dawson.

But Catholics, as Catholics, cannot as yet hope to bring soundness to England. They cannot lead. It is not they who will do the immediate reshaping of England. But they have a work which they can do, and that is learning, themselves, and disseminating among others the Catholic principles of social justice.   For just this purpose a far-seeing Jesuit, Father Plater, in 1909 founded the Catholic Social Guild, which, while filled with zeal, limits itself to an educational mission.   Centered at Oxford, this guild now spreads its membership all over England. It works by means of one hundred thirty or more study-groups, many of which have but nine or ten members, but the study is serious; it enriches itself by correspondence within the groups, and by the common use of a circulating library.   Its direct influence is not on a large public, but by its annual publications, and its summer conferences it keeps itself prominent.   Naturally, those who study social problems are inclined to be reformers, so that the charge that the Social Guild leads to discontent and socialism has been made.   At the same time the radicals bring a charge that saves it, namely, that it does not act, raises no banners, marches with no processions.   There is truly a wise discretion behind the Guild.   It does what it can do.   Its good effects will be seen when Catholics, in no matter what party, will be able to distinguish what is anti-Christian in the various socialistic schemes of reform, from what is not.   And another effect can be looked for.   Perhaps among the working-men the Catholics who have profited by the education for public life offered by the Guild may become among their less-lettered neighbors, leaders.   In 1922 the Catholic Social Guild inaugurated at Oxford a Catholic Workers' College.   Its avowed purpose is "the education of

Catholic working-men in apologetics and ethics, and in the social sciences from the standpoint of Catholic principles." The first three students were a textile operator, a sheet-metal worker, and an engine-driver.

The Catholic Church has not retreated as a teacher. It has provided somehow elementary, secondary, and university education for its children. The task is not easy. In 1902 by the Balfour Act it seemed to be made possible for the churches to continue forever their religious schools, side by side with the council schools, which correspond to our public schools. If the various churches built their schoolhouses, the National Educational Board would see to it that funds came to them to pay the teachers, and pay the current expenses. In other words, the Balfour Act was designed to insure the continuance of religious schooling. But the Balfour Act has been inadequate for that. The difficulties and, above all, the expense of providing schoolhouses when the standard of schoolhouses is high, and the cost of schoolhouses higher, have brought about an increase in the council schools at the expense of the voluntary, religious schools. Between 1896 and 1923 the number of pupils in the Anglican schools had dwindled by 600,000, and the number in the non-conformist schools by 400,000. At this rate voluntary schools, if it were not for Catholic schools, would become extinct. During that same period the accommodation in Catholic schools increased by 36,000, a comparative victory, and there are now in the Catholic elementary and secondary schools in England 425,000 pupils; not a small number out of a Catholic population of two million.

But there are no Catholic universities in England, and some Catholics must go to the universities, and some Catholics must go to Oxford and Cambridge, which are supposed to give that education which opens the most doors. It is the duty of the Church to enable the students at these universities to receive not only an education, but a Christian education. To accomplish this there is only one thing to do, to enter into the universities with the students. This is not so dangerous at the newer universities: Liverpool, Sheffield—but it is dangerous at a place like Oxford, where a man receives not only an intellectual but ethical formation. And besides, now Oxford is the world capital of modernism. Its most brilliant partisans are there, and there the characteristic attitude of the student is to admire two conflicting creeds or theories and not choose. Nowhere else in the world is intellectual dilettantism so perfectly charming.

It has been dangerous to go to Oxford. Catholics have gone there. Before the war they were treated with hospitality, and since the war they have been treated with hospitality and interest. Perhaps it is a passing fashion, but for the moment they are looked upon as exemplars of an ethical quality which others do not possess. There are at Oxford now about a hundred and fifty Catholic students, a more negligible minority than Catholics are in England

as a whole. Around the colleges, to make Oxford
safe and to draw what is good from it, have camped
houses of study of the great Catholic Religious Orders which once indeed made Oxford: Benedictines,
Dominicans, and Franciscans. And there are the
Jesuits too, who were the first to establish a house
at Oxford, after the Catholic revival, and who are
intellectually the most conspicuous of the Religious
Orders in England. And here is, also, a Catholic
chaplain, with a newly built chapel. The Catholic
priests at Oxford do not scowl at the Oxford intellect.
They adopt all that is best in it: its brilliance. Some
of them, like Father Martindale, and Father Knox,
the present chaplain, can out-Oxford Oxford. Under
these circumstances the student who is most intellectual has least chance of losing his Faith. To be
seen walking with the Jesuit, Father d'Arcy, helps
one's intellectual reputation. Catholicism has intellectual audacity at Oxford, and not a few of the
young intellects in revolt—like Christopher Hollis—
have become Catholics.

What in our modern, tame days is more extraordinary than Catholics teaching Catholics, is Catholics trying to teach those who are not Catholics, for
such an act assumed that there are not twenty-five
kinds of truth, one for each temperament, but one
truth for no matter how many millions. An Englishman on religious matters may want to learn, but
he does not wish to be taught. For Catholic Englishmen to inform other Englishmen of what they
should believe would be impossible, but those Cath-

olics have found various ways of telling others of what they, Catholics, do believe. Among their devices they have hit upon two which have had a marked success in England. The Catholic Truth Society has developed the art of printing and distributing pamphlets for those people who are too shy to ask questions, and the Catholic Evidence Guild has developed a rare skill in so speaking to the crowds that they learn in spite of themselves. The Catholic Truth Society "is an organization"—so run their words—"of members of the Catholic faith, clerical and lay, men and women, founded to promulgate the truths of the Catholic Religion by means of the written word." It was founded in 1884 largely through the efforts of Mr. James Britten, but it is since the war that it has had its greatest development. It has sold during the last three years about as many pamphlets as it did during its first twenty years. In the year 1930 it sold over a million and a quarter pamphlets. From the rack in Westminster Cathedral, which is the one church most easily visited by those who are not Catholic, it sold in the same year over seventy-five thousand pamphlets. The rack in that cathedral is replenished three times daily. All this has been done not without the greatest care, both in the selection of writers, and in the methods of selling. That the society has made some progress on public opinion is witnessed to by the fact that whereas ten years ago the greatest demand was for pamphlets of controversy, in refutation, for instance, of the calumnies against monks, now the greatest demand is for devotional pamphlets, and the greatest increase in sales is that in pamphlets on Catholic social principles. The pamphlets that sold best in 1930 are—after a prayer book: "The Soviet Campaign against God" (50,000 copies), then the catechism, "The Christian Education of Youth" (28,000), "The Carfin Grotto" (19,000).

The Catholic Evidence Guild has in comparison with the Catholic Truth Society, a very dramatic appearance. To the eye of him who first hears of it, or who has caught sight of its work by circling around it from a respectable distance, it is a corps of ardent haranguers standing upon so-called "perches" over "seas of faces" and turning them all to Catholics by a fiery eloquence. Nothing could be further from the truth. The speakers have low voices, and the most interested listeners usually turn their backs. In fact the Catholic Evidence Guild is interesting only because it is so patient and ordinary, because it does not at all represent a mere lust for speaking. More truly than of the Truth Society it can be said that its work began after the war, for then it took on its expansion, its limitations, and clerical supervision. It became country-wide, and now counts over six hundred speakers, who are two-thirds laymen, and one-third lay-women, one hundred and twenty of whom speak every week. The persons who speak are almost any type of persons except orators, and they are, of course, all of them unpaid volunteers. They go through a training in

Catholic doctrine, and in explaining a part of it in spite of being heckled and in spite of being interrupted by their fellow-speakers. Then they are allowed to speak for twenty minutes on one subject, in some park or by the cobblestones of some square, and then to answer questions on that one subject. While they speak, they do not exhort, they do not assail. They explain. They teach. They teach in monosyllables. They prove when they must prove. Most of all, they show how ultimately desirable would be such a church as the Catholic Church, if such a church existed.

What progress has the Catholic Church made in England towards its goal of goals, the converting of all England? The angels read this progress in terms of the quality of the spiritual life of Catholics: there have been founded during the last twenty years eight new Carmelite convents for women. Vocations for them abound. But we who are not angels look to the grosser data. Every year for the last ten years there have been from ten to twelve thousand conversions, and usually each new year has shown a greater harvest than the last. Among these conversions are annually ten to a dozen which are those of Anglican priests. This trickle always suggests that a dyke may some day give way, and that at least a small part of the Anglo-Catholic group may become truly Catholic in a body. And apart from conversions the Catholic marriages in England do beget more children than other marriages, so that now the Catholic Church which a century ago was baptizing but one in a hundred and twenty of the children born in England, now baptizes one in every twelve. Such is an indication of one sort of progress. But the progress which is ultimately most important is the progress in preparing the minds of Englishmen for future conversion.

To measure such a progress, one can judge somewhat from the words of those who write, and from the demands of those who read. It is startling, the number of literary men who, during the last ten years, have been converted in England—Chesterton at their head. It can be said that their conversion is but a rocket in the sky, that will fade: a mere affair of artistic temperament. But it can also be said that it is a proof that those who care for the fine things in European culture are turning to the Catholic Church for protection. Many writers, too, who give no promise of becoming converts, show that those who write in England have a new, more Continental attitude towards the Church. Says J. Middleton Murry: "Christianity is Christianity at its noblest, truest and most comprehensive, and that is the Catholic Church. If you desire to be a Christian, join it." (See quotation, p. 215, *Essays in Order*.) Of the demands of those who read, it can only be said that the newspapers, which are supposed to have a sense of what the public wants, print much fuller and fairer news of things Catholic than before the war, and a publisher who wishes to sell his books has seen fit to publish one with the title: *Why I Am a Catholic. Why I Am Not a Catholic*.

The great obstacle to the spreading of the Faith in England is not the old Protestant hostility, but the more new mere indifference. It is not that the Englishman bears an ill-will, but that he is ingenuously ignorant. Once it used to be said that every Englishman had his castle. Now the only castle that he has is a spiritual one, which is not a castle at all but a prison. Into that castle not only no Catholic priest can penetrate, but no one who professes to be a spiritual teacher. The contemporary symposiums concerning religious belief recently conducted in the press in England have not shown that the readers want to be led, but rather that the writers want to follow the readers. The only way that an Englishman can learn religious truths is when he learns them unawares, and in order to enable him to learn unawares the Catholic laymen with whom he associates must be steeped in the lore of their Faith. It is not unfair, therefore, to judge of the prospects of the Church in England by the intellectual enterprise of the laity, or by the growing sense of their intellectual responsibility. Hilaire Belloc in his recently published *Essays of a Catholic* has pointed out the need in England of "a more general press with a Catholic spirit about it." This indicates one thing which Catholic laymen have not as yet supplied. But there are numerous evidences of their energy. It is not amiss to mention, for instance, the establishment in 1926 of such a publishing house as Sheed and Ward, not an ecclesiastical publisher, nor a dealer in church goods, but a house such as takes its position with countless other commercial publishers, and simply supplies books which are written by Catholics, and which sees the world neither through provincial-sectarian, nor through pagan, eyes to a general public. Another evidence of the intellectual alertness of the laity, and of the clerical approval thereof, is the recent founding in London of a Catholic Institute for Higher Studies. This Institute, sponsored by the Cardinal Archbishop, and to be attended by the laity, does not sound in its title entirely novel. But practically it will be something of an innovation; a school in Theology, Philosophy, Scripture, and Church History, where the most learned priests in England will not give a smattering, but a thorough discipline, lasting for three years, to men and women, who must do the study for that school outside the hours when they gain their livelihood.

Finally, can we not say that although England is tending to become less externally nationalistic, that her lot is growing more and more to resemble those of her Continental neighbors, that her special industrial advantages are disappearing, yet those of her people who are Catholic are not, therefore, becoming more foreign, more like members of an "Italian Mission." They are becoming more English. And indeed the English Catholics have good title to appear English. What, for instance, could be more English than their models, the English martyrs, more than a hundred of whom have in the last ten years been beatified; those martyrs, one of whom asked for a pipe in order that through its smoke he might regard with pleasure one town in the offing where he should be drawn and quartered, and all of them so ready with laconic wit on the scaffold? Recognized as English by their compatriots, the English Catholics will not only have daily more chance to draw others into their ranks, but in the pacification, and decent disarmament of Christendom, will serve as a valuable link with the Catholics of other countries. One might say that they are extremely necessary to Europe.

III

THE CHURCH IN CONTEMPORARY FRANCE

Charles L. Souvay

Since the close of the war the Church is, according to places, under two different régimes: in the territory of pre-war France, its legal status continues that of the pre-war period; whereas Alsace-Lorraine is still under the régime of the Concordat of 1804.

The territory of pre-war France which alone will detail our attention, may contain some thirty-six million people. Of this number, two to three millions are said to be of foreign origin, mostly Polish and Italian immigrants, who came to supply to agriculture and industry man-power depleted by the war. These we may leave out of consideration. Of the native population a recent survey [1] estimated that twenty-eight to twenty-nine millions should be regarded as "more or less practical Catholics." This estimate appears to me a little optimistic. But *transeat*. It must be added that all the sections of the country are not uniform in point of the proportion of "more or less practical Catholics" to the whole population. A circle of a radius of some

[1] Dassonville: "La France pays de Mission," in *Dossiers de l'Action Populaire,* October 25, 1926.

70

seventy-five miles drawn around Paris would fairly mark off the region where, except in cities, this proportion is the smallest. On the other hand, the North, Britanny, the Central Plateau, French Lorraine and the Alpine country have the highest proportion of practical Catholics.

The condition of the Catholic Church in France during the period with which we are concerned is the function of two distinct causes: the existing status before the war, and the war itself.

In 1877 the anti-clerical party, ousting President MacMahon, got the whip-hand of political power. Faithful to the battle-cry raised by Gambetta from the tribune of the Chamber of Deputies: "Le cléricalisme, voilà l'ennemi," [2] they began at once to carry out relentlessly the execution of their program of dechristianization, hatched and elaborated by Freemasonry during the last years of Napoleon III. By the year 1906, after the passing of the law of separation, a fair portion of the program had coiled around the Church a net of law, the so-called "lay laws," "intangible laws"; and one of the protagonists of the party could intone this proud pæan of victory: "All of us together have been pledged to the work of anti-clericalism and irreligion. We have snatched human conscience from the belief of the hereafter. Together, too, we have with one sweep-

[2] Gambetta was not the originator of this battle-cry; the doubtful honor must go to the obscure Peyrat; but Gambetta launched it so efficaciously that it has become indissolubly linked with his name.

ing gesture extinguished in heaven the light that shall never be rekindled."

With the same consummate cunning which dictated to the Egyptians of old the policy, *Sapienter opprimamus eos*, they first gave their attention to the primary schools, where the bulk of the country's citizenry is formed and is fed notions well-nigh ineradicable. Primary instruction must be lay, gratuitous and obligatory. That it should be gratuitous and obligatory, no one objected. But it must be lay too. Quite a number of the public schools were taught by Brothers and Sisters; these must give place to lay teachers. There were still in the country quite a few school teachers of the good old type, serious, religious, teaching catechism, lending even a helping hand in the church as sextons, chanters or organists, almost lay assistant pastors. They could not easily be retired; but one could be patient, as the passing of years would soon dwindle their numbers. Meantime, they must stop saying prayers and teaching catechism in the school; they must remove such seditious emblems as crucifixes and holy pictures from the walls of the classrooms, and must sever all connection with any kind of church work. At the same time provisions were made that the young graduates of the normal school should be trained in genuine anti-clerical fashion. And here it must be said that the realization has gone beyond the anticipations: for now many years the new brand of lay school teachers, male and female, formed in these schools have been loud atheists, rank materialists, and their associations are hotbeds of the reddest Communism, giving untold trouble to the anti-clerical hand which nursed them. What havoc the *ipse dixit* of such teachers may cause in the minds of the children is scarcely possible to fathom.

The Church authorities were always keenly alive to such a distressing situation. As long as there were Religious communities to supply teachers, Catholic schools were raised wherever the parish resources permitted. But the defenders of the "lay laws" were watching: a timely regulation excluded members of Religious communities, even approved, from teaching in free elementary schools and from certain State examinations and degrees, so that they could never qualify. Yet many who had anticipated the measure were duly qualified; the Catholic schools continued to operate and even to multiply; for, whereas official statistics for 1886 number 11,754 Catholic schools with 907,346 pupils, in 1897, they acknowledge 16,129 schools with a population of 1,477,310; and it is a significant fact that during the trying period 1892-1897 public schools saw a decrease of 90,867 pupils, while Catholic schools counted 65,821 children added to their ranks. This was intolerable to the party. Then came the law of 1901 against the Religious Congregations; 5,643 of their members sought a new home on foreign soil; and, as if the blow this wholesale forced departure dealt to Catholic primary schools was not enough, the ex-seminarian Combes, then at the helm of the vessel of State, by one high-handed stroke of the pen closed some three thousand of these schools.[8] He had not reckoned on the resourcefulness of the Church. Not all the Religious obliged to disperse went into exile. Quite a number chose, or were prevailed upon, to become secularized, and together with a noble phalanx of duly qualified Catholic young men and women devoted to the cause, kept the schools going. In fact during the school year 1910-1911, there were in France 14,428 Catholic schools with 960,712 children, an increase of 130 schools with 26,933 pupils over the preceding year. At the same time, the public schools numbered 71,-491, and had 4,135,886 pupils, 222 more schools and 71,327 more pupils than the year before. The comparison is quite interesting: public schools showed an increase of 3 per 1,000 schools and 17 per 1,000 pupils, whereas Catholic schools increased at the ratio of 9 per 1,000 schools and 28 per 1,000 pupils. No mean achievement of Catholic zeal and generosity when all the difficulties besetting the financing of the schools and the recruiting of teachers are borne in mind. The progress continued until the war. While there was reason for gratification, still the fact was that for the last forty years half a million boys and girls were every year entering life with no other antidote than that which a weekly hour or two of catechism for one or two years could furnish against the poisonous notions

[8] In all, 5,000 Catholic schools, with a population of 400,000 children (round numbers, of course) were closed, either as the result of the law of 1901 or by decree.

imbibed in the public schools. In view of this fact
there should have been in 1914, all told, scarcely
seven to eight million practical Catholics. Whence
is it that there were at the very least three times
that many?

Two causes account for this: the one paramount
and self-evident, upon which I shall not expatiate,
the untiring zeal of the priests, who, all things often
said to the contrary notwithstanding, did not remain
cooped up in their sacristies to bemoan in despond-
ent solitude the evils of the times; the other, example, or if you prefer, leadership. In times gone by
it used to be said: *Regis ad exemplar totus com-
ponitur orbis.* In our democratic societies, the higher
classes are setting the pace; and despite the mount-
ing of leveling socialism, the rank and file always
did, and do, and will look up, and strive to imitate
those higher up. But it is a well-known social law
that they are lumbering along, lagging fifty years
and more behind their models. Up to almost the
end of the last century, skepticism and Voltairianism
were the fashion among the French bourgeois class;
Musset's *Confessions d'un Enfant du Siècle,* and
Ozanam's letters vouchsafe to us very significant
information on the college and university life of
their time. The people were still fairly religious.
But turn to the close of the century; you find inside
and outside State lyceums and universities men of
the stamp of Brunetière, Ollé-Laprune, Fonsegrive,
Paul Bourget, René Bazin whose sincerity appealed
to intelligent and fair-minded youth. Their disciples

in 1914 were already legion in every profession; leavening the paste saturated with the pseudo-science of the belated "primaires."

Most unfair would it be to omit the part played by Catholic colleges [4] in this revival of Catholic sentiment in the *bourgeois* class before the war. Figures again tell the story. In 1900, Catholic colleges had an attendance of 91,140 pupils, 6,668 more than the State institutions; the law of 1901 against Religious Congregations caused a loss of 104 colleges, numbering 22,223 pupils; but at the time the war broke out the Catholic colleges were again practically on a par with State colleges. The significance of this fact cannot escape anyone. It meant, of course, great monetary sacrifices on the part of the Catholic parents, and also on the part of the Catholic teachers accepting courageously to serve in these institutions for a mere pittance; it meant likewise sacrifices to be anticipated by the pupils themselves, to whom (and they knew it) positions in the civil service were denied or made almost impossible of access, simply because they had made their studies in a Catholic college. Sacrifices like these show the mettle of these men, young and old.

The hard uphill work of these colleges was worthily crowned by that of the five Catholic Institutes

---

[4] The word *Collège* as used in France means an educational institution different from the American college: the course extends over eight years; it follows the primary grades and generally leads to the State examination for the Bachelor's degree. In the Arts department, the culmination is the class of philosophy. No doubt, the thorough study of philosophy is accountable for the change of mental attitude of the bourgeois in regard to religion.

of Paris, Lyons, Angers, Lille, and Tolouse—Catholic Institutes we call them, for the law of 1880 forbade them to assume the title of universities, and took from them the power of conferring degrees. Upon them devolved the duty of training professors for the colleges and seminaries, an élite of laymen creditably filling high positions, nay even an élite of Catholic women. Should I need mention here that the science of experimental phonetics, and the discovery of the principle of wireless telegraphy came from the laboratories of two professors of the Catholic Institute of Paris, Father Rousselot and Professor Branly; and that the highest scientific bodies of France and other countries deemed it an honor to call into their ranks many professors of the Catholic Institutes?

The program of dechristianizing carried out by the anti-clericals culminated in the law of December 9, 1905. This law, sponsored by the then prime minister, Emile Combes, an ex-seminarian—*corruptio optimi pessima*—and reported by Aristide Briand, of whom we hear so much nowadays,[5] recognized no longer the Catholic religion as the religion of the majority of the French people; the so-called salaries of pastors, bishops, and archbishops were denied them.[6] Churches, rectories, episcopal residences and

[5] This was written before the death of Briand, in March, 1932.
[6] Pastors received a yearly salary of $160 or $240 according as they were movable or irremovable, bishops $2,000 and archbishops $3,000. Be it remembered these salaries, totaling about $8,000,000 a year, were in reality an interest of about one per cent on the Church's property lost during the Revolution, and had been repeatedly declared by civil authority intangible and a debt

seminaries were declared "to be and to remain the property of the State, Department, or town," as the case happened to be, but they might "be put gratuitously at the disposal of the Associations of Worship" [7] to be formed. Ill-treatment, confiscation, the Church can stand and has stood often enough in the past; but to dispositions contrary to her divine constitution she has but one answer since St. Peter: *Non possumus*. Of this nature were the dispositions regarding the Associations of Worship, in which all ecclesiastical jurisdiction was ignored. And the lawmakers who introduced these dispositions were perfectly aware of the inacceptable implication: for the remark being made in the Senate that they aimed at destroying the lawful and necessary authority of the hierarchy, "That is just what we want!" was the reply shouted from the left. No wonder, therefore, that on being asked whether the French Catholics could form Associations of Worship as defined by the law, Pius X, with his eyes fully open to the consequences, emphatically answered in the negative. Full well can we, of America, appreciate his answer: we have not forgotten Trusteeism; the Associations of Worship were nothing else than an aggravated form of Trusteeism. It is a matter of record, that in the face of the privations which the papal pronouncement implied, and despite the fact that before

of justice. Their suppression was, therefore, downright confiscation.

[7] The churches without time limit, except in some specified cases (Art. 13); archbishops' and bishops' residences for two years; rectories and seminaries for five years (Art. 14).

all the implications of the law had been fully studied, the majority of bishops and scores of prominent laymen had recommended compliance, the French clergy obeyed the pontiff with practical unanimity —indeed the exceptions could be counted on the fingers of one hand.[8]

Other vexatious provisions of the law, especially those under the title "Police of Worship" might be mentioned, but what's the use? What has been said is sufficient to show the precarious condition of the Church under the law: deprived of its income—still *plaie d'argent n'est pas mortelle*—deprived of its church residences and seminaries, and refusing to form Associations of Worship that might at least have secured the use of the sacred edifices. By the *denier du culte* the Catholics assured to priests and bishops a pittance, paid for the rent of other residences, without prejudice to what they were already paying for the support of their schools.

The priests ignored the law and in contravention of it continued to officiate in their churches. Where the local authorities were well disposed no objection was made, nay even they concurred in the breach of the law. But such was not the case everywhere, and here and there at the beginning there were some molestations. As, however, with the strong support

[8] One of the recusants, personally known to the writer, was a good and pious priest of rather mediocre talent, a royalist dyed in the wool, who had manifested from school days marked proclivity towards odd opinions (*e. g.* the claims of Naundorff to be Louis XVII), with a meek stubbornness which made him impervious to any argument. Why such a *tête fêlée* should have been allowed to reach the priesthood, has always been a puzzle to his former schoolmates.

of Catholic sentiment, the law was everywhere publicly disregarded, opposition had to cease, and the most fiery local tyrants could but grit their teeth in impotent silence. True, in 1907, a *modus vivendi* based on the law of the Associations was drafted by Briand which could have been acceptable to the Holy See; but once more the anti-clerical opposition sent it to the limbo of abortive laws. If anyone should regard the situation resulting from the inapplication of the law as at least a partial victory for the Catholic Church, let him remember this: the priest or his parish could do nothing for their churches in need of repairs, and if the structure became unsafe, it was promptly condemned by public authority. Then again as long as the law remained on the statute book, its application depended after all, on the ebb and flow of politics, the most uncertain of uncertainties.

I have not deemed it necessary, in this rapid endeavor to describe the stifling atmosphere in which the Church of France was plunged when the war broke out, to rehearse the long series of hostile laws and decrees which made that atmosphere so oppressive; but one question must be asked presently: what were the reactions of the Roman authorities to these hostile measures, and what were the relations of the papacy with the government so openly bent on "crushing the sprinkler," to use the picturesque, if inelegant anti-clerical expression?

At the time of Gambetta's flinging of the gauntlet,

Leo XIII had just sat on the Chair of Peter. He
had a long experience in pontifical diplomacy, and
at first adopted the wise policy of watchful waiting.
It was not long before he discovered that anti-clericalism was making capital of the notion that French
Catholics were systematically allied to the anti-
republican parties; they were either legitimists, supporting the claims of the Count of Chambord to
the throne;[9] or Orleanists, favoring the Count of
Paris; or Bonapartists, advocates of Prince Napoleon Victor, grandson of Jerome Bonaparte; but
very few, if any, cared to, or dared declare themselves for the republican régime. To dissociate
French Catholics from these political affiliations
would take the prop from under anti-clerical pretense; let the Catholics declare themselves loyal
republicans before the electorate; once they were
in the house in sufficient numbers, the law-making
machine would cease to grind anti-clerical statutes.
We are in 1890, just on the morrow of the passing
of the law impressing seminarians and priests in the
army. First by his approval of Jacques Piou's efforts to unite the elements of a Catholic Republican
group in the Chamber of Deputies, then by the
mouth of Cardinal Lavigerie, Archbishop of Algiers,

[9] The Count of Chambord, grandson of Charles X, died on
August 20, 1883. As he left no issue, the legitimist party had
no longer any *raison d'être*, and rallied to the cause of the Count
of Paris, the grandson of Louis Philip I, standard bearer of the
Orleanist party. A reconciliation of the two branches of the royal
dynasty had already been effected in 1873. (Cf. Leopold de Gail-
lard, "Les Parties et la Monarchie en 1884," *Correspondant*, May
25, 1884.)

in his epoch-making toast of October 27, 1890, then solemnly by his Encyclical of February 16, 1892, to the archbishops, bishops, clergy and Catholics of France, Leo XIII launched his idea of the *Ralliement*.

The enemy was at first utterly disconcerted by this master stroke and his tactics ill concealed the fright which had actually seized him. Doubts were cast upon the sincerity of the *ralliés* who, it was said, obviously wanted to get in in order to overthrow the Republic. Recent or actual events gave semblance of truth to this contention. Not to speak of the gullibility displayed by the Catholic masses at the time of Leo Taxil's pretended disclosures of the nature and work of Freemasonry, had not many Catholics mixed themselves up in the ridiculous Boulanger affair (1888)? Did not millions of them send messages of congratulation to the Duke of Orleans incarcerated at Clairvaux after his spectacular attempt to enlist in the French army (March 1890)? Later on, their attitude in the Dreyfus affair (1898), and in the childish Déroulède plot (February 23, 1899) was grist for the anti-clerical mill. Why is it, that in spite of the noble sacrifice of not a few, to the many, even among the leaders, the Pontiff's advice was *vox clamantis in deserto?* Had that voice been heeded, the next page of French Catholic history would have borne a different aspect.

Leo XIII never swerved from the direction he had given to French Catholics, and in his relations with France's government went out of his way to promote peace.[10]   But he could be uncompromising when a matter of principle was at stake.   In 1902 Combes pretended to impose upon the Holy See the appointment of bishops and refused to accept bulls until the word *Nobis* was expunged from the formula *Te quem præses Reipublicæ Nobis nominavit*.   In the name of the Pontiff, Cardinal Rampolla replied that the Pope could not accede to the Minister's demands.   The Sees were not filled, nor were in consequence during several years, filled any vacancies which occurred in the episcopal body.

On July 20, 1903, Leo XIII breathed his last. "The Pope is gone; Mr. Combes remains: this alone matters."   This cynical funeral oration made by Clemenceau, was all too true.   Pius X, in the first two months of his pontificate, saw the ex-seminarian Combes at his pet work of expelling from their convents 40,000 nuns.   The saintly Pontiff could then but pray and grieve, and as long as possible, exer-

---

[10] So for instance in 1899-1900, the Congregation of the Assumptionists was dissolved; while declaring himself painfully affected by the rigorous measure and saddened by the attitude openly taken against Religious Congregations, "he was not less outspoken in his disapproval of the manifestations in favor of the Assumptionists." (*Univers, Temps,* January 28, 1900.) Two months later, March 23, 1900, when the laws disbarring from public service all candidates who had not made the last three years of their studies in State Colleges, and that against the Congregations were looming up above the horizon, Leo XIII appealed personally, but in vain, to President Loubet, in favor of religious peace. Less than two weeks after, when Waldeck-Rousseau enjoined the members of unauthorized Congregations from preaching, the Holy See without delay entered a protest.

cise the same longanimity as had been displayed
by his predecessor.[11]

Even the uncivil and brutal ejection of his nuncio
from France in 1904, and the breaking of diplomatic
relations with that country, though protested against,
were suffered in patience and so was the "historical
lie," often repeated by the men in power, that Rome
was responsible for the separation. Only a *White
Book* published by the Vatican after the vote of
the law of Separation reëstablished the truth.
However,

> *Sunt certi denique fines*
> *Quos ultra utraque nequit consistere rectum.*

The law of 1905 had reached that limit; the encyclical *Gravissimo officio* of August 10, 1906, was the
Pope's verdict on the schismatic provisions regarding
the Worship Associations. And when, in December,
1906, the impulsive "Tiger," Clemenceau,[12] had
Monsignor Montagnini, the former secretary of the
nuncio, arrested and deported from France, his house
searched by the police, and a careful selection of

[11] The law of 1901 had left untouched authorized Congregations. Among them were in particular the Christian Brothers,
and the Daughters of Charity, who continued to teach in Catholic
schools. This was a bad breach left open in the citadel of the
lay laws, which Combes in assuming power, had sworn to fill.
In the fall of 1903 the draft of a new law framed to obtain the
desired end was ready for discussion. On the 2nd of December
Pius X, in a letter to President Loubet, deplored the expulsions
accomplished, and protested in the name of religion and "of the
principles of liberty and equality upon which modern constitutions
are founded" against the law contemplated. This elicited from
the president but a disingenuous answer. (Letter of February
27, 1904. *White Book of the Holy See.*)
[12] He had come into power some months before.

his papers published, Pius X could do no less than denounce this intolerable breach of international law.[13] No wonder that the Pope who at first had strongly recommended to the French Catholics the *ralliement* advocated by his predecessor, departed somewhat from that policy,[14] and speaking to a group of French pilgrims upon the solemn occasion of the beatification of Joan of Arc (April, 1909), asked them to unite themselves on the only platform now possible, that of the vindication of religious rights, and not on this or that constitution.[15]

To the clouds amassed by the enemies of the Church there was a silver lining: the Holy See had now a free hand in the choice of the French bishops. Everyone remembers the scene at the Vatican when Pius X consecrated a number of them for the Sees which had remained vacant since 1902.   That in the following years candidates with more or less royalist sympathies were raised to the purple, is not to be wondered at, after his change of heart towards the *ralliement*.

The beginning of the twentieth century witnessed an unprecedented revival of ecclesiastical scholarship among the French clergy, particularly in the fields of positive theology, biblical exegesis and Church history. "No French priest will rest satisfied until he writes at least one book," one of our

[13] *Quinzaine, Chronique politique,* January, 1907; *Correspondant, Chronique politique,* April 25, 1907.
[14] *Mémoires du Cardinal Ferrata,* II, p. 24.
[15] Jacques Rocaford, *Les résistances à la politique religieuse de Pie X,* Paris, 1920.

American priests used to say facetiously. New wine is always fraught with danger. This was led by a priest of great literary talent and wide erudition, whose influence soon became considerable, the Abbé Loisy; and also in a lesser degree, but with a viciousness truly incomprehensible in a man of his calling, and which has been completely uncovered but lately,[16] namely by the Abbé Joseph Turmel. Dazzled by their brilliancy, the Abbé Bricout welcomed imprudently their contributions in the *Revue du Clergé Français*, of which he was the editor, and which was widely read by the French clergy, eager to keep abreast of the times. Soon, however, to the new wine was added in carefully measured, but constantly increasing doses, the poisonous drugs of rash affirmations sapping the foundations and perverting the notions of Christian dogma. This compound of errors is well known to us under the name of Modernism.[17] Something had to be done to stop

[16] Louis Saltet, *La Question Herzog-Dupin*, Paris, 1908; "La suite des Pseudonymes de M. J. Turmel," in *Bulletin de Littérature Ecclésiastique*, 1929, pp. 83-90, 104-125; "L'Oeuvre Théologique Pseudonyme de M. l'Abbé J. Turmel," do. pp. 165-182; "L'Oeuvre Pseudonyme et le Silence de M. J. Turmel," do. pp. 213-223; "Le Silence de MM. P. L. Couchoud, R. Dussaud, et A. Loisy sur M. J. Turmel," do. 1930, pp. 31-36; "Jugement prononcé par S. S. le Card. Archev. de Rennes sur les imputations portées contre M. l'Abbé Joseph A. Turmel," do. 36-40; "Supplément Théologique aux Supercheries Littéraires dévoilées de M. J. Querard," do. pp. 87-96; 124-141; "Robert Lawson- Turmel et la Revue du Clergé Français," do. pp. 151-157; "Supremae S. Cong. S. O. Decretum quo Sac. Joseph Turmel Excommunicatus vitandus declaratur et ejus opera in Indicem Librorum prohibitorium inseruntur" (Nov. 8, 1930), *Acta Apostolicae Sedis*, 1930, pp. 517-520.

[17] Modernism was by no means confined to France. The names of G. Tyrrell, S. Minocchi, E. Buonaiuti and the movement of the *Reformkatholizismus* are sufficient evidence; it is even a question

the evil.   On the 17th of July, 1907, appeared in the *Osservatore Romano* the Decree *Lamentabili*.[18]

Almost to a man, those priests and laymen who, through misguided zeal and imprudence, had partaken of the drugged wine, rallied at once to the standard of pure orthodoxy.   The *Revue du Clergé Français* signified without delay [19] its full and loyal submission.   If here and there some mutterings of dissatisfaction were still heard, they found no echo. Only Loisy, as might be anticipated, remained obdurate.   After a great deal of recrimination and quibbling, on the 19th of January, and again on the 28th of February, 1908, he formally refused to submit.   On March 7th he was declared *excommunicatus vitandus*.   Since then he seems to have lost the last vestige of true criticism; his extreme rationalistic method and subjectivist views excite but a pitying shrug of the shoulders in scholarly circles.

Like all reactions, the reaction against Modernism perhaps went too far.   There were men haunted with the ghost of Modernism, who saw it everywhere and assailed Rome with wholesale denunciations,[20]

whether it was distinctly a French product. Pope Pius X, it is true, spoke of Modernism as *il morbo gallico della Chiesa;* however strong these words, they do not settle the matter of its origin; they intimate at most its wide spread in France. See Jean Rivière: *Le Modernisme dans l'Eglise,* Paris, 1929.

[18] On the part taken by the French theologians and ecclesiastical authorities in the elaboration of this decree, see Paul Dudon, "Origines Françaises du décret Lamentabili" (1903-1907), in *Bulletin de Littérature Ecclésiastique,* 1931, pp. 73-96.

[19] Nos. of August 4, 1907, pp. 225-232 and October 1, pp. 5-16.

[20] In this connection Count Sforza relates *con gusto* a little story, of which, of course, we must leave him the responsibility. The day after his election, Benedict XV found on his desk all the

with the result that scientific research in matters ecclesiastical was regarded by some as too dangerous to pursue, and that it was safer to practise the *altiora te ne quaesieris.*[21]

papers marked "reserved to the Holy Father" which had piled up during the agony of Pius X up to the close of the conclave. Among these papers was a long letter to the late Pontiff written by Monsignor Pellizzari, Bishop of Piacenza, near Bologna, containing a regular denunciation of Cardinal Della Chiesa, "suspected of Modernism." (Count Sforza: *Les Bâtisseurs de l'Europe moderne.* 3rd ed., Paris, 1931, p. 132.)

[21] Archbishop Mignot of Albi sounded the alarm in a memorandum addressed in October, 1914, to Cardinal Ferrata, Secretary of State during the first month of Benedict XV's pontificate: "It is beyond doubt that certain tendencies had become a danger to the faith. It was imperative they should be energetically curbed, as they were . . . But were there not, on the part of the subordinates any exaggerations in the mode of effecting that doctrinal reaction? That sometimes too the impression was conveyed that an opposition to disinterested and honest research was meant, is undeniable. As a consequence everywhere thinkers and scholars have become estranged from us. The Church has lost some of the prestige which it enjoyed under Leo XIII. In its bosom itself discouragement has seized a number of the intellectual or social workers. Denounced, tracked down and vilified by the press of an occult power, suspected by those who, misled by false reports, doubted at times their upright intention, their task had become difficult. Many withdrew forever from the lists, who might have fought useful battles for the triumph of the Christian cause. This uneasiness was unfortunately felt in many theological seminaries, in religious scholasticates, in university centers. Upon this the testimonies gathered are unanimous. Our young men have no longer the sacred fire of intellectual work, and it is well-nigh impossible for the professors to rekindle it. There was, I grant, a craze for the study of apologetics, of exegesis, of positive theology, of philosophy and sociology; now the trend is towards emasculated study and textbook theology. Inborn sloth is, of course, accountable in part for this attitude; but more so in not a few the calculation that this attitude makes their future more secure, and serves better their personal ambition. These dispositions, should they continue, are preparing us an inferior clergy, making more of the externals of worship than of the spiritual relations of interior religion. They will understand neither the intellectual and moral problems confronting them, nor the movement of ideas, to the great detriment of the Church. They will remain at a standstill in the midst of a world which goes forward, the path of which they should illumine. Neither their intellects nor their hearts will seem open to those who, being beset by doubts, would

August, 1914, "Wars and rumors of wars." And amidst the first roar of battles, the cry: "The Pope is dead!" In France, and elsewhere, it was commonly said that Pius X had died of a broken heart, on seeing his powerlessness to stop the catastrophe. This does not appear to be altogether true.[22] Nor is there any particle of truth in the view, widely spread in France that Pius X's successor, Benedict XV was in favor of the Austro-German empires,[23] and hoping for their victory. His note of August 1, 1917, "Aux Chefs des Peuples Belligérants," [24] advocating a peace without victory, increased this impression, due to a total misunderstanding of his aims and of his intentions.

At home, the war proved a powerful check to the continuation of the anti-clerical program. From all parts of the country, the priests subject to military service had unhesitatingly responded to the call of arms; from foreign lands and from missionary countries, Religious, both priests and brothers, had come

have so much need of their guidance." (*Le Mouvement,* May, 1924.)

[22] "I have it from his physician, Marchiafava, my colleague in the Italian Senate, that the disease which carried away the Pope had for many months undermined his constitution, and that the overwork of the last weeks at most accelerated the issue, which he, Marchiafava, had already declared to be inevitable and soon to be expected" (Count Sforza, *Les Bâtisseurs de l'Europe moderne,* 3rd ed., Paris, 1931, p. 127.)

[23] His election had been looked upon with distrust in Vienna and Berlin, as he was regarded as having been all along hand in glove with Cardinal Rampolla, whose election in 1904 Emperor Francis Joseph vetoed. It was not a palinode which dictated to him these words, in 1920, addressed to a group of French war widows: "We regret to be French only in heart, and not by birth. But such is the sincerity with which we are French in heart, that today we share fully in the joy of all native Frenchmen."

[24] *Acta Apostolicae Sedis,* 1917, pp. 417-420.

back to join the colors;[25] and side by side with their fellow countrymen, a great many of whom then learned to know them better, they gave excellent account of themselves. Many priests too old for service in the ranks enlisted as chaplains. In the face of the fatherland's peril, all efforts were knit together in the *Union Sacrée*. The government remembered the powerful moral influence wielded by the bishops, and showed them a consideration to which they were no longer accustomed; they were officially invited to join committees formed for procuring resources for various works rendered necessary by the war; official appeal was made to them to urge their diocesans to subscribe to the war loans; in official ceremonies they were given a seat with the civil authorities.

Extreme anti-clericalism, however, stubbornly refused to lay down arms, to accept the truce of the *Union Sacrée*. To its unquenchable hatred of anything Catholic is due the spread of the *rumeur infâme* and the malicious move to incorporate into the regular military units of the line priests who by law had been assigned to ambulance or hospital service. But this was but a rift on the otherwise peaceful sea of the union which had been created by the unprecedented cataclysm, and was bidding fair to be the harbinger of better days.

[25] The conduct of all, seculars and Religious, was severely criticized and condemned by many non-French Catholics, perhaps "more Catholic than the Church." These well-meaning critics did not realize that their blame really fell upon the bishops, higher religious superiors, and the Pope himself. We have not to enter here into the theological and canonical questions involved.

May it be said that this hope was not disappointed? To expect that, once peace had been restored, the union would persevere in its original fervor, and that the Church and the government would again walk arm in arm as lovers happily reconciled after a quarrel would be to forget the existing conditions. Loud-mouthed anti-clericals did not forget those conditions, and never ceased to urge the full application of the "lay laws." On the other hand, Clemenceau's words of November 15, 1919, about "the legitimate rights of religious liberty," proved that not only "the Tiger" had filed his claws, but also something was changed in France.

In March, 1920, the French government took the initiative of an attempt to restore diplomatic relations with the Vatican. Mr. John Doulcet, entrusted with the delicate commission, was *persona grata* in Rome.[26] On the delicate point of the Associations of Worship, the views of the French government as explained by its spokesman were such that the Congregation of Extraordinary Ecclesiastical Affairs declared that the Associations could be tolerated. But before a definite agreement was concluded, the French cardinals, archbishops and bishops assembled in Rome for the canonization of Joan of Arc, drew up a memorandum to the Holy Father stating

---

[26] The spokesman for the Vatican was naturally the Secretary of State, Cardinal Gasparri, exceptionally well versed in French affairs since he had been for a number of years professor of canon law in the Catholic Institute of Paris.

they were "unanimous in their respectful resistance." [27]   Why and whence this *coup de théâtre?*
The agreement of the memorandum with the tactics
of the *Action Française,* that it was better that the
resuming of diplomatic relations with the Vatican
should fail rather than that it should lose the appearance of a clerical victory, leaves little doubt
as to the spirit prompting the episcopal document.
Thanks to the exertions of the Bishop of Nice, the
conversations were resumed the following year, and
terminated in a tacit understanding, pending a formal agreement to be concluded, on the matter of the
Associations of Worship.   In the meantime the government had obtained for the reëstablishment of the
Vatican embassy the favorable vote of the Chamber
of Deputies, overriding the obstruction of the Senate
committee whose majority [28] had voted the postpone-
ment of the project.   It appointed an ambassador in
May, 1921.

On February 5, 1922, Pius XI ascended the Chair
of Peter.   To the matter of the Associations of Worship, left in abeyance, he soon turned his attention,
gathering from the French cardinals and bishops
and from other sources the information which he
deemed opportune.[29]   What the opinion of some
French prelates was, may be surmised from their

[27] Jules Delahaye, *La reprise des relations diplomatiques avec le
Vatican,* Paris, 1921, pp. 167-179; Msgr. Chapon, *L'Eglise de
France et la Loi de 1905,* Paris, 1921.
[28] Of two votes.
[29] *Osservatore Romano,* Jan. 23, 1924.

action of two years before.[30]   At any rate Pius XI likes to study for himself every important matter; and so during the month of July he reserved the question to his personal consideration.   Eighteen months later, President Millerand must have had some intimation of the conclusion arrived at by Pius XI, for in his answer to the New Year good wishes tendered to him by Msgr. Ceretti, the papal nuncio, in the name of the diplomatic corps, he hailed "the dawn of reconcilation and peace." [31]

Indeed, on January 18, 1924, the Encyclical *Maximam* [32] made known to the French hierarchy and to their people the pontifical decision.   Diocesan associations formed according to statutes annexed to the encyclical may be permitted at least by way of trial.   These statutes, which are not based directly on the law of 1905, are in conformity not only with canon law, but with French civil law, as was unanimously declared by the Council of State.   Thus a juridical status is given to the Church, which since 1906 was legally a nonentity, incapable consequently, among other things, of owning, renting or administering any kind of goods, movable or immovable.

Soon, however, it looked as though the "reconciliation and peace" announced by Millerand were to be nipped in the bud.   The election of May 11 returned to power a radical-socialist and communist legislature.   On June 17, Herriot, the new Prime Minister,

[30] Certain ideas expressed in the Encyclical *Maximam* can be traced unmistakably back to these opinions.

[31] *Correspondant*, Jan. 10, 1924, p. 182.

[32] *Acta Apostolicae Sedis*, 1924, pp. 5-24.

pledged himself to put again in vigor the laws of persecution, to suppress once more the embassy to the Vatican and to work with might and main for the monopoly of the public schools. He was forgetting that the war had brought a change in the public spirit, that the Catholic men of 1924 had learned to assert themselves, that the association with staunch Catholic young men and priests in the trenches had torn prejudices out of the minds, and hatred out of the hearts of many who did not know better, before that experience. The Home Secretary had ordered an investigation on the return of the Religious Congregations. Those of their members who had fought in the war grouped themselves, rose up bravely, and adapting a word now historical, said, to the applause of the majority of the people: "We shall not go!" And they did not go, for the government did not dare to put out of France those who had fought for France. Everywhere meetings of Catholic men, sometimes running into thousands, and often presided over by distinguished Catholic military leaders, protested against the measures announced by the government. Herriot's grand program fell through.

The fantastic drop of the rate of exchange, *la débâcle du franc,* caused the downfall of his ministry. Since then conditions seem to be very much what they were before his coming to power. This does not mean that anti-clericalism has disarmed. On the morrow of the law of separation a socialistic paper said openly:

The fight is only commencing . . . The question of the State monopoly of education has been now studied for years. It is ripe, and it is a duty for free-thinkers to obtain of the future republican representatives pledges that they would introduce it in their program.

Here and there along the line the relative quiet is broken by an advance shot, which forces upon one the conviction that the battle will not be delayed very long. What will be the issue?

Playing the prophet is always a dangerous game. Safer it is to play the historian. Have to this day the French Catholics opposed a united front to the attacks to which they were subjected? Unfortunately no! We have had several occasions of noticing it. Why not? Here a word on the *Action Française* is in order.

What is the *Action Française?* Essentially a political movement bent on overthrowing by all means, lawful or unlawful, the republican régime. Its founder and recognized head, Maurras, is a man without religion, and who, judging from his books, has long since flung Christian morals to the winds. The existence of God he rejects, and, of course, the divinity of Jesus Christ and His teachings in the Gospel; while at the same time by a strange somersault of common sense and distortion of history he extols to the skies the Catholic Church because of the strong social spirit and principle of authority which, he says, it inherited from imperial Rome, and is antagonistic to the anarchy taught by the Gospel.

How is it that the league, founded under such a leader, soon met the support, or at least the sympathy of untold members of the French clergy and of the hierarchy? To begin with, let us notice that not a sentence in the review or the paper edited by Maurras ever betrayed his anti-Christian sentiments. He affected there, on the contrary, the strictest orthodoxy, swore by St. Thomas and the *Syllabus*, and gave warning that a number of his books should not be read by Catholics. Then let us remember the league was born in the opening of the twentieth century. It was the time of the elaboration of the "abominable lay laws"; Maurras' militant attitude naturally made a strong appeal to the victims; it was the time of the spread of Modernism; Maurras' militant orthodoxy in his review or his paper delighted the "integrists," as were called those of the extreme anti-modernist wing, more Catholic than the Church. They took him to their heart and so the *Action Française* and the integrist movement joined hands; and as the integrist movement had in Rome many strong advocates, enjoying the confidence of Pius X, it is not surprising that the Pope manifested towards Maurras a certain indulgent partiality. That there was a relation of cause to effect between this favor and the new policy of the Holy See in regard to the *ralliement,* cannot be affirmed; but certainly Maurras was by no means *un bel difensore della fede.*[33]

[33] This word of high appreciation is so well authenticated that it is impossible to deny or even doubt it was pronounced (Maurras: *L'Action Française et le Vatican,* p. 144; Camille Bellaigue:

Some bishops,[34] however, who were neither royalists nor integrists, were viewing with alarm the growing influence of the *Action Française* and its protagonist. Several of Maurras' books, which he declared ought not to be read by Catholics, were denounced to the Congregation of the Index. On the report of Cardinal Van Rossum they were proscribed by a decree dated January 29, 1914. For motives of expediency, Pius X, who had approved the condemnation, decided to postpone its publication until circumstances would make it necessary.

Pius X died the following August. A long letter of the Archbishop of Albi in October to the Secretary of State voiced the anxiety felt by a few prelates over the increasing evils. Whether as a result of this letter or of other information, Benedict XV declared emphatically that he did not wish to hear any more about "integrism," and in the spring of 1915 took up again the matter of *Action Française*. No decision followed for fear that amidst the turmoil of the war, the Holy See's action should be misinterpreted. Benedict XV did not go down to the tomb however without ordering the dissolution of Monsignor U. Benigni's *sodalitium pianum* which, through its branches in Italy, France, Belgium, Ger-

Pie X et Rome, p. 310; Letter of September 18, 1926, to the *Rappel* of Charleroi). This is a case where "a respectful appeal from the pope ill informed to the pope better informed" was in order.

[34] Among them Bishop Péchenard of Soissons, former Rector of the Catholic Institute of Paris; Archbishop Mignot of Albi; Bishop Chapon of Nice; Bishop Catteau of Luçon, and Bishop Guillibert of Fréjus (Memorandum of December 17, 1913).

many and Austria had become under the preceding pontificate a mighty hunter of Modernism before the Lord, and the apostle of "integrism."

The curtain rose for the last act of the drama when on August 23, 1926, Cardinal Andrieu, Archbishop of Bordeaux, by a letter to the paper *Aquitaine,* condemned the *Action Française.*[35] This letter was published in first page by the *Osservatore Romano,* and the cardinal was congratulated by Pius XI. The latter indeed was not a stranger to the question and, with his habit of studying things for himself, for many months previously, he had read, pen in hand, the paper of Maurras. A definite action was then to be expected. It came in a letter of January 5, 1927, to Cardinal Andrieu, containing, with a historical commentary, a decree of the Holy Office, in date of January 29, 1914 and December 29, 1926, condemning most of the works of Maurras and his paper *L'Action Française.*

Many bishops promulgated at once the papal decree; the delay of others, however, indicated they yielded but reluctantly; one[36] asserted he had learned from unimpeachable authority that the Pope had just declared: 1) that one could be a member of the league; 2) that one could read and subscribe for the *Action Française;* 3) that one could write for that paper. On March 2, an address testifying the obedience of the French episcopate to the action of

[35] He was, it may be said, a convert, for he had in previous years dallied with the *Action Française* and been a staunch defender of integrism.
[36] Bishop Marty of Montauban.

the Holy See contained 104 names; a few days later
a long declaration from the same source was subscribed by 118; the names of three prelates [37] were
missing. Meanwhile there were not lacking priests,
secular and regular, who justified theologically the
refusal to submit, of the leaders of the *Action Française;* the latter at the same time, strengthened by
this support, had launched upon a more intense
propaganda. For these reasons to queries sent to
Rome, as the ordinary canonical sanctions were ignored, the Holy See had to answer, first [38] that not
the ordinary permission to read books on the Index,
but a special permission, rarely to be granted, and
only for grave reasons, was necessary to read the
Action Française; then two weeks later,[39] a rescript
of the *S. Poenitentiaria Apostolica* stated what sanctions, according to the Code of Canon Law, are
incurred by the readers, leaguers and propagandists
of the *Action Française,* especially the ecclesiastics
"who encourage by theological consultations or in
private conversations the people to read its paper, or
contribute to the league; or to absolve without the
condition of purpose of amendment the readers of
the paper or of the works of the leaders of the
Action Française." This drastic action was followed
by a further declaration,[40] issued by the Pope's express orders, that the priests could not depart from

[37] Archbishop De Llobet, Coadjutor of Avignon; Bishop Marty
of Montauban, and Bishop Penan, former incumbent of Moulins.
[38] February 24, 1927.
[39] March 8, 1927.
[40] October 11, 1927.

the line of action prescribed by the Holy See without incurring themselves the vengeance of the Divine Judge.

The chief men of the *Action Française* never submitted, of course. In certain ecclesiastical circles, the rescripts of Rome were either ignored or explained away; many were, and still are maintaining outwardly an attitude of reserve, which warms up into positive sympathy in the security of friendly conversations. Sanctions have been taken, showing that the Holy See will not brook the shadow of resistance. We shall mention only three, which affected men in high ecclesiastical positions. Father Pègues, O.P., who had given on January 20, 1927, a consultation which caused scandal, at last publicly recanted on March 4, and was nevertheless in the fall of the same year relieved of his office of Regent of Studies in the Monastery of St. Maximin. Father Le Floch, Rector of Santa Chiara, the French Seminary in Rome, was for years one of the ardent supporters of the *Action Française* and of integrism: "in order to save him from more rigorous measures, His Holiness Pius XI, kindly suggested his resignation, which he (the Pope) would accept." [41] He left Rome on July 16, 1927. Cardinal Billot's relations with the leaders of the movement and integrist proclivities were long since well known; he, with Father Le Floch, wielded for years a great influence in the appointments of French bishops. After the Pope's approval of the letter of Cardinal Andrieu,

[41] *La Croix*, December 14, 1927.

Cardinal Billot wrote to Léon Daudet, Maurras' *fidus Achates*, a note congratulating the heads of the league for the address sent by them in reply to the Cardinal of Bordeaux. This note created quite a stir in Rome. Maurras' condemnation was to the cardinal a terrible blow. In a letter to the Holy Father he offered to resign from the Sacred College, and the Pope acceded.[42]   Accordingly on September 13, 1927, Cardinal Billot was received in audience and there tendered officially his resignation. The next day Father Ledochowski, General of the Jesuits, accompanied him to the Order's house in Galloro [43] where he lived in absolute retirement until his death in December, 1931.

The league of the *Action Française* is still in existence; its paper still finds enough readers to keep it afloat. Perhaps most of these readers are more interested in its royalist opinions than in the theological views of the party leaders; however, they know its condemnation and yet pretend to be Catholics. In view of this, who would dare assume that French Catholics will oppose a united front, on the day, very likely not far distant, when the battle for which the anti-clericals are openly girding themselves is begun?

A short survey of the present conditions will serve as a conclusion. In relations between Church and State relative peace is now prevailing. Occasionally this quiet is broken by local anti-clerical snipers.

[42] Consistorial allocution of December 19, 1927.
[43] Msgr. Pucci in *L'Europe Nouvelle*, Oct. 8, 1927, p. 1339.

Some small tyrants, for instance, continue to forbid processions; some prefects pay their court to the Masonic lodges by molesting the priests and Catholic laymen who have incurred the displeasure of the sect; civil administrations have not ceased to put up for sale or to turn to lay works of relief, convents and seminaries [44] confiscated by virtue of the law of 1905; a few years ago word seemed to have passed to the mayors to raise unreasonably the rent of rectories; sporadically, too, it happens that public welfare organizations refuse subsidies or help to people in need, for the sole reason these people are sending their children to Catholic schools.

Over against that it is gratifying to see the government leaving certain of the "lay laws" go unobserved, winking at the reëstablishment of Religious houses,[45] and continuing to manifest towards the hierarchy the same regard as during the war, and to send official representation to great religious ceremonies. Contemporary literature,[46] a sure enough sign of the trend of the public mind, has divorced the gross naturalism of a generation ago and the once fashionable false scientism inherited from Renan; it has become more and more impregnated with Catholic spirit. All the forms of Catholic Ac-

[44] Several seminaries have thus been bought back by rich Catholics, who rent them at a nominal price to diocesan authorities.
[45] It cannot be said the government is not aware of the existence of these institutions; complete lists of them are in the files of the Ministry of the Interior, and they are carefully kept up to date.
[46] J. Calvet, *Le Renouveau Catholique dans la Littérature contemporaine.* Paris, 1927.

tion are flourishing; their financial support, of course, has felt the effects of the depreciation of the franc; but trust the thrifty Frenchman to make a depreciated franc go to lengths unknown in other less economical countries. There is, however, one dark spot, to be mentioned in that encouraging outlook. The war took away five thousand priests and Religious, and the priests sixty years of age and over are more than twice as numerous as those under forty. Various organizations have been set on foot to grapple with every aspect of this most serious problem. Their unrelenting efforts are bearing some fruit; during the last few years the number of the young priests ordained was in several dioceses in excess of that of the deaths in the clergy. This is a good omen, and there is reason to believe that the new sacerdotal generations are of the seed of those men by whom salvation will be brought to France. *Faxit Deus!*

IV

THE CATHOLIC CHURCH IN CONTEMPORARY GERMANY

Francis S. Betten

By the World War and its consequences the position of the Church in Germany has both deteriorated and improved.

Changes in the Status of the Church. The provinces ceded by the Empire were either entirely or overwhelmingly Catholic. This changed the proportional strength of the Catholics very considerably. Before the war they numbered 36.69 per cent of the total population, after the war 32.36 per cent. The Center Party, which may be considered the parliamentary representation of the Catholics in the Reichstag, and which before the war had about a hundred and with the Polish and Alsatian groups more than a hundred and twenty members, at present cannot expect to gather more than ninety, or at the most a hundred under its banner. The financial inflation following the war, the reparation payments, the derangement of business, and other causes of distress and poverty affected the Catholics more than the non-Catholics, and thus had a disastrous effect upon Catholic institutions of all kinds. In consequence of the absence of the heads of the families during

the war and later by the prolonged captivity, the
younger generation had grown up rather unmanage-
able and self-willed and had imbibed much of the
poison of exaggerated republicanism and infidel Socialism.   In fact the war and its aftermaths resulted
in a noticeable relaxation of the bonds of religion
and morality.   If at the present time, thirteen years
later, religion can be said to be in a good condition,
it is due to the watchfulness and incessant activity
of the bishops, the intelligent and untiring efforts of
a well-trained priesthood, and to the self-sacrificing
coöperation of volunteer battalions of the Catholic
laity.   The excellent organizations of pre-war times
were not allowed to go to ruin.   They were not only
kept up but developed intensively and extensively.
As a first remedy against the sad conditions caused
by the war, the bishops had missions preached in
almost every parish of the land, to counteract religious indifference and arm the people against the
fierce attacks of Socialism and allied tendencies.

On the other hand, the war and its consequences
improved the legal and civic position of the Catholics.   In the constitutional assembly at Weimar the
Center Party, in spite of its small number, wielded
a great influence for good.   It was almost the only
party that had a definite conception of the nature
and duties of states and their members, and possessed a proportionately large number of able and
industrious men, so that its influence was far beyond
its numerical strength.   The religious enactments
of the new constitution are on the whole not un-

favorable. The remnants of the *Kulturkampf* laws were thrown overboard, and similar laws will be impossible in the future. In particular the galling restrictions on the Religious Orders are gone for the whole territory of the Reich. The appointment of the parish clergy, formerly hampered by governmental control, is entirely in the hands of the bishops. The ecclesiastical affairs of Bavaria are regulated by a new, rather favorable concordat. The free state of Prussia, too, entered into a new agreement with Rome, born of a genuine desire on the part of the government to assist in remedying some very undesirable conditions, which had been complained of for many decades. This agreement provided for the establishment of two new dioceses, raised two more bishops to the rank of archbishop, and organized some border lands into a special administrative district. The German hierarchy now counts seventeen bishops and six archbishops. The revenues of the Church to be paid by the State from confiscated Church property were increased. The bishops are to be chosen by the cathedral chapter from three candidates proposed by the Holy See.

Ecclesiastical Revenues. As the revenues of the Church were mentioned, a word may be in place to clear up the manner in which the Catholic Church in Prussia and other States of Germany is supported. In 1803, all the enormous property of the German bishoprics, cathedral chapters, and monasteries was confiscated and handed over to the secular princes, obliging them, however, to pay a decent revenue to the bishops and to take over whatever obligations the monasteries had. Let it be stated here clearly that no parish property was taken away. At that time all parishes were endowed, that is, they possessed so much property, chiefly in agricultural land, that the parish required no other financial support. Parishes which then existed, still hold their old property. There is, therefore, still a goodly number of Catholic parishes, in which no collections are needed.

But it is different with the dioceses and the clergy of the cathedrals. They have no such endowments. The State has, however, recognized its duty to provide revenues for them. Though these are paid out yearly, it is easy to see that they are not salaries. These revenues do not come from the taxes of the people, but are a small part of the sums accruing to the State from the ecclesiastical possessions confiscated in 1803. In reality this money is the Church's own property.

However, when it becomes necessary to establish new parishes the government contributes no money from the confiscated Church property. In such cases the people must help themselves. This they do either by collections and other voluntary contributions, or by a church tax. Certain parish committees, consisting of ten or more representatives, may impose a tax, to be expressed in a percentage of some State tax. When this is done, the State tax commission of the district is informed, and it determines the amount to be paid by each member of the parish and puts it on the tax bill. There is then not much preaching of money. Nor have the rich parishioners a chance to get by with a smaller percentage than the poorer classes. As already stated these conditions vary greatly. But our explanation applies chiefly to the two largest States, Prussia and Bavaria.

The Center Party. This is perhaps the best place to introduce the Center Party, which in our American papers is commonly called "the clericals." The Center Party was founded in 1871, when the first signs of the approaching *Kulturkampf* began to appear. It is really not a strictly Catholic party. It stands for equality of all before the law, for justice to all classes of people and also to all denominations and for the promotion of all efforts which tend toward general welfare, especially the right relation between employers and employees. These demands are inspired by positive Christianity. Following the lead of Bishop von Ketteler the party worked for the amelioration of the lot of the laboring classes nearly two decades before Pope Leo XIII issued his great labor encyclical, which in fact sounded like a solemn approval of the Centrists' program. It is evident that every sincere Christian can subscribe to such a platform. In the beginning the party always counted some Protestants in its ranks. At present, too, it has non-Catholic members in the parliaments of individual states, in city councils and similar representative bodies. In the Reichstag, however, only Catholics belong to it. Its strength is unfortunately not commensurate to the number of Catholics in the

Reich.   Many Catholics do not approve of its decidedly republican attitude; others find fault with
its practice of combining occasionally with other
parties for the purpose of securing the passage of
desirable measures.   Soon after the war a split occurred in the party.   The Bavarian members separated themselves from the rest and formed a distinct
party.   On matters touching religion they always
vote with the Center, and the other points of difference have so much vanished out of sight that a
reunion is only a question of time.

   The *Kirchliches Handbuch*.   The compilation of
such a survey as is here attempted is greatly facil-
itated by an annual publication issued by the German Catholics under the direction of the bishops.
It is the *Kirchliches Handbuch* (ecclesiastical handbook) which, started in 1907, has appeared regularly
with the exception of several years during the war
and once during the present depression.   (Volume 17
is for the year 1930-31.)   It is issued by a Central
Bureau for Ecclesiastical Statistics, which has its
office in Cologne.   With its regular appearance and
copious information the *Handbuch* has become a
permanent feature of German Catholic life.   It deserves a few words of description.   Some of its sections bear resemblance to our *Catholic Directory*.
Its first part, like the first part of the *Catholic
Directory*, gives the organization of the Church at
large, *i. e.* the Roman authorities and congregations.
But it lists also the papal nuncios in the various
capitals and the diplomatic representatives of the

secular powers with the Holy See; part two gives the German dioceses, with their bishops and officials, like the first paragraphs in the sections on the individual dioceses in the *Catholic Directory*. There is no enumeration of parishes, since another publication called *Schematismus*, issued by each diocese individually, takes care of that very minutely. One part reproduces and discusses the latest decrees and utterances of the Holy See and such new secular laws and regulations as bear on the Church and the religious character of the schools. The most extensive chapter is that on the organizations to which we shall have to refer frequently.

The last fifty or sixty pages are covered by tables in which an astonishingly large amount of statistical material is represented. The data are classified under some thirty heads, such as the number of parishes and quasi-parishes, and of parish clergy; of priests occupied in schools or institutions; Catholic and non-Catholic population; civil marriages of Catholics (obligatory in Germany) and Catholic marriages; mixed marriages; births and baptisms of children of Catholic couples, of mixed couples, of Catholic unmarried mothers; Catholic burials; total number of Communions; Communions outside of parish churches; and Easter Communions. These data are shown as applying not only to the several dioceses but to each and all deaneries, some five hundred in number.

Two causes facilitate the compilation of these countless data. One is the fact that the secular census not only gives the number of civil marriages, births, and deaths, but in each case indicates the religion of the persons concerned. The second cause is the evident willingness on the part of the entire clergy to coöperate with the endeavors of the Catholic Statistical Institute. The priests seem to realize the advantages accruing from this publication. In the latest volume the compiler concludes his short introduction to these tables with the words: "And now let the figures speak. And may the incessant labor of the clergy, which stands behind these figures, be an inspiration to new joyful endeavors for the benefit of the souls of our Catholic people." To this part also we shall have to revert in another section of this paper.

The St. Boniface Society. One of the most difficult problems facing German Catholics is the care of the *diaspora*, that is of those districts where few Catholics are living amid large Protestant populations. In the beginning of the nineteenth century such districts were rare. The several sections of the German lands were either compactly Catholic or compactly Protestant; and, where the religion was mixed, as for instance in the Palatinate, some provision had been made for Catholics. In the nineteenth century industrialism and other conditions caused Catholics to move into Protestant regions in ever-increasing numbers. Most of these Catholics were poor. They had no churches or priests or schools for their children. Since 1849 the *Boniface Society*, founded by Count Stolberg, has come to the aid of these *diaspora* Catholics, by soliciting prayers and alms for them. From alms collected in the Catholic districts the *Boniface Society* assists in building modest churches and sees to it that priests either travel from place to place and look after the scattered Catholics, or that parishes are erected in suitable places. Wherever possible, schools with Catholic teachers are started, and even Catholic orphan asylums and hospitals arise.

One remarkable institution is the First Communion Homes, where children are kept for some weeks as boarders to be prepared for the greatest spiritual day of their lives. The money collected since its foundation, about $36,200,000, has been distributed among 4500 *diaspora* centers. The Society has a special auxiliary organization which collects stamps, tinfoil, and similar articles, and in 1929 gathered the sum of $35,000, which went to the support of the First Communion Homes. Numerous ladies' sodalities form sewing circles, to make clothes for the poor children and sacred vestments for the churches and chapels, all of which represent an annual outlay of about $20,000. Thousands of better-situated priests impose a specified tax on themselves to assist their poor confrères in these districts. There are auxiliary societies of children and of students in higher schools and a very flourishing Academic Union of graduate university students, for the gathering of small sums, although their chief purpose is the training of young minds in generous support of ecclesiastical enterprises and imparting to them a practical knowledge of the needs of the *diaspora*. Since the war there is a branch office of the *Boniface Society* in New York, and the home organization gratefully recognizes the generous support received during this period from the Catholics of the United States. Without this American support a great part of its institutions would not be able to exist.

Foreign Missions. One of the remarkable features of Catholic life in Germany is enthusiasm for the foreign missions. Before Germany embarked on its colonial policy, there existed societies for the support of the missions. Several missionary Orders, too, chief among them the Society of the Divine Word, took care of districts in pagan lands. But the acquisition of colonies by the Fatherland gave a new impetus to all missionary effort. A landmark in the development of missionary endeavors was the National Catholic Congress of 1909. In an eloquent address Prince Aloysius Loewenstein appealed to his Catholic countrymen to devote more effort to this noble purpose. Rarely has a single speech produced more abundant fruit. The appeal evidently found the public mind well prepared, and the problem was taken up by all classes with great enthusiasm. New popular local societies began to contribute regularly to the expenses of the missions. Many "Missions Feste," large and small, fostered and spread the general enthusiasm. The subscriptions to the popular mission periodicals increased by leaps and bounds. Most of these monthlies or quarterlies are not confined to the news from the mission field but carry articles of a more scientific character, relating the cultural conditions and history of the peoples among which the missionaries are laboring. In the University of Münster a chair for Mission Science has been erected. A quarterly review soon served the same purpose. Scientific courses, given in all parts of the country, deepened and widened the knowledge of the history, the character, the inherent difficulties, and the concomitant requirements of missionary endeavor. This scientific viewpoint is one of the causes for the spread of the popular movement and the coöperation of the educated classes, and at the same time marks a true progress in apostolic methods.

The results of these efforts were not small. When the war broke out the German organizations counted 205,000 converts in the German colonies, and 383,-000 in non-German pagan districts. During the war this sturdy stream of enthusiasm continued for several years unabated, nay, with even increasing force. The contributions of the Society of the Holy Child, which is very popular in Germany, increased from 1,400,000 marks in 1914 to nearly two million marks in 1917. But the Peace of Versailles brought a sad disappointment. The colonies were placed under French or English or Belgian mandates, with the result that hundreds of German missionaries, Brothers, and Sisters were expelled. They returned to Germany and crowded the houses of their organizations, not knowing where to put their hand to the plow again. Starvation stalked through the land.

The terrible depreciation of money destroyed merci-
lessly what funds had been collected. It is little
wonder that the missionary movement languished
for several years. About 1925, however, the English
and French governments somewhat relaxed their policy of exclusion, and when conditions at home had
become more nearly normal, the old ardor for missionary zeal gradually revived. All the former scientific and popular methods of spreading the idea of
the propagation of the Faith were soon in full swing
again. New fields were assigned to the German
apostles, though the number of converts under their
care is not one-half of what it was before the war.
What the present years of depression and distress
will bring no one can tell.

The Organizations of Catholic Germany. In the
Catholic life of Germany organizations play an un-
usually important part, and the picture we are to
draw would lack very essential lines unless we devoted a considerable fraction of this paper to the
*Vereine, Verbände, Verbindungen, Bünde, Gesell-
schaften,* and *Arbeitsgemeinschaften* which flourish
in the Fatherland. The brief descriptions and reports of the principal ones cover about a hundred
pages in the *Kirchliches Handbuch.* There are societies of mothers, priests, priests' housekeepers, artisans, master craftsmen, rural laborers, young
merchants and office workers, store clerks, waiters in
hotels and restaurants, school teachers, prison chaplains; societies as we have just seen for the support
of foreign missions; societies for the aid of dis-

charged prisoners, and for the protection of traveling girls. We select only a few of the most characteristic ones to explain their purpose and methods of action.

a) *Organization of Students and for Students.* The German Catholics are unable, for the present at least, to establish a Catholic University. So they do the next best thing. They try efficiently to keep hold of the Catholic graduate students during their university years by uniting them in student societies; these, though varying greatly in order to suit various characters and tastes, have the same essential religious features. All insist on the fulfillment of the Sunday duties, recommend the frequent reception of the Sacraments and the participation in spiritual retreats, inaugurate lecture courses on apologetics and similar subjects. Most of these societies assist in a body at Corpus Christi processions. Each has its periodical, and these papers are on the whole well edited and well patronized. The figures of membership show that ninety per cent of the 23,000 Catholic university students belong to the one or other of these bodies. After leaving the university and entering upon the practice of their vocation most of them remain in touch with their organization under the title of *Alte Herren* (Alumni) and assist their younger brethren by their example, advice, and aid in various forms. All these societies of university students are affiliated with the *Akademische Bonifatius-Einigung* which is both an auxiliary to the St. Boniface Society and an organization for the general promotion of religious life. It inaugurates religious training courses, "religious circles," and educational journeys into the territory of the *diaspora,* and has established a sort of theological university for laymen. The students of undergraduate schools have their own societies. Two should be mentioned, *Quickborn* (Fountain of Life), and *Neudeutschland* (New Germany), with 33,000 and 16,000 members, respectively. Both are well organized under priestly directors and each has several periodicals accommodated to the capacity and tastes of its members. Both participate heartily in the movement for retreats and the liturgical movement, besides laying stress upon physical exercise. They provide for vacation homes among the hills or on the seashore and send their members on long hiking tours.

There are societies, chiefly of laymen, which endeavor to assist poorer students during their stay at the educational institutions. The oldest and probably most important of them is the *Albertus-Magnus-Verein*, which, however, excludes students of theology. The same purpose is pursued for women students by the *Hildegardis-Verein*. Both these societies grant their support in the shape of money. A third organization, called *Caritas für Akademiker*, makes it its aim to take care of the actual needs of students somewhat according to the methods of the St. Vincent de Paul conferences. They provide better spiritual facilities for the Catholic students of smaller universities, assist poor students in case of sickness, in finding suitable lodgings, or opportunities of needful recreation.

Nearly twenty years ago (1913) a number of societies of university graduates, *i. e.* professional men, combined into a federation called the *Katholischer Akademiker-Verband*, a very active organization of 14,000 members, which endeavors to promote the Catholic *Weltanschauung* by numerous large and small lecture meetings, by periodicals and other publications, and last but not least by their own example and the apostolic activity of the individual members. Its special object is the discussion from the Catholic standpoint of burning questions of the day, and the propagation of the retreat movement and of sound piety based on the liturgy of the Church.

This leads us to the great learned society of Catholic Germany, the *Goerres-Gesellschaft*. The Goerres Society is named after the great champion of the Catholic cause who in the middle of the last century raised his voice so eloquently for the liberty of the Church. It is a body of some 5,000 members banded together for the promotion of scientific study among Catholics. Its record indeed is an admirable one, and consists of a long list of highly scientific publications. It has issued the several editions of the scholarly *Staatslexikon,* an exhaustive encyclopedia in five volumes of social and political science, economics, and the theory and practice of government. It has undertaken the publication of the authentic *Acts of the Council of Trent,* now in its twelfth volume. It maintains historical institutes in Rome and Jerusalem and a similar home of learning in Madrid. Fifty volumes have appeared of its *Historisches Jahrbuch*. It grants stipends and other helps to promising young men especially for original historical research, in order to assist rising young Catholic scholars. Similar in scope to the *Goerres-Gesellschaft* is the *Leo-Gesellschaft* in Austria, which looks back upon forty years of successful activity. Unlike its German sister it lays more stress upon propaganda by word of mouth; hence its extensive lecture service on subjects chosen from sociology, philosophy, pedagogy, history, arts, and natural sciences. But it also has to its credit a long array of learned and popular volumes on almost all branches of human knowledge, which without its able direction and liberal subsidies could never have appeared. In spite of the poor financial condition of the little country, it carries on its work to a remarkable degree.

b) *Volksverein.* The need of a more vigorous instruction of the Catholic population against the fallacies of Socialism is the reason of the existence of the *Volksverein,* "The People's Society," a well-organized union of some 500,000 members of all classes, chiefly of working-men. It is not a federation of societies, though the members form local, regional and diocesan units. Its headquarters at München-Gladbach (Rhineland) are a combination of administrative offices with study rooms for writers, lecture halls for teachers on social and apologetic science, a library of some 80,000 volumes, a commodious reading room, the sanctums of the editors of several periodicals, and a well-equipped printing establishment. The 500,000 members are individually kept in touch with headquarters by local officials, *Vertrauensmänner,* who six times a year put one of the society's pamphlets personally into the hands of every member. Some 200 million pamphlets, leaflets, and books have been distributed by the People's Society since 1890, when at the suggestion of Windthorst it began its work.

Literature is a chief instrument of the *Volksverein* for the social and apologetic instruction of the people. But propaganda by word of mouth is another. Astonishingly great is the number of assemblies held year after year. During the year 1930-31 the headquarters and its supreme branches supplied speakers to 4500 local units, and in still more cases the units provided their own speakers. Needless to say, papal utterances form the backbone of all discussions. Special conferences for the study of

social and apologetic questions are held for priests, and
for leading men of the different occupational classes. Of
late the *Volksverein* has vigorously endeavored to counteract the *Landflucht*, or the tendency of country people
to move into the cities. Its aim is the renovation of village life in the Catholic spirit. A crusade, started for
this purpose, reached no less than 15,000 farmers in one
year, not counting the participants of the 150 conferences
for the training of rural leaders.

The headquarters at München-Gladbach are a bee-
hive of activity. Men from all parts of Germany and
other countries flock together for conferences of several
days or several weeks, or for longer courses on special
subjects and on special problems. Without having the
title, it is a university of a very honorable standing.
But all this brisk labor could not be as efficient and as
telling on the Catholic population, were it not for the
multitude of volunteer workers in the country at large.
In fact the *Kleinarbeit*, carried on in city and village as
well as in the branch meetings of other societies, is the
aim and purpose of all the work persistently and indus-
triously pursued by this central administration, which
supplies the units in the field with suggestions, direction,
and information for their procedure. If the Socialists
of all classes have found the Catholic districts impregna-
ble against their doctrines, it can hardly be questioned
that this is to a very great extent the effect of the untiring activity of the *Volksverein*.

c) *Gesellenverein.* In 1845, Father Adolph Kolping
founded the first Catholic *Gesellenverein*, a society for
young artisans, to safeguard them from the dangers of
youth and the perils of their travels, to give them religious assistance, and to provide for them chances of fur-

ther instruction in useful branches of knowledge. The society now enrolls 128,000 active members, divided in two thousand sections; its organ, the *Kolpingblatt,* has an edition of 108,000. It maintains 430 "Journeymen's Homes," which may be compared with the institutions of the Y. M. C. A. These houses provide lodgings for traveling workers, have schoolrooms for instruction, and halls for lectures or recreation. In 1929, they granted 220,000 free night lodgings and distributed 402,000 free meals. They assist the traveling young man to find employment, and inspect the places where their charges are going to work.

d) The *Caritas-Verband.* Perhaps the grandest achievement of the German Catholics is the *Caritas-Verband,* a confederation of all societies and institutions which are active in the field of Catholic charity in Germany. Besides the members thus indirectly affiliated with it, there is a considerable number of members joining it directly and not through membership in another charitable organization, the total of all members being 600,000. The central administration is located at Freiburg in Breisgau, with secondary headquarters at Munich and Berlin. Each diocese has its branch organization which supervises, supports, and directs the charitable agencies of that part of the Church and, if necessary, starts charitable action under its own direct control. Though all these branches are under the management of the central office at Freiburg, they are supposed to take care individually of the needs of each place and district and to proceed by using their own means or by obtaining aid from other Catholic or non-Catholic agencies. Thus the Berlin secondary headquarters for several years assisted the numerous German-Russian refugees. Under papal direction a special section was created under the title, *Papal Assistance Committee for Russians in Germany*. It received liberal assistance from the Near East Welfare Association and from the Holy Father. The central bureau of the *Caritas-Verband* is more like a university where all the questions of Catholic charity are studied both theoretically and practically, with a preponderence, however, so it seems, on the practical side. A number of set courses is offered, lasting from a semester to two years in length, on the various phases of charity, and differentiated according to the character and needs of persons occupied in the field. Most of these courses lead to state certificates. A special school is opened for chaplains, physicians, and officials of hospitals. An office for statisticians not only cares for the tabulation and discussion of the charitable actions of the affiliated societies and of the results of new researches, but also manages a variety of enterprises which require extensive and specially accurate bookkeeping. There are among others a section for the Catholic science of charity and one for the protection of dependent children. This latter section is in constant correspondence with the local societies, agencies and institutions which are engaged in the care of delinquent children. It devotes special attention to securing Catholic guardians for Catholic orphans, and offers study courses for questions of guardianship. This section studies the laws referring to this field and points out the legal means which might be useful to reach results. It keeps a watch on the legislatures and tries to prevent unfavorable enactments and to avert the progress of the control of charity by the State, which is a menace wherever the Socialists or Communists have influence. A similar department surveys and assists the

activity of those societies which support families finan-
cially or morally endangered, or which care for mothers
in critical times. A library of 50,000 volumes is at the
disposal of these committees, of the teachers in the schools,
and of all those interested in charity. The central bureau
issues publications on the subject of charity both theoretical and practical, and has a department for camera
slides and moving pictures. In consequence of its influence an Institute for the science of Catholic charity is
now attached to the theological faculty of the Freiburg
University.

The diocesan branches of the *Caritas-Verband* hold a
similar position to the organizations of their respective
dioceses, though their activity naturally is far more
directly practical than that of the central bureau at Freiburg. In reviewing the condensed reports of these
branches, one notices a great variety of purposes brought
about partly by the special needs of different localities,
and partly by the historical development of charitable
action. In these organizations the most elementary kind
of charity, judicious almsgiving, is prominent, though
the care for mothers, for young men and women and
young children assumes a large proportion in the reports.
Individual societies work for children's recreational homes,
for convalescent children and mothers, for poor families
with many children, for crippled children, for tubercular
children and adults, and for poor sick persons in their
homes. There are numerous hospitals (numerous because
many of them are small and situated in country places,
to accommodate the rural population); and the St. Vincent de Paul conferences, which are far spread, attend to
a great deal of this work. Very numerous and enterpris-
ing are the St. Elizabeth societies of women, which are

modeled upon the type of the St. Vincent de Paul conferences. The St. Francis-Regis societies, which have been
adopted from France after Germany introduced civil
marriage, try to rectify invalid marriages, to assist in
securing the necessary papers and testimonials, and see
that the children are baptized and sent to Catholic
schools, though this is also very extensively done by
other organizations. The members of the Third Order
of St. Francis exert an incredibly large influence in all
the fields of charity. And there are schools and courses
of lectures everywhere for the training of the workers.

The short descriptions of these charitable societies in
the compact reports of their activities cover forty pages
in the *Kirchliches Handbuch*. Then follow other organizations working for the direct assistance of parish priests
and parish interests or for the promotion of priestly vocations and the assistance of the rural poor. Catholic
employment bureaus and societies for the protection of
girls form each a close network over the whole land.

Of the several other such federations of societies we
mention only those embracing the organizations of young
men and women. The *Katholischer Jungmänner-Verband
Deutschlands* has a membership of 387,000 young men,
and the *Zentral-Verband der Katholischen Jungfrauen-
Vereinigungen Deutschlands* counts 780,000 girls within
its ranks. Both these federations together with several
others, nearly all with tens of thousands of members,
are again consolidated in the *Katholische Jugend
Deutschlands*, a central organization with about a million and a half young Catholics of both sexes. The
headquarters of these three *Verbände* are located at Düsseldorf, and like those of the *Caritas-Verband* and the

Volksverein are the home of theoretical and practical studies.

General Characteristics of the German Catholic Societies. This may be the place to point out some peculiar features of the German method of organization. In the *Volksverein* and *Gesellenverein* there are large societies in which, though they are divided into sections, every member is directly affiliated to the supreme administration. The *Caritas-Verband* is essentially a federation of societies and branches, most of the individual members belong to it through an affiliated organization. Another method of combining several organizations which pursue similar purposes, is the *Arbeitsgemeinschaft,* or Labor Group. The individual societies agree to send delegates at regular intervals to a conference in which common interests and aims and the methods of procedure are discussed with a view to arrive at a more perfect understanding of the conditions common to all, and also to prevent duplication of effort. The plan of the *Verband* and the *Arbeitsgemeinschaft* is commonly followed in all the Catholic organizations in Germany.

Another feature of the organized activity of these Catholic societies is the practice of arranging lectures and other more systematized means of spreading Catholic information. We have seen that the *Volksverein* alone has inaugurated in one year some ten thousand assemblies with one or two or more lectures on social or apologetic questions. The *Caritas-Verband* and its branches maintain an equally brisk activity in lectures on Catholic charity with its many problems and achievements. More important probably, though attracting less attention in public, are the schools—schools of real university rank, and schools in the elements of the doctrine the respective society represents; schools for priests and ambitious laymen and members of the Sisterhoods; schools of several daily lessons for three days and of extended courses for a month or several years; schools for the leaders of the crowds, for the officials of hospitals including the chaplains, doctors, and administrators; schools on general Catholic principles and on particular problems of the day or on peculiar tasks of individual institutions. We should mention also the stress laid everywhere on the spiritual aspect of life. In the constitutions the provision that the society's activity is to be pursued for the purpose of realizing in the members the principles of their Catholic faith is common, and where it does not appear in so many words, the whole tendency of the society is oriented in that direction. Not rarely the constitutions expressly recommend spiritual retreats or the practice of liturgical devotion. Finally there are the periodicals. Nearly each of the larger unions of Catholics publishes its own weekly or monthly or quarterly to keep its members informed of what happens within the ranks, to outline methods for the various phases and features of the common activity, to discuss questions and problems which arise, and to unfold the Catholic doctrine on which the whole activity is based. The organs of the great *Verbände* and *Arbeitsgemeinschaften* are literary publications of a high class, those of the smaller societies being more directly aimed at the work in hand.

Problems. With this elaborate machinery of societies, federations, and conferences German Catholics endeavor to solve the serious problems which are before them and to fight the mighty hostile powers which oppose the Church in their land. One of these problems we have already seen: the Catholics of the *diaspora*, which is successfully handled by the vigorous St. Boniface Society and its several branches. Another problem is the unrelenting *opposition of Protestantism* through the Evangelical Alliance. The number of believing Protestants, for instance, orthodox Lutherans, is not very great; but all those who go in any way by the name of Protestant persist in their attacks on anything that comes from Rome, and take hold of every weakness, of every unfortunate happening which may occur in Catholic circles in and out of Germany. One of its most effective weapons are the *mixed marriages*, which harm the Church not only by the apostasy of many of the children but also by the fact that mixed marriages are remarkable for their small number of offspring, and that divorces are remarkably large in the case of mixed marriages. Until post-war times these losses, though not insignificant, did not prevent the regular increase of the Catholic population, nor are they now the worst obstacle in its growth. Much more dangerous are the modern enemies, the several classes of Socialism, namely, Communism, Social Democracy, and National Democracy, which especially in hard times deceive the common people by their denunciations and glittering promises. In numberless meetings and in private intercourse they talk boldly against God and scatter their leaflets and pamphlets broadcast. They particularly aim at the young, even young children. It is for this reason that the *Volksverein,* which was originally founded against social evils, expressly put the teaching of popular apologetics upon its program. Probably the principal means the Catholic body at large uses against these enemies is the well-developed Catholic press.

In spite of all defensive measures, however, it cannot be doubted that these enemies cause no little damage to the Catholic body. The *apostasies,* as they appear from the reports of the official civil census, amounted, in 1929, to 40,000, while the number of converts was only 8,762. (It is remarkable that a very considerable part of these apostasies take place in connection with mixed marriages, and that this is even the case with those caused by Communistic agitation.) Judging from a comparison of the record of births with the record of baptisms, the loss by mixed marriages alone was about 40,000 in 1928. Both these causes together, therefore, result in a yearly loss of more than 70,000 souls for the Church of Germany. This is certainly deplorable enough. If there were no other cause, however, it would not affect very noticeably the yearly increase in num-

bers.   In former times the number of German Catholics grew every year by several hundred thousand.
But gradually another influence set in, the curse of
race suicide.   Long before the war it had appeared
in the non-Catholic districts in increasing force and
had begun to show in the Catholic regions.   But
even after the war, the increase of the Catholic population went on, though in diminishing percentages.
As late as 1928 there was still in the state of Prussia
alone a surplus of 118,408, which for the whole
Reich would mean some 170,000, a rather creditable
showing in view of the existing economic crisis.
This yearly number has still more decreased.   And
although a very competent authority assures us that
the estimates on this item (they are no more than
that) given in the *Kirchliches Handbuch* are too
pessimistic, and though the surplus is still considerable, the Catholics entertain no rosy hopes for the
future.   They begin to figure with the eventuality
that birth rate and death rate will be equal in their
ranks.   Steps have already been taken to counteract
this sad tendency.   The charity societies grant extra
support to families with many children, and the
State allows tax reduction to the heads of such house-
holds.   Above all, the vigorous religious life of the
nation, which we shall consider presently, gives the
German Catholics a reason to expect victory in their
struggle against the evil of race suicide.   The present economic conditions of the Fatherland, however,
which in many circles amount to misery, for the time

being seem to form a powerful obstacle against the success of such a crusade.

Let us now look at another vital problem with which the German Catholics are confronted: the school problem. Under conditions vastly different from ours, our German brethren have to fight for the religious character of their schools and teachers in order to secure the heirloom of Catholic faith to their offspring. For this purpose they have created another organization—the *Katholische Schul-Organization* with headquarters at Düsseldorf.

This body assists Catholic municipalities, large and small, in obtaining their rights concerning schools and teachers by giving legal advice or making practical proposals for the solution of difficulties. Above all, it voices the Catholic educational principles before the public and the educational offices and ministries of the Reich and the individual states. It issues two notable educational periodicals which enjoy the best reputation, and when necessary it appears in the field with other publications. It is frequently consulted by the secular authorities on general and particular questions of education. In the Constitutional Assembly at Weimar, in 1919, the Center Party, as stated elsewhere, succeeded in having the Constitution shaped in such a way that on the whole it is not unfavorable to the life and development of the Catholic faith. However, the provisions concerning the school, as finally passed, did not satisfy its desires. The Constitution indeed prescribes denominational schools according to the demands of the parents, and in case of doubt the parents are expressly to be consulted; but in practice this leads to complications. Nor are the parents always given a chance to express their preference. The matter was to be determined by a special school law. An attempt, made in 1927, to enact such legislation failed. And in the present constellation of political parties there is no prospect that another attempt will be successful. The Catholics, therefore, prefer meanwhile to leave the question alone and to utilize to the full the legal means they actually possess. But the existing indefiniteness is fruitful of much annoyance and gives the Catholic School Organization many questions to discuss and numerous entanglements to unravel.

The Catholic Press. This important subject, which has been alluded to in several places, cannot unfortunately be given the treatment it deserves. The *Katholischer Literatur-Kalender* of 1926 furnishes the names of the Catholic dailies; the prominent ones number twenty-two. The subscribers to eleven of these amount to 265,000, and the most powerful ones are not among these eleven. Thirty pages of the *Katholischer Literatur-Kalender,* closely printed, are filled with titles of and information about the Catholic periodicals, which are classed under no less than thirty headings. There are for instance twenty-eight periodicals on theology; nineteen on pedagogy; eight on history; nine on sacred music; fourteen for sodalities; fifty-two for foreign missions; eighty for young people, including twenty for children; and seventy-eight similar to our Sunday papers.

It is interesting to know that Germany has 197 Catholic publishing houses, that is, firms which will refuse to print or issue anything objectionable to the Church.

Several organizations have for their purpose the spread of good literature. The largest of them is the *Borromaeus-Verein,* the Society of St. Charles Borromeo. Its aim is both the establishment of Catholic loan libraries and the building up of libraries in the homes of the people. According to the amount of his membership fee, every member yearly selects one or several books from a list furnished to him. Local branches to the number of 5,400 maintain as many Catholic libraries, especially in smaller localities. At the present time these contain more than four million books, and recently had a circulation of eight million volumes. The society publishes several periodicals on library science and bibliography and keeps a system of library schools for the benefit of its 15,000 volunteer attendants.

The Practice of Religion. We have now considered the Catholic life of Germany under several aspects. The Catholics support domestic and foreign missions; they band together in an almost uncountable number of societies for the assistance of the helpless, for the defense of Catholic doctrine, for the furtherance of Catholic interests in every field. But are they real Catholics in their hearts? Do they practise their religion by such activities as refer to their own personal piety? In other words, is their Catholicism for show only or is it sincere? Is it the result of their intimate conviction? Do they use those means which tend in the first and last end to the perfectioning of their own private life?

a) To answer this well-justified question, let us first view under another angle what has been said about the Catholic organizations, the *Vereine, Bünde, Verbände, Gesellschaften, Arbeitsgemeinschaften, Vereinigungen,* etc., with their distribution of literature, collection of contributions and other alms, gathering of postage stamps, cigar ends, and old clothes—all of which has left in us the impression that large numbers of scientific workers and administrative officials are necessary to keep that complicated and yet well-articulated world a-going and progressing. Let us hope that those who give their whole time to this activity are drawing a decent salary. The overwhelming majority are certainly volunteer workers who contribute their labor gratis. But paid or unpaid, all this work is inspired by charity, the greatest of Christian virtues, the virtue by which Christ recognizes those who are really His disciples. Behind the dry figures of the reports of these devoted bands there lies hidden a truly astonishing amount of this Christian virtue of supernatural charity. Without doubt these countless acts of charity draw down upon the workers themselves and upon the Catholic population an abundance of heavenly graces and blessings, and will help efficaciously to stop the spread of pernicious customs, as indeed they have already assisted the Church successfully in holding its own against powerful adverse influences.

b) *Spiritual Retreats.* One of the efficient means to promote a genuinely Catholic spirit is no doubt the practice of spiritual retreats, and these are extensively applied in the Germany of today. Germany has more than seventy retreat houses, that is, homes which have no other purpose but to harbor those who wish to go through the spiritual exercises in the so-called closed retreats. Besides these, a great number of other institutions, such as boarding schools, convents, recreation homes, etc., accommodate retreatants for a limited time during the year. Closed retreats are given for all classes of people, including soldiers. During the last year, one retreat house of Berlin saw two thousand retreatants within its walls. The whole number of men, women, and young people who go through this renewal of spiritual fervor amounts to more than a hundred thousand a year, and it is noted with gratification that the number of the men and young men is rapidly on the increase. This total of course does not include the religious of either sex, or those who participate in the "open retreats" given in parish churches and institutions in the manner of missions. Most dioceses have their own diocesan secretary for retreats, and these secretaries meet yearly in connection with the National Catholic Congress for a day of conference and consultation. For many years three separate assemblies take place at the Catholic Congresses for the sole purpose of retreat propaganda. National conventions of retreat masters have met several times and conventions on a smaller scale are held frequently. Retreat leagues of laymen and laywomen are spread over the whole country and keep alive the spirit conceived in the days of holy retirement; and by personal contact or public addresses their members pass on to others the knowledge of this unique experience. Books and booklets abound both for retreatants and retreat masters, and two periodicals repeat regularly their message and invitation. In close connection with the retreat movement goes the inculcation of frequent Communion. About 750,000 men, a million young people of both sexes, and a million of adult women, have expressly pledged themselves to receive Communion at least once a month, and no doubt many of these receive much more frequently. Nor are these nearly three millions the only ones who practise frequent Communion.

c) *Liturgical Movement*. We must not omit the strong and ever-increasing force and expansion of the *Liturgical Movement*. "Prayer in the spirit of the Church," "Piety in connection with the Church," "Prayer in the words of the Church,"—these are watchwords met with everywhere in the religious literature of Germany. The Benedictine Fathers are the chief, though not the only, promoters of this special feature of piety. The movement is furthered by word and writing, by various editions of the Missal in Latin and German, each edition serving a different purpose, and by popular and scientific explanations of Church ceremonies. Travelers in Germany have expressed their surprise at the large number of people who when hearing Mass use Missals instead of other prayer books. In Germany it goes without saying that liturgical societies have been founded. Other societies, too, frequently mention the promotion of the liturgical movement as one of their objects.

d) *Pilgrimages*. Age-long traditions draw the German Catholics to their places of pilgrimage. Nearly every larger Catholic district has one or several shrines, usually of the Blessed Mother of God, which have been the goals of the pious wanderings of generation after generation. In modern times the custom of pilgrimages has been strongly on the increase. Whenever one of the great conventions of Catholics takes places in the neighborhood of such a sanctuary, a pilgrimage to it is commonly part of the program. The total number of pilgrims is surprisingly large. Altötting in the South and Kevelaer in the North alone are visited year after year by nearly a million, and the pilgrims who frequent the less famous places, or Lourdes in France, or the sanctuaries of Switzerland and Austria may amount to another million. The peace and happiness of soul, true penance, confidence for the future life, and religious enthusiasm, which are the fruit of these pilgrimages, are well known to those who have had the good fortune to witness the scenes occurring at these places. May Catholic Germany ever preserve the precious heirloom it possesses in its shrines and pilgrimages. On the occasion of the jubilee of 1925 Catholic Germany, in spite of its poverty, furnished a larger number of pilgrims to Rome than any other nationality.

e) *Holy Communion.* The *Kirchliches Handbuch* draws for us a very accurate picture of the use of the greatest means of personal salvation and piety, the participation in the sacraments, especially the reception of Holy Communion. How detailed this picture is I shall show by giving the data for the deanery in which I myself was born. In the year 1929 the deanery of Arnsberg had 40,000 Catholics and 5,000 non-Catholics. During that year 322 Catholic and 18 mixed marriages were concluded. One Catholic marriage and eight mixed ones remained without the blessing of the Church. There were born 838 children of Catholic couples and 23 of mixed couples, beside 22 illegitimate children of Catholic mothers. All these children with the exception of one child of a Catholic couple and six of mixed couples were baptized. 421 Catholics died and all these received a Catholic burial. The number of Communions amounted to 440,799, of which 67,000 were received in monastic or other institutions. To turn to the number of Communions, the number of the Catholics in this and every other deanery or district is rather exactly known from the civil census. The number of Communions can easily be made out by the number of the species required. In the deanery of Arnsberg there were 10.88, practically 11, Communions to every Catholic person, man, woman, and child.

Of course the number of Communions varies very greatly in the several deaneries or districts of the whole Reich. It depends on a number of conditions, only one of which is the personal zeal of the individual Catholic. It depends on the distance of his home from his church, on the number of times Holy Communion can be distributed in church, on his occupational duties, his family duties, etc. In some of the political units there are 10, or 11, or 9 or 5 or fewer Communions a year to one Catholic. The average for the whole Reich, however, is 10 yearly Communions to every Catholic, man, woman, and child, which certainly is quite a good showing.

f) *Easter Communions.* After just learning the number of Communions in the whole Reich, the percentage of the Easter Communions comes like a shock. According to the tables only 60 or 61 percent of the German Catholics make their Easter Communions. Happily, however, the matter is not quite so bad as it would appear. In the number of Catholics are included also the children, who have not yet been admitted to the sacraments. These children, the compiler of the tables tells us, would amount to some 15 percent of the whole number of Catholics. Besides, the number of Catholics is pretty accurately known from the civil census, in which they figure as Catholics, until they have notified the civil authorities that they have left the Catholic Church. The twenty million Catholics therefore include also all those who have not taken this official step, though they have not participated in the active practices of the Church for many years, and in other countries would not be known as Catholics at all. There are moreover the Catholics of the *diaspora*, who often cannot receive their Easter Communion with the best of will, and are easily led, by their non-Catholic surroundings, to attach little importance to this special test of their affiliation with the Church. There is above all the difficulty of counting the Easter communicants with anything approaching accuracy. This difficulty is so great, especially in the larger cities, that many prominent ecclesiastics advocate the dropping of this item in the statistics. It is probably better to retain it, though not without pointing out at the same time that it would be absolutely unwarranted to count all those as apostates who fail to appear at the Holy Table during Easter time. While all these circumstances are bound to change materially the percentage of the Easter communicants, the most consoling fact is its slow but steady increase. In 1924 it was 57.00; in 1927, 59.72; in 1928, 60.33; and in 1929, 60.95. In these five years, therefore, there was an increase of practically 4 percent. The state of misery through which Germany is going at present is not favorable to a sound religious development. But let us hope that the German clergy will succeed in keeping up this improvement until that limit is reached which is set by human frailty and the particular difficulties of the Fatherland.

g) *The number of priests.* In this connection we should also bear in mind that by the war and for many years after the war the ranks of the priesthood were badly thinned. Though the priests had not served as soldiers many of them had served and fallen as chaplains. All the seminarians had been drafted, and long were the lists of those who did not return. Then came the deflation which destroyed the endowments of the seminaries and preparatory schools and made it hard for the impoverished population to supply the means necessary to run them in a satisfactory manner. With all this went the demoralization which extended to the remotest villages. So gloomy was the outlook that men envisaged a time not too far distant when Germany would need missionaries from abroad. Happily these fears have not been realized. For many years indeed the *Kirchliches Handbuch* had to report not only that the number of priests remained stationary or even decreased slightly, but also that the students of theology were not numerous enough to justify the expectations of the necessary increase of the clergy. The later issues of the *Handbuch,* however, report a steady rise in the numbers of theological students, and the very latest, of 1930-31, can state that the present student body of the seminaries and the theological faculties in the universities warrant the hope that in the course of several years there will be priests enough for all the now existing ecclesiastical positions.

This latter statement, however, needs an explanation. In consequence of the peculiar German conditions there is a definite number of priestly positions such as pastors, assistants, chaplains, etc., for which a revenue is provided, either from some ancient endowment, or the church tax, or some other source. As far as these places go, there will soon be no lack of priests in Germany any more. Unfortunately this number of priests is not by far large enough to take efficient care of the Catholics. And the establishment of new positions, which are badly needed, meets with the obstacles raised by the impoverishment of the Catholic population. The present economic situation, which is going from bad to worse, renders such an increase of the priesthood for a long time impossible. This condition of things leads to strange happenings. Thus in 1932 in the diocese of Münster 190 *Abiturienten* (college graduates) applied to be admitted to the study of theology, and the bishop could not accept more than a hundred.

Let us conclude our presentation of Catholic life in Germany with a hearty congratulation to people, priests, and bishops of the Fatherland. Under the protection of its great Apostles, St. Boniface and St. Peter Canisius, Catholic Germany bids fair to hand over its most precious possession, the Catholic faith, unimpaired and in ever-increasing perfection to the coming generations.

V

THE CATHOLIC CHURCH IN CONTEM-
PORARY IRELAND

James F. Kenney

In the county of Antrim, on the north coast of
Ireland, about ten miles to the east of the Giant's
Causeway, lies the little town of Ballycastle. It
grew up in a valley running inland southwest from
a small bay, not far from one of the castles of the
MacDonnells of the Glens. To the north the town
is sheltered from the sea by high ground, where the
Catholic church and other religious institutions now
stand; to the south rises the dark mountain of
Knocklayd, 1,695 feet high, one of the more prominent of the Antrim hills. The MacDonnells of the
Glens were a branch of the family of the Lords of
the Isles, who, about the beginning of the fifteenth
century, obtained by marriage a domain in this
northeast corner of Ireland. Ballycastle is an out-
settlement from the Glens, and, like them, has a considerable Catholic population. The MacDonnells,
earls and marquesses of Antrim, although becoming
Protestants themselves, protected their Catholic de-
pendents, with the result that today, in Protestant
northeast Ireland, this extreme northeast corner,

the Glens of Antrim, is held by a Catholic community.

A short distance to the east of Ballycastle are the ruins of the abbey of Bun-na-mairge, or Bonamargy, a Franciscan house, founded, it is said, about 1475 or 1500. It was destroyed, according to local tradition, during the wars of the Elizabethan conquest, towards the end of the sixteenth century. The friars retired into Glenshesk, the glen that leads into the interior at the foot of the eastern slopes of Knocklayd, and maintained a poor shelter at a place called Ardagh until that too had to be abandoned under pressure of persecution. The story is still told around Ballycastle of Julia MacQuillan, "the Black Nun of Bonamargy," who, after the friars had fled, took possession of the convent and there amid the ruins devoted herself to prayer and penance and the care of the deserted sanctuary. A curious old cross is pointed out as marking her grave at the western church door. Be this as it may, the cross itself, a rude stone monument of unusual character, with a disc at the intersection through which a round hole has been perforated, must be many centuries older than the abbey of Bonamargy, and may well be a relic of the first ages of Christianity in Ireland. An equally noteworthy relic of a later era is preserved in the new abbey of Bonamargy, built—with the cornerstone transferred from the ancient ruins—on the "Catholic hill" overlooking Ballycastle from the northward. It is an altar stone of the penal days, an oblong of mottled black marble, bearing the inscription: *Fr. Bonauentura Boylan ordinis S^tt.^ Francisci me fieri fecit Anno Dni 1725.* Of Father Boylan we know little, except that he was one of the priests who braved the worst of the penal laws in order to maintain the Faith on the slopes of Knocklayd and through the glens of Antrim, but his altar stone could, doubtless, tell many a story of Masses said in strange places in the days when priest-hunting, and more particularly friar-hunting, was a profitable industry.

Towards the end of the eighteenth century the restrictions on Catholics began to be relaxed. In 1795 Hugh Boyd, a wealthy local magnate to whom Ballycastle owed much, donated a plot of ground at the southwest of the town for a Catholic "chapel." A small wooden building was erected; the statement is made that it was the first Catholic church built in Ulster since the penal days, which is as it may be. The building, although much altered, still stands, and is now used as a parochial school. Slowly through the nineteenth century the Catholic people, though losing in numbers, gained in wealth, power and independence. In 1874 the present imposing church of Sts. Patrick and Brigid was built on the hill above the town; in 1880 a commodious presbytery was constructed near by, and in 1905 a parish hall; in 1924 the abbey convent of the Sisters of the Cross and Passion, dedicated to St. Brigid and linked spiritually and materially to the ancient

Bonamargy, was completed, a beautiful and impressive addition to the Catholic "city on the hill."

Thus the Catholic who stands on the streets of Ballycastle has, almost within a stone's throw of him, visible monuments of the history of his Church in every age. So it is throughout Ireland. Each step one takes is planted on historic, indeed on holy, ground. In any survey of Catholicism in Ireland, first consideration must be given to the pervading presence of this background of fifteen hundred years of Catholic history, history in which glory and disaster alternate, but struggle and exaltation are never absent. By reason even of purely secular, though non-material, influences the Irishman cannot but be loyal to the Faith of his fathers. Religious apostasy is, broadly, as unthinkable in Ireland as national apostasy in, shall we say, the United States of America.

In one of the early years of the nineteenth century a certain Catherine MacAuley was born in Ballycastle. As it happens, she was my maternal grandmother, and to seek information about her I, some time since, visited Ballycastle. My search was in vain; as in so many Irish parishes, the extant registers begin only towards the middle of the nineteenth century. Parenthetically may it be remarked that in a large measure the priests of Ireland do not seem to realize of what priceless historical importance their parish registers are to the far-flung Irish race, even in our day, and still more in ages to come!

So I went back to the little weather-beaten frame building where my grandmother had worshipped, and wished she could have been at my side. Doubtless she rejoiced in her day that once more, after so many generations, her people had a church in which to bend the knee, but it must have been wormwood to see, standing in the middle of the town-green and towering above that little chapel, the lofty stone edifice of the then Established Church of Ireland. Could she have lived to behold the magnificent group of Catholic buildings that now dominate the whole community her prayer assuredly would have been *Nunc dimittis*.

Ireland, a poor country, has, it is said, indulged in one foolish extravagance, her churches. Such comment misses the spiritual inspiration of which they are the outward and visible sign; misses the economic philosophy of

Give all thou canst: high heaven rejects the lore
Of nicely calculated less and more—

and quite fails to comprehend the past of Ireland and the reaction thereto of a high-spirited people. The churches, monasteries and convents with which the Irish people, at great sacrifice, have adorned their land are not unconnected with the sentiment of the Irish poet:

Sound the loud timbrel o'er Egypt's dark sea,
Jehovah hath triumphed, his people are free.

Though Irish Catholics won religious liberty, in theory, and with certain limitations, by various measures culminating in Catholic emancipation in 1829, in practice they continued handicapped in many ways, and particularly by their political disabilities. The Irish revolution of 1916-1921, the supreme political upheaval of the present generation, has had powerful repercussions on all phases of Irish life, and not least the religious.

Of the causes and progress of the Irish revolution this is not the place to speak. It must suffice to say that on Easter Monday, April 24, 1916, the workers' "Citizens Army," led by James Connolly, and a section of the Irish Volunteers, led by Padraic Pearse, seized a considerable portion of the city of Dublin and proclaimed an Irish republic; that the insurrection was crushed by the British army after a week's fighting; that fifteen of the insurgent leaders were shot by order of the military tribunals; and that, by the time the fifteenth man had gone down before the firing squad, the majority of the Irish people had been won to latent, if not open, support of the revolution. In 1919 and 1920 the war broke out again, but there was no repetition of the tactics of Easter Week. The Irish resorted to guerilla warfare and assassination, and the British forces to a terrorism which rapidly lost them sympathy not only abroad but even in Britain. In June, 1921, negotiations for peace were opened; on July 11 an armistice was arranged; and on December 6 a treaty of peace was signed. The Irish Free State came into being, consisting of all Ireland except six counties in the northeast. There followed the usual aftermath of revolutions, a civil war among the Irish themselves in 1922-1923, and sporadic outbreaks of violence in subsequent years.

The six counties excluded from the Free State, in which, taken as a whole, there was a large Protestant and Unionist majority, had in 1921 been, by British legislation, created a principality with restricted self-governing powers. The result has been that for the last ten years Ireland has had two governments, that of the Irish Free State with the great majority of its members practical Catholics, that of Northern Ireland with all its members either enrolled in or acknowledging political adhesion to a secret society whose *raison d'être* is opposition to the Catholic Church.

The Irish revolution has been remarkable, if not quite unique, among European revolutions in that it had no anti-Catholic flavor. The anti-Catholics were on the other side. A careful observer wrote of the rising of Easter Week, when the later phase of the struggle was still in the future: "To speak of a Catholic Revolution is practically an oxymoron. Yet Pearse's movement inevitably claims the epithet. Since the days of the *Chouans* so many practising and believing Catholics, aided by so few who were not, never set out to combat an established government. . . . And—what would if possible be less believable to a continental observer—the Freemasons were found well-nigh to a man on the side of con-

stituted authority engaged in putting down the insurrection." [1]

The labor movement in Dublin contained a small
ingredient of Socialism: James Connolly, it is said,
had, under socialistic influences, fallen away from
the practice of his religion, but at the end he returned to the Faith. Sometimes its opponents accused the Sinn Féin party of being anti-clerical: the
only foundation was that Arthur Griffith, its leader,
criticized equally unsparingly priest and layman who
did not square with his ideals of duty to country.
A few insurgent leaders, and a relatively smaller
number of the rank and file, were Protestants.

Easter Week inaugurated the revolution in the
grand manner. Its history reads like a romance of
chivalry. Its gesture was successful with the Irish
people, but its methods would never have forced
negotiations from an imperial government. Over
Ireland after 1916 came a change like that which
passed over Europe after 1914: when the war broke
out again, to the ideals of chivalry and sacrifice were
joined those of "blood and iron" and the "will to
conquer." The wholesale assassinations, ordered by
the Republican military headquarters and executed
by the Irish Republican Army, presented a serious
moral problem. The Catholic Church in Ireland
made no official pronouncement on the subject, and
was in consequence severely criticized by her, and
Ireland's, enemies. The Catholic Church is always

[1] Arthur E. Clery, *Poets of the Insurrection* (Dublin: 1918),
p. 59.

loth to invoke her spiritual authority in political struggles. It is only recently that she has taken definite action condemning the organization that is believed to be mainly responsible for the occasional but persistent outrages which have marred the tranquillity of the Free State during the past eight years, and also condemning a number of very small but active Communistic societies in league with the Bolsheviks of Russia. Every revolution carried by violence has its evil influences, and the Irish revolution was not an exception.

The Irish revolution was a political, not a religious, struggle. This statement holds true, from Easter Week to the Treaty of London, for the twenty-six counties in which Catholics form an overwhelming majority. It does not hold true of northeast Ulster. There the upheaval became a fight between Catholics and Protestants, a Twelfth-of-July riot turned into civil war. The Ulster Orangeman defines political issues on religious lines. When the Republicans attacked a policeman because he was a government official the Orange mobs retaliated by assaulting their Catholic fellow citizens because they were Catholics. Belfast, an industrial city of over 400,000 inhabitants, of whom slightly less than one-fourth were Catholics, living, for the most part, in segregated enclaves, became for two years, from July, 1920, to June, 1922, a scene of horror. During this period 420 people were killed and over 1,600 wounded. On July 21, 1920, riots began in the shipyards, as a result of which all Catholic workmen were expelled, many of them after receiving serious bodily injuries. Henceforth the Catholic sections of the city were in a state of siege, subject to systematic terrorism, to bursts of rifle-fire, sniping, and bombing, and to frequent raids in which men, women and children were butchered with almost unbelievable savagery, and whole rows of houses destroyed. The connection with the war going on in the remainder of Ireland was little more than nominal; there, hostilities ceased with the armistice, while in Belfast they grew worse, and reached their climax after the treaty.[2]

That agents of the Irish Republican Army were operating in Belfast, at least till the truce, may be regarded as certain; that some of the Catholic people who were not of the I. R. A. resisted attack and occasionally struck back fiercely at their persecutors is also certain; but the statement of the Catholic archbishops and bishops assembled at Maynooth on April 26, 1922, cannot be gainsaid:

No reasonable man will believe that Catholics, who form only one-fourth of the city's population, or Sinn Féiners, who form a much smaller percentage, are the instigators or originators of riots in which they are always the chief sufferers.

To this may be added the resolution of the Irish Protestant Convention held at Dublin on May 11, 1922:

[2] Cf. Patrick J. Gannon, "In the Catacombs of Belfast," *Studies*, June, 1922.

We abhor and condemn as unchristian and uncivilized the murders and outrages which have been committed upon men, women and children as a result of sectarian hatred, as well as the forcible depriving of any Irish citizen of his means of livelihood because of his conscientious opinions. We place on record that, until the recent tragedies in County Cork,[3] hostility to Protestants by reason of their religion has been almost, if not wholly, unknown in the twenty-six counties in which Protestants are in a minority.

The supreme test of persecution even to death has not been lacking to Catholicity in the Ireland of our day.

It is not to be inferred, however, that the Protestant or even the Orangeman of the northeast of Ireland is a cross between a Bashi-Bazouk and an Iroquois scalp-hunter. The average Orangeman is a kindly person who would do no harm in the ordinary intercourse of life to his Catholic neighbors. But he is an outstanding example of social atavism: on politico-religious topics his mental processes are those of the seventeenth century. He believes that civil and religious liberty, which are the peculiar glory and monopoly of Protestantism, depend on his own individual vigilance against the machinations of the Pope; from the cradle to the grave his ears are made familiar with "putting down the Fenians" and "slaughtering the Papists"; and twice a year,

[3] On April 27, 1922, five Protestants were murdered in Cork county, apparently in reprisal for the killings in Belfast. If these were reprisals, the universal execration with which they were greeted brought them to an immediate stop.

on the anniversaries of the battle of the Boyne and the relief of Derry, he falls a victim to an epidemic brain-storm. The fever of the revolution wrought a brain-storm long drawn out, under which the wild fanatics and the hoodlums of Belfast reverted to their type and their teaching. Only a very small minority was actively concerned in the pogroms, but the vicious system of sectarianism, like the vicious system of nationalism in a world war, blocked respectable citizens from taking any action that might be interpreted as sympathy for the enemy.

However, brain-storms pass, whether after a day or two years, but the atavistic politico-religious principles remain. Even in his periods of "normalcy" and good will the Orangeman is absolutely determined on one thing: to maintain his own political supremacy. In politics his attitude towards Catholics is not unlike that of the whites of the southern United States towards the negroes in the years following Reconstruction. It is the opinion of careful observers that in public and municipal affairs Catholics in Northern Ireland are today in a considerably worse position than they were twenty years since. Of the six counties and two boroughs that were incorporated in this new state two counties, Tyrone and Fermanagh, and one borough, Derry, had each a Catholic majority. One of the first acts of the new parliament was a reorganization, in 1922, of the municipalities in what was, it is asserted, a barefaced gerrymander against Catholic voters. Since then Protestants have had a substantial majority on the councils of these three Catholic municipalities. In 1929 the parliamentary constituencies were rearranged, again, it is charged, by gerrymandering methods; and the system of proportional representation, enabling minorities to win a fair number of seats, was abolished. Catholics are almost entirely excluded from the public service, and a new educational system gives serious dissatisfaction.

Prior to 1921 there was a single system of education for all Ireland, but it was amorphous and more or less inefficient. From the religious point of view, however, it was generally acceptable to Catholics. Governmental control was exercised through various boards on which, for the most part, Catholics were well represented. The national primary schools were nominally non-sectarian, but practically those that Catholics attended were, normally, Catholic in character, owned by Catholic trustees and administered by managers who, almost always, were the respective parish priests. Secondary schools were subsidized by the State, but privately owned—those for Catholics, by Religious Orders or diocesan trustees.

The Northern Ireland Education Act of 1923, modified by later amendments, centralized governmental administration in a Minister of Education, and greatly increased its range; required that all schools receiving full state aid must be transferred to the ownership and local control of the municipal councils; permitted schools not transferred to continue to receive a subsidy, relatively smaller, at the discretion of the Minister; and authorized public payment for "simple Bible instruction" in the newly provided and transferred schools. The Catholic bishops at once declared "the proposed schools are impossible for our children"; Catholics have not transferred their schools; and there has been constant friction over the discretionary aid granted by the government.

When the boundary of the Irish Free State is crossed we are in a different world. Politics here are not based on religious differences. The State is maintained as a strictly secular institution, and the spirit as well as the letter of the constitution (based on the treaty of 1921) is rigorously observed: "Freedom of conscience and the free profession and practice of religion are, subject to public order and morality, guaranteed to every citizen, and no law may be made either directly or indirectly to endow any religion or prohibit or restrict the free exercise thereof or give any preference or impose any disability on account of religious belief." A small number of good Catholics have been highly critical of such a policy pursued by a government whose members, with one exception, are practising Catholics.[4]

But there are fields in which religion and politics necessarily overlap. One of these is the restraint of the public presentation of matter which may lead to sin or crime or may give serious offense to a large body of well-deserving citizens. The Censorship of Films Act, passed by the Oireachtas, or Free State Parliament, in 1923, provided that no motion-

[4] This was written in December, 1931.

pictures should be exhibited in public unless cer-
tified by the Official Censor appointed by the Minister of Home Affairs. The Censor was required
to certify any film presented to him "unless he is
of the opinion that such picture or some part thereof
is unfit for general exhibition in public by reason
of its being indecent, obscene or blasphemous or
because the exhibition thereof in public would tend
to inculcate principles contrary to public morality or
would be otherwise subversive of public morality."
The Censor may also allow only portions of a film
to be shown, or restrict its exhibition to certain
classes of people or certain geographical districts.
An appeal was allowed to an Appeal Board of nine
members, appointed by the same Minister. In general, the censorship has been applied more rigorously, and much more in accord with Catholic ideals,
than in other countries. During the year 1930, out
of 1,321 "Drama and Variety" films submitted, 185
were rejected and 202 received expurgatorial cuts;
of the 185 rejected the Appeal Board admitted 13
as submitted and 15 others with cuts. The situation
has called forth threats of boycott from the film-
renters of London, and the sarcasm that "theatre
architects in Ireland must have a troublesome time
designing theatres so that the audience can see stage
or screen over each other's haloes." On the other
hand the story goes that when one of the renters
pointed out that he had no Free State rules similar
to those of the British censors the Irish official replied: "Our rules are now the oldest and the shortest

in the world; you will find them in any catechism. They are generally known as the Ten Commandments." [5]

In 1929 a further Censorship of Publications Act was passed. It was introduced as a result of Catholic agitation, but was opposed by some Catholics and received only moderate support from the government. The Act may be divided into an optional section and an obligatory section. Under the first the Minister of Justice may, after complaint has been received, and on the recommendation of a majority of five members of the Censorship of Publications Board, prohibit the sale and distribution of a book that is indecent or obscene or promotes birth control. Periodicals come under the same regulation, with the addition of such as "have devoted an unduly large proportion of space to the publication of matter relating to crime." The obligatory portion of the Act places restrictions on the reporting of judicial proceedings, particularly those relating to conjugal relations, and prohibits the printing, publishing, sale and distribution of literature setting forth methods of birth control. During 1930 the ban was applied to forty-four books and twelve periodicals. The Act is so recent that discriminating information as to its effects is not available.

Divorce, as distinguished from separation, cannot be granted by the Free State courts, and the attempt by private member's bill to introduce judicial divorces has been decisively defeated. It would

[5] *Manchester Guardian Weekly,* November 13, 1931, p. 395.

appear that a majority of Protestants as well as of Catholics is opposed.

By the Intoxicating Liquor Acts of 1924 and 1927, the government, in the face of an influential opposition, made drastic reductions in the hours for the sale of intoxicants and, what was more important, in the number of licensed houses. In neither respect, however, did they go quite as far as the parliament of Northern Ireland in its legislation of 1923.

In education, nearly as extensive a revolution has been wrought in the Free State as in Northern Ireland, but by administrative methods rather than radical reconstruction. As in the North, governmental control has been increased and concentrated in the hands of a responsible minister, but the local management is still, for Catholic schools, in the hands of the Catholic priest; for Protestant schools, of the Protestant minister or his representative. It may be noted that the department declares that of all subjects taught religious instruction is "by far the most important." In the case of secondary schools, increased grants towards salaries and more rigorous requirements as to teachers' qualifications have resulted in a growth in the proportion of lay teachers.

University education is provided for Catholics by the National University of Ireland, with its chief center in Dublin, but having constituent colleges in Cork and Galway. It remains, as it was created by the British Government in 1908, a non-confessional institution, but is Catholic in control, personnel and atmosphere in much the same way as the average state university in America is, in these respects, Protestant.

In affiliation with the National University is St. Patrick's College, Maynooth, Ireland's famous seminary. About six hundred students are enrolled there: in 1930 seventy-three of its graduates were ordained to the priesthood. There are other smaller seminaries in Ireland, which, assuredly, does not lack vocations.

The Free State government has met with strong criticism because of its Irish-language policy. Irish is made compulsory in the primary schools, in the National University matriculation, and in the first years of that university's Arts course; and a necessary qualification for teachers' certificates and appointments to the civil service. On Catholic grounds there should be no objection; the Irish language bears the impress of Catholicity even more than English does of Protestantism; and for a time Irish may be some offset for Catholics to the tremendous cultural, social and financial advantages that non-Catholics still possess throughout Ireland.

This inferiority of potential opportunity for Catholics is a matter of some consequence. According to the census of 1926 Catholics formed 92.6 per cent of the population of the Irish Free State, yet they numbered only 85 per cent of civil servants, 83 per cent of employers, managers and foremen in industry, 80 per cent of railway officials, 78 per cent of physicians, 73 per cent of farmers holding over two hundred acres, 71 per cent of male clerks not in government employ, 70 per cent of lawyers, 64 per cent of civil engineers, 55 per cent of chartered accountants and 47 per cent of bank officials. This is, of course, in the main the heritage from centuries of anti-Catholic rule. It may be noted that there is still some legal débris of disabilities and discriminations against the Catholic Church. The majority are curious rather than important, but it is remarkable that even yet neither the Church as a whole nor the separate dioceses have any legal corporate existence, but must hold property through the troublesome and expensive system of trustees.

It should be added that the Irish Free State maintains a minister at the Vatican and receives an apostolic delegate representing the Pope.

It is now time to present a brief statistical and factual summary of the condition of the Catholic Church in Ireland. By the census of 1926, Catholics in the Free State numbered 2,751,269 out of a total population of 2,971,992, and in Northern Ireland 420,428 out of 1,256,561. They experienced a slight relative gain in the Free State since 1911, and a slight loss in the North, probably in each case resulting mainly from conditions connected with the Revolution. In all Ireland there are four archbishoprics and 24 suffragan sees; 1,115 parishes with 2,473 parochial and district churches, increased by chapels to over 5,000. Statistics now some years old give the number of priests engaged in diocesan work as 3,923, of whom 736 were of the regular clergy. There are some 22 Orders or Congregations of priests, with about 115 houses in Ireland; five Congregations of teaching Brothers; and about 45 different communities of nuns with some 478 convents.

Attention should be directed to the recent development of interest in the pagan mission field. The missionary spirit has been active in Ireland since the early middle ages; in the nineteenth century, however, it expended itself chiefly in supplying priests and Religious institutions to the growing Catholic populations of Britain, the British dominions, and the United States. Even today it is estimated that there are nearly 3,000 Irish priests and over 5,000 Irish sisters serving abroad in English-speaking lands. But in these the need is no longer so great, and Ireland is turning more and more to work among the heathen. A recent article in the periodical, *Pagan Missions*,[6] gives the following statistics of Irish Religious now so engaged: priests, 385; teaching brothers, 259; sisters, 1,063; and in each case the lists are incomplete. In number of priests, Ireland stands seventh among the nations, following France, Belgium, Italy, Holland, Spain and Germany, and preceding the United States and Canada. Special fields assigned to Irish missionary institutions by the Congregation of the Propaganda are as follows: to the Irish province of the Fathers of the Holy Ghost (established in Ireland in 1860),

[6] Use has been made of a summary published in *The Eikon* (Toronto, Canada) for October, 1931, it having been found impossible to obtain a copy of the original publication.

the Vicariates of Sierra Leone, Southern Nigeria, Zanzibar, Kilimanjaro and Bagamoyo, with a population of about 4,000,000; to the Irish province of the Society of African Missions (first introduced into Ireland in 1876), the Vicariates of Western Nigeria and Benin, and the Prefectures of Northern Nigeria and Liberia, in all a population of some 17,000,000; to the Maynooth Mission to China (a purely Irish organization, founded in 1916, just a few weeks after the Dublin insurrection), the Vicariate of Han Yang and the mission of Kien Chang, containing over 5,000,000 persons. The Irish Redemptorists have important charges in the pagan sections of the Philippine Islands, and other Irish congregations are working in various parts of Africa, India and China. Father Gavan Duffy is known throughout the English-speaking world for his work in and his propaganda in behalf of the missions of India.

And what of the Irish laity? In the first place, they supply the men and women and the money that make possible all ecclesiastical effort. But the following headings may be noted of more peculiarly lay Catholic Action, devotional, educational, charitable:

The retreat movement, especially among the working-men of Dublin, is growing steadily. The Third Order of St. Francis is peculiarly strong in Ireland. Many confraternities, especially those maintained by the Dominican Fathers, flourish. There are over 600 sodalities of the Blessed Virgin. In the Apostleship of Prayer, Ireland ranks sixth among the nations in the number of prayers and intentions offered for the Holy Pontiff. The *Irish Messenger of the Sacred Heart* has 253,000 subscribers, besides 3,000 for the edition in Gaelic. In 1927 the *Messenger* office published 469,077 books and pamphlets. "The League of Daily Mass," founded in 1915, has more than 50,000 members, a total which includes the membership throughout the world. The Catholic Truth Society of Ireland is well known beyond the bounds of the Green Isle for its popular doctrinal and controversial publications, but we are not so familiar with its other wide and diversified activities—public lectures, Catholic weeks, study clubs, national pilgrimages, and Catholic press service. Two special organizations have recently been founded, in 1923 the Rescue Society of Ireland to fight non-Catholic proselytism, a not very serious but extremely persistent feature of Irish religious conditions, and the League of the Kingship of Christ, to inculcate Catholic principles in public affairs. The Catholic Young Men's Society, founded in Limerick more than eighty years since, still has a number of large branches, but, in the opinion of some observers, is neither so well organized nor so vigorous as the peculiar conditions of the present day demand. The Saint Vincent de Paul Society in 1927 counted 350 conferences and some 5,650 active members: 27,824 families were visited and 108,938 persons benefited from its assistance. Like the Catholic Truth Society, its activities are more diversified than in other countries, and include the maintenance of an orphanage, a class for deaf-mutes, sailors' clubs, penny-savings banks, restaurants for the poor, a night refuge for men. The Roomkeepers Society, an organization some 140 years old, assists poorer workmen who are temporarily in difficulties. The temperance propaganda of the famous Father Mathew has been revived in recent years by various organizations, of which the most important is the Pioneer Total Abstinence Association, founded in 1899 and now numbering over 300,000 members. Due to this movement, to government legislation, and, it must be added, to economic depression, there has been in the last two or three years an extraordinary decrease in the consumption of spirituous liquors.

Two movements of recent origin should, perhaps, be selected for emphasis because they seem so well designed to meet the special needs of the present day. One is the Central Catholic Library, founded in Dublin in 1922 to provide "a representative collection of Catholic literature on all subjects bearing on the Faith . . . intended primarily as an aid to students, journalists, teachers, social workers, professional men, writers, and inquirers," but open to all who wish to use it. Already, in large measure because of the energetic work of the Rev. Stephen J. Brown, S.J., it has gone far to attaining its aim. The other movement is that of the Legion of Mary, founded in Dublin in September, 1921, chiefly through the instrumentality of a man who should be described as a worker of wonders in our time, Mr. Frank Duff.

It has a somewhat elaborate organization, modeled on that of the Roman military legion, and with its ideals of action those of the Roman legionaries: fearlessness in the face of the moral enemy, self-sacrifice, discipline. Its object, as stated in the handbook, is "the sanctification of its members by prayer and active coöperation in Mary's and the Church's work of crushing the head of the serpent and advancing the reign of Christ." It seeks especially such tasks, open to the laity, as seem impossible. Its standards and its aims appear to be perilously high, and yet, as Professor Alfred O'Rahilly recently wrote, "I made a great discovery, or rather, I found that the discovery had been made, that there is a latent heroism in seemingly ordinary men and women; an unknown source of energy had been tapped." [7] Mr. Duff states: "No branch of the Legion has yet failed. . . . Its members have specialized in the attacking of situations and problems—and places—voted impossible, and have gained a uniform success." In Dublin, three concrete monuments show part of its achievement: the Morning Star Hostel, for the permanent rehabilitation of "down-and-out" men; another for "down-and-out" women; and a third for derelict women who can also be described as "fallen." They have been maintained entirely by voluntary workers, and have had extraordinarily good results. The Legion now numbers 130 branches, including many established abroad; is increasing at the rate of about two

[7] *The Irish Press*, September 15, 1931.

branches a week, and has received the stimulus of the expressed wish of our Holy Father that it may spread over the whole world.

Such are some of the factual records of Catholicity in Ireland as they appear to an onlooker from abroad. They seem good. And they do not include the intangible evidences of spirituality, the Catholic attitude of mind evidenced in casual speech, the matter-of-fact devotion that sends city housewives in crowds to the eleven o'clock Mass that is said daily for their accommodation. At least two men who died in our time may, we hope, be some day classed by the Church as of heroic virtue: Father William Doyle, Irish Jesuit who was killed while serving as chaplain in the Great War, and Matt Talbot, poor day-laborer of Dublin. The record, I have said, seems good; but the average Irish Catholic of today has not the "guid conceit" of himself as offspring of a chosen people that possibly characterized his father. The average elderly Irish priest will tell you that spiritually the country is going to the dogs. There is change in the things that the priest has loved; the modern world is pressing more and more into the green fields of Ireland; a great revolution has shaken the country morally as well as materially to its foundations. God in His own good time has seen fit to give to some of the Irish people some of the secular blessings they have prayed for during seven hundred years. To our blurred vision it would seem that He is likewise reviving old or raising new forces to meet changed

needs.   Certain it is that from Ballycastle to Skib-
bereen the average Irishman is faithful still as he
has been faithful since Patrick brought the Faith
fifteen hundred years ago.[8]

[8] The book which comes nearest to covering the matter of this
paper is *Le Catholicisme en Irlande*, by Dom Thomas Becquet,
O.S.B. (Liége, La Pensée Catholique).   Some help has been obtained from the Rev. George Stebbing, C. SS. R., *The Position
and Prospects of the Catholic Church in English-speaking Lands*
(Edinburgh and London: 1930), from Denis Gwynn, *The Irish
Free State: 1922-1927* (London: 1928), and from M. F. Liddell,
Irland (Leipzig and Berlin: 1931).   The most valuable repertories
of source-material are the various Irish Catholic periodical publications, in particular the annual *Irish Catholic Directory and Almanac*.   Other such are *The Irish Ecclesiastical Record, The Irish
Rosary, The Irish Monthly* and *Studies*.   *The Dublin Review*,
published in London, also contains occasional articles on contemporary religious conditions in Ireland.   The writer has
consulted many individual issues of these publications, but
has not been in a position enabling him to make use of complete
series.   He has also used the following pamphlets: The Rev. T.
Corcoran, S.J., *Notes sur l'enseignement secondaire catholique en
Irlande* (Brussels: 1930) and *Les écoles catholiques en Irlande*
(Louvain: 1931); the Rev. M. J. Browne, *Legal Disabilities of
the Catholic Church in Ireland* (Dublin, The Catholic Truth Society of Ireland); *The Morning Star: the theory and practice of
a great experiment;* and the provisional handbook of the Legion
of Mary.   Official statistics and other information are to be obtained from the publications of the governments of the Irish Free
State and Northern Ireland, more especially the statutes and
parliamentary debates, the census reports and the reports of the
departments of education.   Finally, the writer is indebted for
suggestions given personally by the Rev. Stephen J. Brown, S.J.,
the Rev. Myles V. Ronan, and Mr. Frank Duff.

VI

THE CHURCH IN CONTEMPORARY ITALY

Wilfrid Parsons

There are certain factors, social, historical, and religious, that distinguish Italy from other European countries, and certain others which it has in common with some but not with all. They must all be taken into consideration for a proper understanding of the Church's position in that country.

1. Social and Physical Factors

The first of these factors special to Italy is, of course, the presence within its boundaries of the seat of the central government of the Catholic Church, the Holy See. This presence has contributed to politico-religious events a color which is entirely lacking elsewhere. The second factor is what I might call a concentration of history within it to an extent which can be said of no other country. Rome has really been at the end of most roads in Europe for twenty centuries. This concentration of the past at times works with an almost explosive force in the present; nowhere more than in Italy. The third is its special central geographical position: a peninsula which has two frontiers—one Gallic and one Germanic—and which is the crossroads of the South, as Belgium is of the North. No social, political, or economic movement happens in Europe without leaving its imprint on Italy. The fourth is the social awareness of its people—a racial trait that has always made it the immediate victim or the close forerunner of revolution or reaction alike. One special economic factor which reacts on social problems is Italy's total lack of coal or oil, and its relative lack of water power. A country without such natural resources cannot embark on Communism in the midst of a capitalistic Europe.

Besides these special and distinctive factors, there are others which Italy shares with some European countries, but not with others. Like Germany, France and England, Italy suffered heavily in the war in young-man power and in wealth. As with France, new territories were won which added to national and religious problems. As in Belgium, a high density of population makes for social solidarity. As in Germany, a high birth rate makes for adventure abroad, with the outlet to the United States closed. Unlike Belgium and Spain, but like France, a homogeneous population makes for racial peace. As in all the Latin countries, a long association with the Church in official relations creates special paradoxical conditions of friendliness and unfriendliness together: anti-clericalism and the political power of Freemasonry moulded its recent history, while nationalism gave a special character to religion. Like all Europe, the post-war economic depression has exercised a cramping effect on both national and religious policies.

The geographic and demographic facts about Italy are soon recalled. It is a peninsula 760 miles long and nowhere more than 150 miles wide. It has an area of 119,744 square miles, a little more than that of New England and New York combined, and more than 36,500 square miles less than that of the State of California. For this area it had in 1929 a population of 42,115,606, a density of 343.9 persons to the square mile, as compared with a density of 131.7 for New England and New York, our most densely populated area, and of 35.5 for the United States. It has the highest birth rate in Europe (29.27 per 1,000 in 1929), and with the exception of the Netherlands (in 1930, 140 per 10,000) the highest excess of births over deaths in Europe: in 1930, 123 per 10,000.[1] In that same year Italy increased its population by excess of births over deaths by 515,027, which has been a fairly stable figure for fifteen years.[2] This growing population has had a large influence in shaping Italy's foreign policies, especially in the Near East, and bids fair to be a determining factor in the future.

The ecclesiastical figures are no less interesting and distinctive. The country is divided into 275 dioceses, of which 75 are immediately subject to the Holy See, and the remaining 200 constitute 37

[1] Statistics from *World Almanac*, 1931.
[2] *Journal Officiel*, Paris, May 10, 1931, annexe. Cf. *Dossiers de l'Action Populaire*, July 26, 1931, p. 16.

Provinces.[3]   A well-known demographer, Abbé
A. d'Espierres,[4] estimated in 1929 that of the population that year of 42,115,606, there were 40,009,-
826 Catholics, 351,617 Protestants (mostly Wal-
densians), and 1,717,622 of no religion.   It is
admitted by candid Italians that Catholicism in Italy
presents, in the period under consideration, the usual
double aspect of Latin countries: an instinctive and
widely uninstructed, and at times fervent, Catholic
population in rural areas, and in the cities an un-
digested mass of anti-Catholicism, largely among the
industrial population, along with much indifferentism,
existing side by side with a splendid enlightened
Catholic élite among poor and rich alike.   This situation is not surprising, when one considers the long
official estrangement of Church and State, and the
intensive anti-religious propaganda to which the
Italian people were subjected for many decades.
Not the least among recent changes is the practical
cessation of this propaganda, and the introduction of
compulsory religious instruction into elementary and
secondary public education.

More potent than any of these statistical factors,
however, and indeed overwhelming in its influence,
is the adoption by Italy, after 1923, of an entirely
new—for modern times—theory and practice of pub-

[3] By the Lateran Concordat, Arts. 16 and 17, the Holy See binds
itself to reduce the number of dioceses, as they become vacant,
so as to make them correspond with the number of State Provinces; there are 92 of these Provinces.

[4] A. d'Espierres, *Les religions dans les différents pays du monde,*
cited in *La Documentation Catholique,* vol. 26, August 29, 1931,
col. 311.

lic government. This new system—Fascism—has transformed both the public and private relations of Italy and the Italians with the Church. It will be part of my difficult task to place this system in its proper historical setting, and to estimate its probable influence on present-day Italian life.

2. THE HOLY SEE

After the death of Pius IX (1878) and the coming of Leo XIII, it might have been expected that skilful diplomacy on both sides would more or less quickly dispose of the impossible situation created by the occupation of Rome by the Italian State, and by the Law of Guarantees. Such, however, was not the case; and modern writers have been wary of placing the responsibility. One of Leo's first acts was to protest to the world against the unnatural situation of the Papacy in his Encyclical *Inscrutabili*, April 21, 1878.[5] He also continued in force the *non expedit* of 1868 of Pius IX with regard to the participation of Catholics in political life, and the *ipso facto* excommunication of members of the government. The Vatican and the Quirinal were hopelessly deadlocked up to the end of the World War. A surcharged emotional atmosphere kept "The Roman Question" continually to the fore, but impossible of solution. Yet in view of the extreme simplicity of the solution when it did come, it seems curious to us

[5] In his Encyclical *Dall'alto dell'Apostolico Seggio* of 1890, Leo XIII laid down the terms of settlement as he conceived them.

now that the formula had not emerged long before. I think it fair to say that this formula was present actively in the Vatican itself for a long time; on the other hand, before the break-up of the so-called liberal-democratic, that is, Masonic, hegemony over Italy, no acceptance of it was possible on the part of the government.

Certain external events prepared the way after 1919. The war had destroyed many false assumptions. In spite of French accusations of Vatican friendliness to Germany, the Italians had had before their eyes the spectacle of the vivid patriotism of the papal entourage, while understanding better than any others the fact that the Pope himself, as the Father of all the faithful, was committed to neutrality and peacemaking rather than to partisanship and war. It can now be seen that the day the war ended, the solution of the Roman Question was inevitable, in spite of the notorious fact that Italy had exacted, in the Treaty of London, the promise that the Pope would be excluded from the Peace Conference.[6] To anyone who lived in Rome, as I did in the two years following 1918, signs of a breakdown of the deadlock were apparent. The sight of Cardinal Van-nutelli on foot in the street, though in black; of religious processions in some localities; of a practising Catholic, Filippo Meda, in the Cabinet; of a Catholic party in the Chamber: all these were merely symbols of what was passing in people's mind. Premier Or-

[6] Former Premier Nitti, in his *Bolshevism, Fascism and Democracy* (p. 208), says that even the Cabinet was kept ignorant of the terms of this Treaty.

lando has related the conversations he had had with Msgr. Cerretti, now Cardinal, through Bishop (then Msgr.) Francis C. Kelley of Oklahoma at the Paris Peace Conference and the cause of their failure.[7] In 1920, Premier Nitti held conferences with Cardinal Gasparri on the Roman Question.[8] Periodically, the inspired newspapers were allowed to speculate on the formula of a solution. There was literally an air of expectancy in Rome that the solution would not long be delayed.

Then began the era of "solutions." At one time the Catholic press, inspired from Rome, broke out with a renewal of Leo XIII's suggestion of 1888 to Francis Joseph, that the Roman Question could be solved only by an international agreement of the world powers, guaranteeing the sovereignty and neutrality of the Holy See.[9] This suggestion aroused violent opposition in Italian State circles up to the end.[10] This was followed by suggestions of the territory to be allotted to the Vatican. The most favored was the "corridor scheme" allowing it access

[7] Vittorio Orlando, "The First Agreement Between Italy and the Holy See," *Saturday Evening Post*, May 4, 1929. Also *Vita e Pensiero* (Milan) for August, 1929, as translated for the N. C. W. C. News Service for the week of September 2, 1929, gives large extracts from the diaries of both Cardinal Cerretti and Bishop Kelley.

[8] "Pertinax" (André Geraud), *Le partage de Rome* (Paris, 1929), p. 22.

[9] For an echo of this, cf. *America*, 21: 7 (May 24, 1919), pp. 174-76, Reville, "The Prison of the Pope." The *Corriere della Sera* of April 16, 1929, told the story of Leo's letter. Cardinal Gasparri, in his letter of June 28, 1915, scouted the idea of an international pact, but Pertinax (*op. cit.*, p. 22) states the idea came up again almost at the last minute.

[10] Mussolini, in his speech on the Treaty on March 14, 1929, said that the Holy See had never asked for it from him.

to the sea.[11]   But little by little opinion was crystallizing, and an understanding of the true nature of the
Holy See's case was beginning to dawn on the minds
of the people.   When Pius XI ascended the papal
throne in 1922, his first act was to appear on the
balcony of St. Peter's for the benediction *urbi et
orbi*, and in his first Encyclical, *Ubi Arcano*, he said:
"It is scarcely necessary to say here how painful it
is to Us to note that from this galaxy of friendly
Powers that surround Us one is missing, Italy, Our
own dear native land, the country where the Hand of
God, Who guides the course of history, has set down
the Chair of His Vicar on earth."

3.   The State

Meanwhile political events in Italy itself had,
unknown to the world, hastened the "solemn and
auspicious hour," to use the words of Pius XI himself on December 23, 1922.   A new system of government had taken possession of Italy's destinies,
which was, in every sense of the word, a revolution.
The war left Italy a chaos of conflicting economic,
social, and political forces, utterly uncontrolled by
the corrupt and inept politicians who succeeded each
other in power.[12]   In 1919, the rise of a new Catholic

[11] Cf. R. L. Buell, *Europe: A History of Ten Years*, p. 359.
Erzberger, in his *Memories of the War* (1920), recalls that he had
proposed the same scheme to the Holy See.   A commission appointed by Benedict XV in 1915, reported many schemes on
December 6, 1923.   *"Ainsi,"* says Pertinax, *"Vatican et Quirinal
étaient encore hantés par des fantômes."*   (*Op. cit.*, p. 115.)
[12] *Europa Year Book, 1929*, pp. 378-79: "Parliamentarianism in
Italy is less than two generations old, and almost from its origin

party, the *Partito Popolare,* founded by a Sicilian priest, Don Luigi Sturzo, Mayor of Caltagirone, seemed destined to change the face of Italy. At its first election in November, 1919, it polled 1,100,000 votes, and gained 120 seats in the Chamber. It had a progressive and even radical social and agrarian platform; it numbered men of real ability, but contained, perhaps, too wide a spread of social thought from left to right.[13] Its mistake, as seen now by looking backward, was in coöperating with the so-called Liberal and democratic parties which had misgoverned Italy for so long. It went down with them in 1924 in the general reprobation of parliamentary government.

Those who lived, as I did, in Italy during 1919-1921, know how imminent was a social revolution. But the paralysis of government seized the Socialists as well as everybody else. It is this paralysis, as manifested in the State, which was the real cause of Fascist success. Democracy, as exercised through parliament, was thoroughly bankrupt in Italy. The steady evolution of Mussolini himself, from anarchical Socialism through republicanism to his present position, shows how unerringly his instinct led

it succumbed to poisonous abuses, chronic, critical and deep rooted. . . . Parliamentary life in Italy . . . was of bad quality. . . . In the midst of post-war misery, turmoil and broken promises, the State was in danger of foundering under the attack of unorganized and unauthorized Socialist depredations." Two old-time politicians, Salvemini, *The Fascist Dictatorship in Italy* (pp. 19-40), and Nitti (*op. cit.,* pp. 48-53), unconsciously bear witness to the same facts.

[13] For the program of the Popular Party, see *Documentation Catholique,* vol. 2, cols. 443-4, and Luigi Sturzo, *Italy and Fascismo,* p. 19.

him to this fundamental fact. Italy itself was thoroughly ready to be governed no matter how, so long as it was governed. In the face of that fact, it is sterile to discuss whether Fascism saved Italy from Communism.

Mussolini, at the age of thirty-six, on March 23, 1919, formed his Black Shirts of some young men who shared the common disgust and distrust of parliamentarianism. To him flocked a heterogeneous crowd of malcontents and idealists. In three years of agitation marked by much violence and bloodshed, the new party was strong enough to march on Rome, where the weak Facta Government succumbed without a blow. Mussolini was called by the King to be Premier. Within three more years, in 1925, Mussolini was strong enough to strike the decisive blow, the proscription of the Freemasons,[14] whom, in a long speech in May, 1925, he had accused of having governed Italy in the interests of France and of having kept the country in a ferment of religious turmoil. From then on, his reorganization of the State was rapid. On April 21, 1927, there was promulgated the Charter of Labor, and the State began definitely to be organized on a genuinely syndicalist basis adapting to Italy the ideas of Georges Sorel and Rossano.

While the new régime was slowly fashioning itself, Italy was held by a rigid dictatorship that reached into every corner of Italian life, which, in Mus-

[14] Law of November 26, 1925, *Gazetta Ufficiale*, No. 277, November 28, 1925, p. 4714.

solini's eyes, was nothing more than an armed guard holding the fort while behind it a new régime was being formed and ingrained into the souls of young Italians.[15]

The new Italian State system is called by its authors the *Stato Totalitario Corporativo*. It is governed on a basis of economic units, not political. Every citizen is to be enrolled in these units, or syndicates, of which there are fourteen: seven for employers and seven for employees, representing industry, agriculture, commerce, banking, inland transportation, air and sea transportation, and professional men and artists.[16] Each set of employers' and employees' syndicates is unified into a corporation, under a Ministry of Corporations (founded in July, 1926) and the National Council of Corporations (1930), of which the Premier is President. These corporations have both an economic and political function. Within themselves they provide for a complete system of compulsory arbitration of disputes, with collective contracts, strikes being forbidden by law; and one of the sixteen Courts of Appeal is a special labor court for these disputes.

Such a system, of course, could exist without in any way affecting the political constitution of the

[15] The dictatorship, or the office of *Capo del Governo*, was legalized by the law of December 24, 1925, and extended by the law of January 31, 1926. *Gaz. Uffic.*, No. 301, December 29, 1925, p. 5067, and No. 25, February 1, 1926, p. 426.

[16] For a good description of the Italian syndicalist State, see *Foreign Policy Reports*, 7: 3, April 15, 1931, "Fascist Rule in Italy," by V. M. Dean, pp. 73-79. See also Carmen Haider, "The Italian Corporate State," *Political Science Quarterly*, 46: 2 (June, 1931), pp. 228-247.

State. In Italy, however, the syndicates are destined
to play a predominant rôle in governing the country
in its internal affairs. The legislative section of the
Italian Government consists of two houses: a Chamber of Deputies and a Senate. The Senate is ap-
pointive by the King from among twenty-five
specified categories, one of which is the archbishops
and bishops. Its functions are largely deliberative.
The Chamber of Deputies, however, is a legislative
body elected in the following manner: The candidates are 1,000 in number for a body of 400. A list
of 800 is sent up to the Grand Council [17] from the
National Confederation of Fascist Syndicates: each
syndicate is assigned a quota in proportion to its
importance; employers and employees in each category receive the same number.[18] Besides this, 200
candidates are named by other recognized associations, cultural, educational, charitable, or propagandist. From these the Grand Council selects 400
names, and the whole list is submitted to the country
in the form of a plebiscite every five years. The
country is made into one electoral district and the
list is accepted or rejected *in toto*. If the people
reject the list, the syndicates present lists, and the
list with the highest vote is elected, other lists receiving seats in proportion. In March, 1929, the
present Chamber was elected in this fashion, and

[17] For the nature of the Grand Council, see *Foreign Policy
Reports, loc. cit.,* pp. 60-62. It is the governing body of the
Fascist Party become the highest State body.

[18] For the inequality of this provision, see *Reports, loc. cit.,*
p. 67.

89.5 per cent of the electorate took part, 8,663,412 out of 9,673,049 registered voters casting ballots, with only 135,761 voting against the list; many bishops and priests urged their people to vote "yes."

It is highly important to note that in the Fascist design there is only one political party and no party warfare; or rather, that the party system is done away with altogether as having been responsible for most of Italy's ills for fifty years. In that sense "Fascist" is not a party tag, but synonymous with "Italian." Fascism is the Italian system of government, the Italian mentality, not a party platform, and enemies of Fascism are branded as enemies, not of the party, but of the fundamental national economy, just as monarchists in Spain were by the group in power there, and as it was proposed to do with opponents of the Free State in Ireland. Thus the division between Fascists and non-Fascists is more fundamental than party.[19]

It has been freely said that Fascist theory owes its origin to Machiavelli's *Prince,* and to Sorel, Hegel and Nietzsche. This theory was succinctly put forth by the Italian Ambassador to the United States in a speech in Philadelphia in 1928, in which he declared: "It was once said that the State exists for the citizen: we have changed all that. For us the citizen

[19] Mussolini had written in 1922: "I do not doubt that Fascism and the State . . . are bound to become 'one entity'": M. Sarfatti, *Life of Benito Mussolini* (1925, p. 297). "The Italian State is the Fascist State," is his formula (speech of May 13, 1929, Chamber of Deputies).

exists for the State." It is true that this neo-Hegelianism is the theory enounced by the philosopher Gentile, who was Minister of Education before 1927.[20] On the other hand, the reaction to this doctrine is led by Alfredo Rocco, Minister of Justice, and a practising Catholic.[21] As for Mussolini himself, I was told late in 1928 by one very close to him that he has no philosophy, no theory, that he is a man of action purely, "who does the next thing that comes along to do."

Fascism, however, has developed along definite lines that should imply a theory, however variable. It does not deny the idea of popular sovereignty, as has been alleged, but it does reject the so-called democratic method of exercising it, that is, through the party system.[22] Primarily, the Fascist theory is said by its adherents to be a moral one, stressing the ideas of discipline, responsibility, loyalty, expressed in concerted action. Negatively, it rejects *laissez-faire* and all forms of European Liberalism. Politically, it sees the State governed by the people in its economic functions, not by parties. One must not forget that it has been evolving constantly, that consistency from one year to another is not made a

[20] Cf. M. Vaussard, "Fascisme et bolshevisme en face du supranationalisme catholique," *Revue Apologétique*, Jan. 4, 1928.

[21] Alfredo Rocco, "The Political Doctrine of Fascism," *International Conciliation*, Carnegie Endowment for International Peace, October, 1926, No. 223, p. 394: "Fascism as an idea is indefinable. It is a fact which is taking place."

[22] Mussolini, *Discorsi della rivoluzione*, p. 21: "You know that I do not endorse that new divinity, the masses. It is a creation of democracy and Socialism. 'Only because they are many, they are right.' Nothing of the kind. The opposite is true: numbers are contrary to reason."

virtue, that last year's statements must not be taken as this year's position.[23]

4. CHURCH AND STATE

Of course Fascism came up against the religious factor almost at once. At first, Mussolini seemed inclined to a thesis almost like that of the *Action Française,* a purely pagan position that welcomed the Catholic religion for its traditional place in popular psychology and its moral firmness. Under certain influences, however, he abandoned this position, and approached more nearly the Catholic position.[24] In any case, he early saw the necessity of regulating the religious question. He was met with the blunt assertion from the Vatican that there were two questions, not one: the *Italian Question,* or the regulation of the affairs of Italy with the Church, and the *Roman Question,* or the regulation of the juridical position of the Holy See in Italy and the world.[25] The latter must precede any attempt to deal with the former. The Vatican, also, publicly made clear its position and the possible terms of solution. It did not seek territory, but independence from secular powers, in order to exercise its spiritual functions unhampered. In this world, such independence can

[23] Cf. Sarfatti, *op. cit.,* p. 71.
[24] Pertinax, *Le Partage de Rome* (pp. 198-9) recounts having heard at the Vatican in 1929 that he is a practising Catholic, and had made his Easter duty for the last three years; he also tells of his long-standing friendship with Father Tacchi Venturi, S.J.
[25] Cf. Letter of Pius XI, *Si è annunciato,* to Cardinal Gasparri, of February 18, 1926 (*Oss. Rom.,* February 22-23, 1926).

be had only by the possession of real sovereignty, an inherent ruling power not subject to any other. The Law of Guarantees was unacceptable precisely because it was a law, an act of a legislature, and hence subject to change, no fit base on which to found sovereignty, not a treaty between equals.[26] As for land, only such small territory as was barely sufficient for a sovereignty to exist in was demanded.[27] It was on these terms that the Roman Question was settled through the Treaty of the Lateran on February 11, 1929, followed by the signing of a Concordat on the same day, settling the Roman Question.[28] The old idea of Temporal Power ended on that day. It was a real revolution in Church polity.

The Treaty and Concordat introduced a profound modification into the religious life of Italy. The old

[26] For a fuller statement of this position, see Wilfrid Parsons, S.J., *The Pope and Italy*, pp. 31-35.

[27] Letter of Cardinal Gasparri on October 6, 1926, as quoted by Mussolini in his speech of May 13, 1929.

[28] The principal documents for the Treaties are: (1) *Treaties:* three documents, Lateran Accord with three annexes, Concordat, Financial Convention, in *Acta Apostolicæ Sedis,* June 7, 1929, and in *Atti Parlamentari,* Camera dei Diputati, Legislatura XXVIII, la sess., 14 maggio, 1929, pp. 171-341. (2) *Acts of the Holy See:* "Laws and Dispositions of the State of Vatican City," in Special Supplement of *Acta Apostolicæ Sedis,* June 8, 1929; 7 laws: fundamental law, sources of objective law, citizenship, administration, economic, commercial, and professional provisions, public safety, and right of entry, with annexes giving the official flag, seal, and shield. The postal convention followed on July 29. *Religious administration:* by creation of a Vicariate and parish of St. Anne of the Vatican, Apostolic Constitution of May 30, 1929, *Ex Lateranense pacto, in Oss. Rom.,* June 11, 1929. (3) *Acts of the Italian Government.* Three Acts of May 14, 1929: Execution of the Treaty, Application of the Concordat to the Marriage Laws, and Disposition on Ecclesiastical Bodies and Goods. Royal Decree of May 27, 1929, on the financial convention. *Gazz. Uffic.,* June 5 and 8, 1929.

laws calling for a secular marriage ceremony before the religious one were done away with, and the religious ceremony was made legal. Says the Concordat in Article 34:

The Italian State, wishing to reinvest the institution of marriage, which is the basis of the family, with the dignity conformable to the Catholic tradition of its people, recognizes the Sacrament of Matrimony performed according to Canon Law as fully effective in civil law.

Obligatory religious instruction was introduced into secondary public education. Article 36 of the Concordat uses these striking words:

Italy considers the teaching of Christian doctrine according to the forms received from Catholic tradition as the foundation and crown of public education.

In his speech on May 13, 1929, defending this Article Minister of Justice Rocco said: *"Lo Stato cattolico non può non educare i suoi cittadini alla fede cattolica*—the Catholic State cannot but educate its citizens in the Catholic Faith." Religion had already been introduced into primary education under Minister of Education Gentile in 1923, in what Mussolini called the "most Fascist of all reforms." [29] Anti-religious propaganda was more sternly repressed, and the proselytizing activities of Protestants severely restricted. The number of chaplains

[29] Royal Decree of October 1, 1923: "The teaching of the Christian doctrine in accordance with the Catholic Faith shall form the basis and aim of elementary education in all its grades." (Art. 3.) Parents who impart this instruction themselves and those who do not wish it at all are exempt from the law.

in the army was increased and they were given larger facilities. Public religious processions were fostered and protected. On many occasions the public authorities pronounced on the patriotic necessity for Italians of practical Catholicism. Private holders of confiscated Church property were granted title to it by the Holy See "to appease their conscience," by Article 28 of the Concordat. The "purification" of the public services from the presence in them of Masons was completed. The inner conflict of Italian loyalty and Catholic faith was dissipated.

On the other hand, the reconciliation of the Church and Italy went through many dark days at first. The ink was hardly dry on the Treaties when Mussolini, in his speech of May 13, 1929, introducing the Treaties to the Chamber of Deputies, spoke as follows on the subject of education:

Another régime than ours, a democratic-liberal régime, one of those régimes that we despise, can deem it useful to renounce the education of the young generations. Not we. On this ground we are intractable. Education must be ours. These children must be raised in our religious Faith, but we must complete this education, we must give these young people the sense of manhood, of power, of conquest; above all, we must transmit to them our faith, our hopes.[30]

To this the Pope took emphatic exception. In several audiences, notably to the students of the College of Mondragone on May 14, he rebuked the idea

[30] *Messaggero* (Rome), for May 14, 1929.

of State monopoly of education, and put forth the
rights of the family and the Church. He said:

Where we can never agree is when men wish to oppress,
lessen, deny this right which nature and God have given
to the family and to the Church respectively in the domain of education. On this point we are, I do not say
intractable, for to be intractable is not a virtue, but intransigeant. . . .[31]

To which Mussolini replied on May 25 before
the Senate:

Instruction is one thing and education is another.
Are we Fascists partisans of a fierce monopoly of instruction? No! Must I recall that it was under the Fascists
that the first Italian Catholic university was opened?
But there is one side of education on which we are, if I
may not say intractable, at least intransigeant. . . .
What is then this education to which we claim the right
in full? The education of the citizen. . . . If the contemporary world were not this world of savage wolves
that we know (wolves even when they dress in the height
of fashion and in funeral tail-coats), then we might renounce such an education, to which we will give a name,
for hypocrisy is repugnant to us: a warlike education.[32]

The Pope replied on May 30 in a long letter to
Cardinal Gasparri in which he threatened to revoke
the Treaty if the Concordat was not respected.
"They will stand together," he said, "or they will
fall together, even should Vatican City as a consequence fall along with the state which it consti-

[31] *Oss. Rom.* for May 16, 1929.
[32] *Corriere d'Italia* (Rome), for May 26, 1929.

tutes." [33]   Meanwhile, however, he was forced to see
the *Giovani Italiane,* the Catholic girls' club, 500,000
in all, follow the way of the *Giovani Esploratori,*
the Catholic boy scouts, into the ranks of the official
Fascist organizations. He did this, he said, to avoid
a greater evil.[34]

Up to 1931 the conflict smouldered. It suddenly
broke out again when the young men's clubs this
time were abolished by decree. The Pope had, on
December 31, 1929, in his Encyclical *Rappresentanti
in terra* on Christian Education condemned the distinction between religious instruction and State education along with the Fascist theory that the addition
of religious instruction to a secular education constitutes Christian education:

The mere fact that a school gives some religious instruction (often extremely stinted) does not bring it
into accord with the rights of the Church and of the
Christian family, or make it a fit place for Catholic students. To be this it is necessary that all the teaching
and the whole organization of the school, and its teachers,
syllabus, and textbooks in every branch, be regulated by
the Christian spirit, so that religion may be in very truth
the foundation and crown of the youth's whole training,
and this in every grade of school, not only the elementary, but the intermediate and higher institutions of
learning as well.[35]

[33] *Oss. Rom.* for June 6, 1929.
[34] Pertinax, in *Le Partage de Rome,* pp. 54-56, gives a résumé
of this struggle.
[35] *Catholic Mind,* 28: 4 (February 22, 1930).

On May 15, 1931, the Pope published his Encyclical *Quadragesimo Anno* on the Reconstruction of the Social Order, in which he claimed the right to determine the answers to social and economic problems.[36]   This challenge was immediately accepted, and the young men's organizations depending on Catholic Action, a national federation, were suppressed on May 30.   This brought the conflict to an acute point, and on June 29, 1931, the Pope issued his Encyclical *Non Abbiamo Bisogno* on Catholic Action, which was smuggled out of Italy by air and cabled over the world.[37]   Again the issue of State monopoly of essential education apart from religious instruction was raised, in spite of Article 43 of the Concordat which reads:

The Italian State recognizes organizations dependent on *Azione Cattolica Italiana*, inasmuch as they, as the Holy See has declared, exercise activity outside all political parties and are under the immediate direction of the hierarchy of the Church for diffusion and propaganda of Catholic principles. . . .

The dispute was settled for the time by the agreement of September 3, on which date the government issued a *communiqué* in which, contrary to cabled reports, the Pope yielded nothing; the right of the Church to pronounce on social questions and to influence their solution was not denied, the central board of Catholic Action was not abolished, while the abstinence of Catholic Action as such from politics was reaffirmed, as was the essentially local and diocesan character of its constituent parts.[38]   Msgr. Pizzardo, its General Assistant and a resident of Vatican City, had already resigned this position on June 10.

5. CATHOLIC ORGANIZATION

In accordance with its official definition as the "participation and coöperation of the laity in the apostolate of the hierarchy," Catholic Action has been looked on by Pope Pius XI as the most immediately necessary factor in his program for the Christian reconstruction of modern society.[39] With insistent pressure he has from the beginning of his pontificate dwelt on its value as an organization for personal sanctification, as an educational instrument, and as a channel of indirect influence on the State.   He took a personal and unflagging interest in the formation and growth of Catholic Action in Italy under the name of *Azione Cattolica Italiana* and secured the inclusion in the Concordat

[38] Cf. Yves de la Brière, in *Études* (Paris) November 5, 1931.
[39] The important documents on Catholic Action, previous to 1929, can be found in Cavagna, *Pio XI e l'Azione Cattolica,* in which it is stated that only in three months from 1922-1929 did Pope Pius XI fail to speak on the subject.   Other texts are collected in *Documentation Catholique,* 23: cols. 323-384, 579-639. The principal Papal documents are Pius X, *Il Fermo Proposito* to the Italian Bishops, May 11, 1905; Pius XI, *Ubi Arcano,* December 23, 1922, and *Quas Primas,* December 11, 1925.   Beside Papal texts, important are the letters of Cardinal Gasparri to Bishop Skwireckas of Kaunas, December 12, 1928, and to Cardinal Hlond, Primate of Poland, February 1, 1929, and April 10, 1929; and the speech of Cardinal Pacelli at Magdeburg, September 5, 1928.

of a provision safeguarding its liberty, as he had in the Lithuanian Concordat.[40]

This Italian society has two branches, masculine and feminine: the masculine is composed of three organizations: the Italian Federation of Catholic Men, the Association of Italian Catholic Youth, and the Italian Catholic University Federation; the feminine section, called the Italian Catholic Feminine Union, is divided into three parts—the Union of Italian Catholic Women, the Italian Catholic Feminine Youth, and the Italian Catholic University Women.[41]   To these are added various professional groups, whose interests are specialized.   In 1931, the *Azione Cattolica* numbered 4,000 sections.   These associations are at bottom parish bodies, each under parochial councils; these councils in turn function under a diocesan council, and all the diocesan councils are coördinated under the Central Committee, with headquarters at Rome, near Vatican City. Each parish has an ecclesiastical assistant, to safeguard orthodoxy of action, but the officers of the councils are laymen.   Each diocesan council has a similar assistant, as has the Central Committee at Rome.   The use of the organizations for political purposes is forbidden, but there is assured the smooth carrying out of Catholic Action's threefold function of personal sanctification and higher religious instruction, of

[40] Pertinax, *op. cit.*, p. 161, n. 6; cf. pp. 127-163, chapter: "La place du concordat italien dans la politique générale de l'église."

[41] Cf. "Statuto de l'azione cattolica italiana," *Monitore ecclesiastico*, November, 1923, pp. 330-340.

interaction among Catholics themselves, and of an ultimate influence on society itself. It was at this latter aspect that Mussolini took alarm, determined as he is that Catholic youth, men and women, be thoroughly imbued with Fascist principles.[42] Peace between the two sides can only be assured at last by confidence on the part of the State of the essential patriotism of the members of Catholic Action, and on the part of the Church that the Fascist State is not anti-Catholic or non-Catholic in its aims and actions. Personal relations will do more than public protests.

6. The Future

Italy, then, is not at all what it was in 1913, still less what it was in 1900. There is also a sharp contrast between Italy before the Treaty in 1929 and Italy today. For fifty-nine years faithful Catholics were torn between their allegiance to the new Italy and to the Church which that Italy openly oppressed, and negligent Catholics were the prey of a never-ceasing anti-Catholic propaganda, which in the growing ranks of Socialism before and after the war reached the height of fanaticism. The divided allegiance was wiped out by the Treaty, and the anti-religious forces are driven out or forced under

[42] Speech of May 13, 1929: "The Fascist State lays full claim to its moral character. It is Catholic; but it is also Fascist; it is even before all, exclusively, essentially Fascist. Catholicism completes it, we declare it openly; but let no one take it into his head, under cover of philosophy, of metaphysics, to shuffle the cards in our hands!"

cover.[43]   The Catholic faith is taught in the public
elementary and secondary schools, and the crucifix
is in each classroom as the symbol of the Faith of
the nation.   Relations between Church and State
are regulated by a Concordat, which is the most
favorable ever negotiated by the Church.   The Catholic laity have an organization in *Azione Cattolica,*
which is a perfect instrument for forging the Catholic
spirit in the nation.   There is only one Catholic
University for laymen, that of the Sacred Heart at
Milan, though there is also an Institute for Higher
Studies for the laity at the Gregorian University in
Rome.   The courses at the other universities vary
from our own familiar naturalism to the best of
Catholicism.   All other things being equal, Catholicism in Italy has the best chances in Europe to
flourish and grow.

The Church, however, is functioning under a régime which is above all others jealous of its own
moral power and influence.   Mussolini is intelligent
enough to know that the preservation of his régime
depends above all on education, and to understand
that all education is not confined to the schoolroom.
All the Fascist organizations are primarily educa-
tive.   But so is Catholic Action.   If the government
continues to observe the Concordat which allows
Catholic Action full freedom, there will be no further
conflict along this line.   In that case coöperation

[43] On June 30, August 7, and December 25, 1930, Pius XI protested at the laxness of the government in dealing with Protestant
anti-Catholic propaganda in Italy.   He does not seem to have
protested since.

between the two systems will be an ideal one: the official organizations stressing the natural virtues of courage, loyalty, self-sacrifice, and coöperation, and the Catholic bodies informing all this with supernatural principles. The task of the Catholic authorities for the next few years is a delicate one. But they will be strengthened by the unshakable determination of Pius XI to see that the Catholic idea prevails in Italy and everywhere.

VII

THE CHURCH IN CONTEMPORARY POLAND

LEONID STRAHKOVSKY

ON the plain between the Baltic and the Carpathian Mountains bordered by the rivers Elbe, Boug, and San, a Slavonic people named the Poles have organized their State. Their original history is obscure. Like most of the primitive people who migrated into Europe they were ruled by a patriarchal system and, in the early times of their existence, their chief occupations were hunting and agriculture. Until the tenth century they remained pagans like the primitive Russians or Teutons, worshipping gods representing the forces of nature.

The first historical ruler, Mieszko (960-992), accepted the Christian faith, in about 969, from Rome, thereby bringing the country within the sphere of influence of Western Europe. The first bishopric was established in Poznań and the most famous missionary of that early time was Bishop Wojciech (St. Adalbert) who preached Christianity in Pomerania and who was murdered, about 997, while endeavoring to introduce the Christian faith into Prussia. In the year 1000, under the reign of Boleslas the Brave, the first Polish archbishopric was established at Gniezno, then Poland's capital. During this time, Poland was desperately fighting for its independence from Germanic influence and even conquest. Professor Paul Kehr of the University of Berlin has finally proved that the alleged papal bulls making the See of Poznań dependent on the Archbishop of Magdeburg were fabrications intended to prevent the creation of an archbishopric in Gniezno in order to keep the church in Poland under German influence [1] However, after the year 1000, the Church in Poland was emancipated from any foreign influence.

The Archbishop was assisted by bishops with their sees in the principal Polish towns of that epoch: Breslau, Cracow, and Poznań. In 1130, a new bishopric was created in Julin, Pomerania. In 1207, through the intervention of the Pope, the Polish clergy obtained the right, together with other privileges, to elect the bishops. In the fourteenth century with increasing influence of the Polish nobles, the church dignitaries received seats in the King's Council. But in 1460 the situation was changed: the clergy had to pay taxes; and thereafter all bishops were nominated by the king to be later recognized by the Pope. Although losing many of its former privileges the clergy continued to perform its great missionary work in Eastern Europe, and converted the heathen population of Lithuania after the union of that country with Poland, in 1386. This missionary work of the Polish clergy differed considerably from that of other religious and semi-religious

[1] Stefan Karski: *Poland, Past and Present*, Warsaw, 1927, p. 26.

groups because it was fundamentally opposed to the
method of spreading religion by force.[2] At the famous Council of Constance the rector of the University of Cracow, Paul Wlodkowic, defended the rights
of the pagans and claimed that they ought not to be
converted by the use of the sword as did the German
knights of the Teutonic Order.[3] In his defense of
the pagans, that distinguished Pole was somewhat a
forerunner of Francesco de Vittoria who, as it is
known, established the foundation of modern international law. Religious tolerance was strictly observed during the rule of the Piast and Jagiello
dynasties. During the greatest persecution of Jews
in the middle of the fourteenth century in Western
Europe, Casimir the Great permitted them to come
freely to Poland. In 1442, the Greek Uniate Church
received in Poland all the rights enjoyed by the Latin
Church.

When the waves of the Protestant Reformation
spread all over Europe, Poland did not remain exempt from the influence of new ideas. However, it
was only the aristocratic families who passed over
to the creed of Luther. With the exception of a few
Northern towns and the City of Danzig, the reformation did not penetrate into the mass of the people.[4]
The then-reigning last kings of the Jagiello dynasty,
though profoundly Catholic, did not use any but
spiritual weapons in their fight against Protestantism.

[2] Antoni Choloniewski: *The Spirit of Polish History,* New York,
1918, p. 35.
[3] Stefan Karski: *op. cit.,* p. 27.
[4] Stefan Karski: *op. cit.,* p. 28.

King Sigismund I used his power in certain instances when after the issue of the Bull *Exsurge* (1520) he forbade by the Edict of Torun (Thorn) the introduction into the country of Luther's works and when, in 1534, he prevented the nobles from sending their sons to the University of Wittenberg.[5] His son and successor, Sigismund August, the founder of the Union with Lithuania (Union of Lublin—1569), manifested even a greater spirit of toleration when he addressed to his people these memorable words: "I am not king of your consciences."[6] As for Stephen Batory, elected King of Poland, in 1576, his reign was supported by wise support of Catholicism and an open struggle with anarchy. Still even during this time, no force in religious matters was ever used. His great chancellor of State, Jan Zamoyski, best expressed the attitude of the king when he said: "I would give half of my life if I could thereby reclaim for Catholicism those who have abandoned it, but I would rather give my whole life than to see them converted by violence."[7] Throughout the religious wars of the sixteenth century and the Thirty Years War in Germany as well as the Huguenot persecutions in France, not a drop of blood was shed in Poland on account of religious differences.

This spirit of religious tolerance remained alive so long as religion was detached from politics. The loss of popularity of Protestantism in Poland in the

[5] A. Leman: *The Church in Modern Times*, St. Louis, 1930, p. 59.
[6] Antoni Choloniewski: *op. cit.*, p. 36.
[7] Stefan Karski: *op. cit.*, p. 28.

seventeenth century was due perhaps to the marked tendency of its followers to combine religion with political purposes, even more so than to the growing influence of the Jesuits who were brought to Poland in 1555. Unfortunately, this tendency of the Polish Protestants was soon followed by the Catholic Poles as well, reaching its apex when, in 1733, the Sejm legislated that non-Catholics should have no right to be elected to law courts or any administrative post.[8]

After the third and final partition of Poland, the Church began to be definitely connected with politics by playing a national rôle in those portions which were taken by Prussia and Russia. Due to this fact, the governments of these respective countries, in their pursuance of assimilation, adopted a policy which often led to intolerance and religious persecution. In some cases, however, the precedent was created by the Poles themselves. Thus in judging the persecutions of Greek Catholics (Uniates) by the Russian Imperial government and their forced reunion with the Greek Orthodox Church, one must not forget that the Union of Brest, of 1595, by which the Ruthenian population of Poland returned to the Catholic Communion, was not achieved by agreement or peaceful persuasion, but through imposing it upon the mass of the population by the nobles. As to the persecutions of the Roman Catholic Poles by the Russian government, inexcusable as they are, they were the result of the undaunted spirit of the

[8] Stefan Karski: *op. cit.*, p. 30.

Polish clergy, members of which used even the Church pulpit for national propaganda.

But not only did the Poles attack Greek Orthodox in their political struggle against Russian domination, they fought even their co-religionists for the sake of nationalism. During the author's research for a study on Emperor Alexander I of Russia, he has come across some material which gives a strong indication that it was Prince Adam Czartoryski's subversive activity which precipitated the expulsion of the Society of Jesus in 1816. Prince Adam, then curator of the educational district of Wilno, desired to subordinate all Catholic education in Russia to the great idea of a complete restoration of Poland. But the Jesuit fathers having always been true internationalists were unwilling to serve any national needs. So long as their college of Polotsk was subordinated to the Catholic University of Wilno they were sometimes forced to yield to some of Czartoryski's orders, but when Emperor Alexander granted their college the rank of a university on the eve of the War of 1812, they were automatically withdrawn from the jurisdiction of the University of Wilno and freed from Prince Adam's influence. This the ambitious patriot could not suffer and he used all his personal influence on Alexander to obtain his aim. And he succeeded, thus deepening the rift between the Russian Church and State and the Catholic world.

However, the Concordat of 1847, concluded in the reign of Emperor Nicholas I by the Russian

Ambassador to the Vatican and the representatives
of His Holiness Pius IX, established a quite liberal
modus vivendi giving freedom to the exercise of the
Catholic faith within the territories of the Russian
Empire and recognizing the rights of Catholics equal
to those of other religious denominations as stipulated by the laws of the Russian state.[9]   Certain restrictions which still existed were abolished after the
Russian revolution of 1904-1905.[10]

During all this period the Catholics in Austrian
Poland enjoyed full rights.   They did so in the Polish
territories annexed by Prussia with the exception of
a brief period when Bismarck had instituted his
famous *Kulturkampf*.

When the World War began the Polish question
was once more put in the foreground.   On August
14, 1914, the Commander-in-Chief of the Russian
armies, the Grand Duke Nicholas, announced his
desire to unite all Polish territories as an autonomous
entity under the Russian Imperial Crown.   This
started the fight for Polish sympathies between Russia and the Central Powers.   After the occupation
of Warsaw by the German armies, on August 5,
1915, the Central Powers spared no effort to secure
Poland as their ally.   Finally, on November 5, 1916,
Poland was proclaimed an independent state with a
constitutional monarchy as its form of government.
Since then, the Polish patriots have endeavored to

[9] R. P. Louis Lescoeur: *L'Eglise Catholique en Pologne sous le
Gouvernement Russe,* Paris, 1860, pp. 434-439.   Text of the
Concordat.
[10] Stefan Karski: *op. cit.,* p. 32.

bring about the practical realization of that theoretical independence. When the Treaty of Brest-Litovsk of March 3, 1918, ended the hostilities on the Eastern front, Poland's independence still remained a dead letter. It was only after the defeat of Germany that, under the pressure of the governments of the Allies, the temporary Regency Council, instituted by Letters-Patent of the German Emperor, surrendered its authority to Joseph Pilsudski, on November 14, 1918. On February 9, 1919, the first Constituent Diet met in Warsaw, thus marking the beginning of Poland's independence which received its final sanction in the Treaty of Versailles, of June 28, 1919.

On March 17, 1921, the Constituent Assembly enacted and confirmed the Constitutional Charter of the Polish State, which was declared to be a republic.[11] This Constitution, which was modeled in its main outlines on the Constitution of May 3, 1791, in its Chapter V dealing with the General Rights and Obligations of Citizens, regulates the religious rights as follows:

Article 111. The freedom of conscience and of religion shall be guaranteed to every subject. No one may be denied the rights granted to other citizens on account of his religion or his religious convictions.

All inhabitants of the Polish Republic shall have the right to profess freely their creed in public or in private and to follow the canons of their religion or ritual, so

[11] F. B. Czarnomski (ed.): *The Polish Handbook,* London, 1925, p. 13.

long as such practices are not contrary to public order.

Article 112. It shall be forbidden to have freedom of creed which is not in agreement with the law. No one may be kept from the performance of his public duties on account of his religious convictions. No one may be compelled to take part in a religious act or ritual, unless he be subject to paternal or tutelary authority.

Article 113. Every religious association recognized by the State shall have the right to organize its religious services in public or at private meetings; it may freely conduct its internal affairs, own and acquire, administer and dispose, of its movable or immovable property, have the possession and benefit of its funds and endowments, equally with institutions of a religious, charitable, or scientific character. No religious association may be formed in disagreement with the laws of the State.

Article 114. The Roman Catholic Creed, being the creed of the majority of the people, shall have a preponderating authority in the State among other religions which shall enjoy equal treatment.

The Roman Catholic Church is governed by its own laws. The relation between the Church and the State shall be determined on the basis of a Concordat with the Holy See, which shall be ratified by the Diet.[12]

Thus, though not recognizing any established State religion in Poland and granting equal rights to all denominations, the Constitution recognizes, nevertheless, to the Roman Catholic Church "preponderating authority in the State." This is only natural when one realizes that the great majority of the population professes Roman Catholicism. According to

[12] F. B. Czarnomski: *op. cit.*, p. 28.

the census of 1921, there were in Poland 17,368,352 (63.8%) Roman Catholics; 3,032,636 (11.2%) Greek Catholics (Uniates); 2,846,508 (10.5%) Russian Orthodox; 2,849,020 (10.5%) Jews; 1,014,577 (3.7%) Protestants; 73,743 (0.3%) others.[13] These are the only exact figures that we possess because the figures of the census taken in December, 1931, are not as yet available. However, the following official estimate for 1930 may be worth while quoting: 23,025,000 (74.9%) Catholics (including both the Roman Catholics and Uniates); 3,802,000 (12.4%) Russian Orthodox; 2,978,000 (9.7%) Jews; 842,000 (2%) Protestants.[14]

In fulfillment of Article 114 of the Constitution, a Concordat was negotiated between the Holy See and the Polish Republic. It was finally signed in Rome, on February 10, 1925, by Cardinal Gasparri, representing His Holiness, and Ladislas Skrzynski and Stanislas Grabski, representing the President of the Polish Republic, and ratified in Warsaw, on May 30, 1925. This Concordat included twenty-seven articles and an annex regulating the compensation of the clergy. It guaranteed a complete freedom of the Church in its existence within the limits of the Polish State as well as in its relations with the Holy See. Article IX declared that no part of the Republic of Poland will come within the jurisdiction of a bishop whose See may be situated outside the frontiers of the Polish State. The same Article estab-

[13] *Statesman's Year Book*, 1926.
[14] *Statesman's Year Book*, 1931.

lished the Catholic hierarchy in the Republic of Poland as follows:

A. LATIN RITE. I. *Ecclesiastical Province of Gniezno and Poznań:* Archdiocese of Gniezno and Poznań, Dioceses of Chelmno and Wloclawek.

II. *Ecclesiastical Province of Warsaw:* Archdiocese of Warsaw, Dioceses of Plock, Sandomierz, Lublin, Podolsk and Lodz.

III. *Ecclesiastical Province of Wilno:* Archdiocese of Wilno, Dioceses of Lomza and Pinsk.

IV. *Ecclesiastical Province of Lwów:* Archdiocese of Lwów, Dioceses of Przemysl and Luck.

V. *Ecclesiastical Province of Cracow:* Archdiocese of Cracow, Dioceses of Tarnów, Kielce, Czestochowa and Silesia.

B. GREEK-RUTHENIAN RITE. *Ecclesiastical Province of Lwów:* Archdiocese of Lwów, Dioceses of Przemysl and Stanislawow.

C. ARMENIAN RITE. Archdiocese of Lwów.[15]

This ecclesiastical organization comprises 5,965 churches and 8,373 priests of the Latin rite; 3,275 churches and 2,144 priests of the Greek-Ruthenian (Uniate) Rite; 12 churches and 27 priests of the Armenian Rite.[16]

Article XI of the Concordat states:

The choice of archbishops and bishops belongs to the Holy See. His Holiness agrees to confer with the Presi-

15 *Dziennik Ustaw,* No. 72, 1925, p. 1086.
16 *Statesman's Year Book,* 1931.

dent of the Republic before appointing archbishops and diocesan bishops, coadjutors *cum jure successionis,* as well as the army bishop, in order to obtain the assurance that the President has no objections of a political nature to this choice.

It may be of interest to compare this Article with Article XII of the Concordat of 1847 between the Holy See and Russia which reads:

The designation of bishops for the dioceses and the suffragances of the Russian Empire and of the Kingdom of Poland will take place after a previous consultation between the Emperor and the Holy See in each case.

It seems that the political reasons of state in Church matters have not much changed since 1847.

In addition to the restrictions established by Article XI of the Polish Concordat, Article XII specifies that all prelates must take an oath of fidelity according to the following text:

Before God and the Gospel I swear and I promise as is fitting for a bishop, fidelity to the Republic of Poland. I swear and I promise to respect in all loyalty and to demand that my clergy respect the government established by the Constitution. I swear and I promise also that I will not participate in any accord or assist any council which might cause prejudice to the Polish State or to the public order. I will not permit my clergy to participate in such action. Being solicitous of the good and interest of the State, I will try to protect it from any danger that I may learn of.[17]

[17] *Dziennik Ustaw,* p. 1087.

The remaining articles of the Concordat regulate the following questions: (1) religious education in schools and universities; (2) property rights of the Church and of the clergy; (3) the right of patronage; (4) the right of the State to extend its criminal jurisdiction to the clergy; and (5) the right of the hierarchy to call on the civil authorities for the execution of ecclesiastical decisions and decrees.

Thus the Concordat of 1925 established the legal basis for the relations of Church and State in Poland. Its Article III regulated the diplomatic relations between the Polish Republic and the Holy See with the following words:

In order to maintain friendly relations between the Holy See and the Republic of Poland an Apostolic Nuncio will reside in Poland and an Ambassador of the Republic will be accredited to the Holy See.[18]

However, this stipulation did not bring about any new situation because, since April 25, 1918, a "Visitator" and since June 5, 1919, an Apostolic Nuncio had resided in Poland.[19]

It might strike one that the Concordat of 1925 did not regulate the status of Catholic societies and associations as was the case in Lithuania.[20] This situation is taken care of by Article 108 of the Constitution, which declares full freedom and exer-

[18] *Dziennik Ustaw,* p. 1085.
[19] V. Meysztowicz: "De Conditione Juridica Ecclesiæ in Polonia," *Jus Pontificium,* 1930, p. 279.
[20] "Concordatum cum Republica Lithuania," Art. XXV, *Acta Apostolicæ Sedes,* 1927, p. 426 ff.

cise to societies and associations, not only *de facto* but also *de jure*.[21] "Proinde et 'Actio Catholica' libere in Polonia evolvitur." [22]

Another important phase of the relation between Church and State is the religious education in schools and universities. Article XIII of the Concordat stipulated that in all public schools, primary as well as secondary, religious education is obligatory.[23] The number of hours of religious instruction in primary and secondary schools is not fixed by the religious authorities but by decrees of the Minister of Worship and Instruction. In practice it varies between two and four hours a week. The teachers of religion are appointed by the civil authority but only after they have obtained the necessary diploma from a seminary. If the hierarchy revokes the right of instruction from a teacher of religion, he is automatically suspended. This rule applies not only to teachers in primary and secondary schools but also to professors, their associates and assistants of the theological faculties in the State universities. It is not only to be found embodied in Article XIII of the Concordat but also in a circular of the Minister of Worship and Instruction, dated April 24, 1926.[24] As far as the religious instruction in universities and graduate schools is concerned there is no obligation attached to it with the exception, of course, of the Catholic University of Lublin. However, the four

[21] F. B. Czarnomski, *op. cit.*, p. 28.
[22] V. Meysztowicz, *loc. cit.*, 1931, p. 8.
[23] *Dziennik Ustaw*, p. 1087.
[24] V. Meysztowicz, *loc. cit.*, p. 13.

leading State universities have theological faculties. These faculties were created at the University of Cracow, in 1369; at the University of Wilno, in 1578; at that of Lwów, in 1661; and in Warsaw, in 1815. The University of Poznań, founded in 1919, has no theological faculty.[25] With regard to the religious education of minority groups in primary and secondary schools, the instruction is being done in the maternal tongue of the children if such be the desire of the parents, and at the expense of the State in each case when there are at least twelve children of that denomination.[26] On the whole it is apparent that the religious education of Polish children and youth is well assured and guaranteed not only by the Concordat but also by State legislation.

There is, however, one domain in the relations of Church and State that presents a fertile field for constant friction, and this, notwithstanding the fact that an amicable agreement on the subject is not only possible but would be greatly desirable for the welfare of the entire Polish nation. This is with regard to the existing laws of marriage. First of all, they are not uniform. Central Poland, which, after 1815, became the Kingdom of Poland under the Russian Imperial Crown, follows the law regulating marriage, dated June 24, 1836. Still, even in this part of Poland, the eastern territories, which formed part of Russia before 1815, are regulated by the laws of the Russian Imperial Code. In former Austrian

[25] *Ibid.*

[26] "L'instruction publique en Pologne," *Varsovie*, 1929, pp. 143-144.

Poland, marriage laws are those of the Austrian Civil Code (Paragraphs 44-136) and of the Hungarian Matrimonial Law of 1894 (Articles XXXI and XXXIII). And the parts of Poland that were annexed by Prussia are subject to the German civil code. In order to bring more harmony with regard to these different regulations, the Polish Government instituted a law of August 2, 1926. But the initiators of this law gave more consideration to the rights of the State than to those of the Church. Thus under this law a civil court can break a religious marriage. This is but one of the provisions which are unsatisfactory to the Church, and V. Meysztowicz, speaking in authority as a former Minister of Justice, strongly advocates the necessity of a new law concerning this matter.[27]

Notwithstanding the existence of this domain of friction, the *modus vivendi* established by the Concordat and the subsequent State legislation places the Church in Poland in a very favorable and independent position. The situation would be quite ideal if it were not that a certain part of the Catholic population, together with its clergy, Religious Orders, and the hierarchy, has found itself involved in a deep political struggle, not only with the Polish government, but with the entire Polish nation.

This study would not be complete if no mention were made of the Separatist Movement in Eastern Galicia, populated by Ruthenians. The Ruthenians do not form a definite nation. As a member of the

[27] V. Meysztowicz, *loc. cit.*, p. 9.

Slavonic race they are equally related to the Russians, Poles, and Slovaks. They belong to the same group as the Little Russians, or Ukrainians in Russia, and the Carpatho-Russians in Czechoslovakia. Their nationalism is of a recent date and since its beginning has been kept alive more or less by foreign influence. As far as their religion is concerned, the Ruthenians of Eastern Galicia are Uniates, *i.e.*, Catholics in communion with Rome but retaining the Greek rite and the married clergy. In the present, as in the past, they are passionately attached to their rite and very much more afraid of Latinization on the part of the Poles than of proselytizing efforts of Orthodox Russians. They form a compact group of over 3,000,000 people whose religious direction has been entrusted to Mgr. Andrei Szeptycki, Archbishop of Lwów and Metropolitan of the Uniate Church in Poland. Soon after the World War the Separatist Movement among the Uniate Ruthenians began to take definite proportions. Politically, these Separatists are divided into many groups, which have only one aim in common: freedom from Polish rule. In quest of this aim the Separatists have adopted terroristic measures which have recently disturbed the whole political and economic life of Eastern Galicia. "All through the autumn of 1930, over the wide expanse of southeastern Poland, the lurid glow of conflagrations was continuously to be seen. They were lit by Ukrainian parties, and all efforts made by the Polish authorities to induce the Ruthenian Uniate clergy to

condemn such acts came to nothing. This clergy,
up to and including Archbishop Andrew Szeptycki,
its highest authority, kept silence, looking with indifference upon what was going on, or, as was shown
by judicial inquiries, even taking an active part in
this action. This disposition among the clergy is to
be explained by the fact that the ecclesiastical seminary at Lwów, which is maintained by the Polish
government, is completely in the hands of the anti-
Polish and pro-German party." [28] In response to
the terroristic activity of the Ukrainian military organization the Polish government has taken strict
measures to protect its citizens and the property of
the State in Eastern Galicia. These measures
brought a wave of protest from Ukrainian organizations the world over. A curious situation is to be
observed with regard to this problem. It is that
the measures of "pacification" taken by the Polish
government were not extended to the important
Province of Volhynia, the eastern part of the Province of Lublin and the south of the Province of
Polesia, in all of which there are communities of considerable size of Greek Orthodox Ruthenians who
are absolutely loyal Polish citizens.

In viewing this situation, one is prone to draw a
parallel between the present and the past. As it has
been demonstrated, the outstanding manifestation of
the Polish character has been religious tolerance.
The exercise of that tolerance has been considerably

[28] Stanislas Srokowski: "The Ukrainian Problem in Poland,"
Slavonic Review, March, 1931, p. 595.

hampered in the past whenever religion mixed with politics. It seems that this grave danger exists in present-day Poland as well. The only hope that one can express is to see that the Polish Catholics in their present enjoyment of freedom will not close their eyes to the experiences of the past.

VIII

THE CATHOLIC CHURCH IN CONTEMPORARY RUSSIA

Edmund A. Walsh

There is being waged in Eastern Europe at this moment an ancient conflict in which the protagonists are not men but principles. The arena, as befits titanic adversaries, is that one-seventh of the earth's surface which stretches from the Arctic Circle to the Hindu Kush Mountains and from the Polish frontier to the Sea of Japan. The stake is twofold. First, the soul of a great nation whose exhausted body has been bludgeoned into passive submission by ten years of terrorism. But ultimately the prize is the soul, the body and the spiritual allegiance of the entire human race. He who visualizes the Russian scene solely within the frame of the Five-Year Plan and limits his inquiry to its political, economic and social accidents has but scratched the surface of the Communist mind. He has not seen the woods because of the trees, has not pierced the first of the seven veils of propaganda that obscure the basic issue between two clashing civilizations.

Soviet Russia is no longer a geographic expression. It is an idea. Those roaring factories built by American engineers, those gigantic collective farms with

their Detroit equipment, those imposing hydro-elec-
tric plants likewise constructed under American supervision, have so intrigued and fascinated the casual
tourist that he generally misses their true, and for
the Bolshevik, their only permanent, significance.
For the midsummer visitor to Moscow, hungry for
romance, they are thrilling poems of industrializa-
tion—busy marts of trade—stately temples of commerce—daring flights of a new-fledged freedom.
But to the calculating builders and masters thereof
they are steely instruments of a far-flung purpose
and the latest concrete expression of Lenin's dream
of universal empire.

The objectives of the Communist State are not
confined to domestic prosperity and security, nor
limited by national frontiers. Their militant political philosophy leaps these traditional limits of sovereignty, since their claim is to rule mankind in the
mass. A line is drawn through human kind hori-
zontally, separating men into two strata—all who
are not of the Communist faith are against it and
are to be regarded as enemies. The Bolshevik victory of November 7, 1917, was not merely revolution
in the accepted sense as historically understood—
that is, a re-allocation of sovereignty—but revolution
in the domain of economics, religion, art, literature,
science, education and all other human activities. It
sought to create a new archtype of humanity, a
"collective man" and a new culture adapted to the
impersonal "mass man," who should displace forever the "soul-encumbered individual man." It was

meant, and so proclaimed, by its protagonists, to be a challenge to the modern state as constituted not merely in imperial Russia, but throughout the entire civilized world. It is philosophic materialism in arms, the most radical school of thought that has yet come on the stage of human affairs. War, implacable war, with no mercy shown, direct action, terrorism, complete annihilation of the bourgeois opponent—such is the all-inclusive strategy of this impatient Hotspur of the nations.[1]

The Bolshevik has a complete philosophy of action

[1] The opening paragraph of the present Soviet Constitution reads as follows: "Since the formation of the Soviet Republics the world has become divided into two camps, that of Capitalism and that of Socialism. . . . The very structure of the Soviet power, which is international in its class character, calls the toiling masses of the Soviet Republics towards a unity of one Socialist family." It will be noted that boundary lines seem to be done away with. Nationality is destroyed. "Capitalism and Socialism," all states automatically fall into one or other of these groupings. The first states that have joined the Union (whether they wanted to or not) are described in the closing words of the paragraph as forming "a decisive step towards the union of the toilers of all countries into a World Soviet Socialist Republic."

Here is formal proclamation embodied in the organic law of the Union to the effect that the Soviet system begun in Russia is to spread to the entire world. Moreover, the inclusion of the first states of this new Union is interpreted in the language of the Constitution not as an isolated historic fact but as an advance, a decisive step in the accomplishment of a definite policy. To symbolize this progression, the previous seal of Soviet Russia, adopted after the revolution of November, 1917, was modified, and Article 70 of the new Constitution provides for the new insignia which we began to notice in Moscow in the summer of 1923. It consists of a sickle and a hammer mounted on a terrestrial globe, on which the two hemispheres are visible; a certain number of the countries are depicted in red, the implication being that the redness is to envelop all other countries in due time. The whole is surrounded by sheaves of grain bearing the inscription in six languages: "Proletarians of all lands—unite." Article 72 provides that the capital of this World Union shall be the city of Moscow.

—is, in fact, far more dialectical and metaphysical than his enemies credit him with being.[2] He has certain first principles which he assumes to be true, not subject to discussion and, for him, incapable of refutation. He will argue their application and extension, debate their success or failure, but he will not permit question of their validity. Seriously attacked, even in a purely intellectual way, he will not hesitate to kill an opponent with a cold, satisfying sense of duty done that has had few counterparts in recorded history. Such impersonal fanaticism can be explained only by a great love or a great hatred. For him there is but one categoric imperative: *Thou shalt communize the world, or else destroy it*. He is wound up on that mainspring.

Bolshevism is Monism in every connotation of the term, but Monism enthroned in the seats of Autocracy and supported by an established government and a Red army. It has set its hand to the creation —first in Russia, then throughout the world—of the "mass-man," a collectivized human machine that will dispense with those attributes of personality that distinguish one individual from another. Form, figure, countenance, strength of body and mind, name, gifts, graces, rank, and age are all weighed in the one balance of economic productivity. To that standard Communism levels all things, known and unknown, and estimates their value by the common denominator of extreme materialism. That done, it

[2] Lenin's collected works, ranging from Logic and Metaphysics to Ethics, Political Science and Economics, form a library of thirty volumes.

organizes the resultant energy into ranks and files of mechanized martinets, obviously devoid of all taint of spirituality, for the eventual conquest of the world. So the peasant is driven to the waiting tractors, the city worker to the lathe and dynamo, all indentured to the service of a State geared to the production of types, not individuals. The universal triumph of the collective impersonal will be achieved by organization and measured by dynes, ohms, kilowatt hours and metric tons of exportable merchandise.

Soviet political theory and its resultant proletarian culture, *Proletkult*, form a complete system of centralized social control exercised from above downwards, denying all limitation to the power of government. The State claims not merely the legitimate field of temporal rule but unlimited jurisdiction over the entire inner life, the intellects and consciences of its massed citizenry. Whatever challenges that single domination, or divides allegiance, is incompatible with Marxian Monism and unthinkable in practice. To rationalize this sweeping postulate and lay the axe to the roots of any possible duality, the religious instinct, obviously, must be rooted out of humankind. Any conception of Deity, from the crudest totem worship to the sublimest spirituality of the Fourth Gospel, implies the existence of something alien to Marxian theory. It is not in the bond. In fact, Lenin is on record as having warned his followers that the purer the belief, the more dangerous to the Soviet State.

That religion in Marxian philosophy is considered *"opium for the people,"* a narcotic which deadens man's intellect, induces fantastic dreams, and retards his economic development, will not be denied by any serious and attentive student of Communist classics, from the *Communist Manifesto* of Marx and Engels down to the *A-B-C of Communism*, which is used at present in Soviet schools as a prescribed textbook. The slogan is openly affixed to a government building just outside the entrance of the Moscow Kremlin. Nicholas Lenin, accepting in fullest measure the integral teaching of Marx, needed no compulsion to accept the militant atheism of his preceptors. It is reported that as early as 1886, while yet in his sixteenth year, he had torn from his neck the cross, the emblem of Russia's traditional faith usually worn by Orthodox youths, trampled it under foot, and declared himself forever a rebel against God and society.

This precocious revolt is attributed to the influence exercised on the immature mind of Vladimir Ulianov (Lenin's true family name) by his older brother, Alexander, who was executed by the Czarist Government for attempted regicide in 1887. Through thirty-one subsequent years of exile, imprisonment, and clandestine agitation characterized by ceaseless brooding on materialism and economic determinism, Lenin's youthful bitterness gradually froze into his "horrible mania of certitude."

"Religion," he writes in his work *Socialism and Religion,* "is an opiate for the people, a sort of spiritual vodka meant to make the slaves of Capitalism tread in the dust their human form and their aspirations to a semi-decent existence." In his petulant letter to Maxim Gorky, whom he suspected of an "underhand religiousness," he warned his friend: "Is it not horrible to think what you will come to in this way? God-seeking differs from God-creating or God-making and other things of that kind much as a yellow devil differs from a blue devil. . . . I am reading your article again and trying hard to understand how you could fall into this error. Why do you do it? A thing like that hurts a man devilishly."

Comrade Zinoviev, when president of the Third International, more than once voiced the official attitude of the Soviet State. Thus, on June 17, 1923, he declared to a group of visiting English and Swedish Protestants: "Our programme is based on scientific materialism, which includes unconditionally the necessity of propagating atheism."

Again at Christmas, 1924, he fulminated against the Deity: "We shall pursue our attacks on Almighty God in due time and in an appropriate manner. We are confident we shall subdue him in his empyrean. We shall fight him wherever he hides himself, but we must go about such a question as religious propaganda more carefully in the future. Our campaign against God and religion must be carried out only in a pedagogic way, not by violence or force."

Madame Krupskaya, Lenin's widow, who is reverenced highly as continuing the tradition of her husband, speaks as clearly: "The need is imperative that the State resume systematic anti-religious work among children. We must make our school boys and girls not merely non-religious, but actively and passionately anti-religious. . . . The home influence of religious parents must be vigorously combated."

Lunacharsky, when Soviet Minister of Public Instruction, was franker still, and speaks with an authority that precludes further argumentation. In setting the powerful and subsidized "Association of the Godless" on its way in 1925, he declared: "With all my heart I wish the 'Godless' every success in its fight against the repugnant spectre of God which has caused such diabolic harm to all humanity throughout history."

One may safely rest his contention on these official pronouncements of responsible members of the Soviet Government. Wherever the spearhead of Communism penetrates, its shaft is clutched by an iron fist sworn to smash all the altars of Christendom. It requires complete liquidation of the "God-idea," whether expressed by Christianity, Judaism, Mohammedanism, or, in short, by any form of belief which admits the existence of a Supreme Being. The present Russian Government has repeatedly declared its intention to extend integral Communism to the entire world, including political jurisdiction over all lands and peoples. And it is not permissible to separate the religious from the political and economic content of Communism, which must be accepted as an indivisible system. Consequently the anti-religious programme considered as a prime tenet of Communism, has been executed consistently within Russia since the revolution as a prelude to its imposition on the non-Communist world.

It is clear that there exists on Russian soil an implacable, an organized, and a militant atheism, supported and sponsored by a sovereign State and designed to be imposed by force on the entire civilized world. If collectivism is the body of Communism, atheism is its soul, and internationalism the be-all and end-all of its external operation. As the nature of fire is to burn, of water to moisten, and of pitch to contaminate, so the characteristic functions of Communism consist in the triple activity of collectivizing the human race, despiritualizing the human soul, and dominating human kind. As a man lives by the simultaneous functioning of heart, lungs, and brain, so Communism lives and functions only in maintaining its three vital activities. Life is dependent on the success of the three; death results from failure of any one.

Without the informing spirit of active irreligion, world revolution, for the Bolshevik philosopher, becomes stale, flat, and unprofitable. And the domestic revolution of November 7, 1917, is conspicuously incomplete so long as God remains on Russian soil. Therefore He is to be hunted out of His last hiding place there and then pursued relentlessly through Europe, Asia, Africa, and the two Americas. "We have dethroned the earthly Tzars, now we shall destroy the heavenly ones," ran the opening slogan in the very first number of the notorious atheist magazine, *Bezbozhnik*. It is an error, therefore, of the deepest hue—an error deliberately fostered by Soviet apologists—to conceive or speak of the anti-religious campaign in Russia as an isolated conflict between Church and State regarding their respective rights and jurisdiction; or as revolutionary vengeance visited on the Orthodox Church for alleged failure to meet its social obligations; or as legalized suppression of "counter-revolutionary" elements; or as stern "liquidation" of kulaks opposed to collective farming.

For your orthodox Leninist, nourished on class hatred and controlled by the master idea laid down in the programme of the Sixth Congress of the Komintern, moral principles do not exist, just as there is no music for a deaf person. His ethical faculty has been completely destroyed by the opium of Marxian materialism. Hence, for him, human acts are good or bad only in the relation they bear to the inevitable class struggle, not to any objective norm or morality which Lenin taught him to despise. The agency that transmutes evil into good, and renders vicious acts that are intrinsically noble and sacred, is the simply query: "Does it help to advance Marxian Communism and world revolution?" As in ancient days, even in otherwise enlightened Athens, the term "stranger" was synonymous with "barbarian" or "hostile," so, for Moscow, not to be a Communist is to be a marked enemy.

Lenin, in a posthumous work on religion, clearly teaches: "Whatever serves to advance class warfare is moral."

In a commentary on Communism intended principally for the young (*Komsomol*) and published as a State edition in 1927, we find the following:

> If an individual is excessively harmful, if he is dangerous to the revolutionary fight, you have the right to kill him, obeying the order of your legal class organ. In moments of acute danger it is useless to await this order. The murder of an incorrigible enemy of the Revolution is a legal, ethical murder, a legal death sentence, for Communism does not recognize the metaphysical value of human existence.

This aspect of Bolshevik philosophy is admirably exposed in Fülöp Müller's *The Mind and Face of Bolshevism*. It is as freely admitted by responsible Soviet authorities. Thus Latzis, one of the originators of the Terror, stated with brutal frankness:

> We exterminate not merely individuals but the bourgeoisie as a class. Do not search out records for evidence of the criminal actions of accused persons. Their fate is decided by the class they belong to and what education they have received. That is the essence of the Red Terror.

Trotsky published a dissertation in defense of terrorism. The thesis is that by murdering one person, though he be innocent of any specific crime, the State will intimidate thousands.

In its official fury against God, whom it considers a personal enemy, the Soviet State pretends that belief in the Deity is incompatible with Communism. That will depend, of course, on your definition of Communism. Christianity could accept free Communism as readily as it accepts democracy or monarchy; in point of fact, Christians welcomed and practised the common way of life eighteen centuries before Karl Marx came upon the scene. The author of this chapter has voluntarily lived a community life for twenty-eight years and needs no Lenin or Stalin as interpreter of its advantages or occasional inconveniences. But what neither Christianity nor the individual believer can ever submit to is Bolshevism —obligatory Communism enlarged into an international dictatorship which claims to impose on us by force its Hegelian philosophy of the equivalent non-existence of an objective, personal Deity and the substitution in His place of a necessitarian State.

The State, in Hegel's philosophy, is the perfect embodiment of his idea in its social manifestation— mind objectified. Lenin's descent is from Marx, and Marx sat at the feet of Hegel. Realizing, however, that Nature abhors a vacuum, and realizing too that the human intellect, as Professor Millikan recently demonstrated, is borne by reason itself to fulfill its religious destiny, the pragmatic philosophers of Sovietism have supplied emotional substitutes. Hegel's transcendental idealism, which

substitutes becoming, *das Werden,* for Kant's un-
knowable substratum of appearances, *Ding-an-sich,*
would have left the Russian moujik as cold and un-
moved as it leaves men generally. A God he could
understand, but not an unending process of becoming
which results in divinity only at the third stage of
every triadic development. A God made man and
crucified on Calvary he accepted as the supreme
podvig (expiatory suffering), but he could not be
expected to understand the Hegelian postulate that
progressive negation is a creative act resulting in
more perfect being. So the prophets of the Bolshevik dispensation descended to the concrete and the
tangible. Nicholas Lenin became God of the Russian land, his words sanctified as holy writ and the
sickle and the hammer erected as the cross of salvation.[3]

It does not fall within the scope of the present
report to present a complete study of religious persecution in Soviet Russia, but only of the latest phase
so far as it coincides with the adoption of the Five-
Year Plan. Briefly, the story may be divided into
four phases. The first period (1917-1920), covering
the earlier years of revolution and civil war, was
marked by shocking brutalities and excesses that
constitute a revolting page in the long annals of
man's inhumanity to man. No pretense of "counter-
revolution" can avail to justify the animal fury exhibited. From 1918 to 1920 not less than twenty-six

[3] As Marx applied Hegel's philosophy to economics and utilized
it for an attack on Capitalism, so Strauss and Feuerbach employed
it against Christianity.

archbishops and bishops and twelve hundred priests were massacred.   (Orthodox clergy.)

The period 1920-1924 may be described as the era of governmental attack on ecclesiastical institutions under cover of legal proceedings.   The universally respected Bishop Benjamin of Petrograd was put on trial for propaganda purposes in 1922; the evidence, however, developed so favorably for the courageous prelate that the authorities whisked him from public sight and murdered him in secret.   Obstruction of famine relief was alleged in its turn, although the Patriarch Tikhon offered sincere coöperation in stripping churches of their ornaments for conversion into funds for famine relief and only resisted the confiscation of the Eucharistic vessels.   Those familiar with Soviet practices can have no delusions about the ultimate intent of the iconoclasts during the long struggle with the Orthodox Church.   When offers were made to redeem the sacred vessels by ransoming them with equal sums of money, the offers were refused, or else accepted, only to have the objects confiscated anew so that they might be ransomed all over again.   In the meantime the government was spending large sums on foreign propaganda and exporting wheat even from famine regions.   In short, confiscation of church property under cover of famine relief furnished an admirable starting point for the elimination of the physical equipment of the churches.[4]

---

[4] The Soviet Government had other treasures immediately available—the crown jewels, the value of which was then estimated

In this connection the present writer speaks from personal knowledge, having been witness to confiscation activities in 1922. Likewise he witnessed the exportation of large supplies of foodstuffs, having made a study of this subject at a certain port in South Russia at a moment when similar supplies were being received from charitable sources through northern ports. The sailors of the foreign ships then taking on cargoes of grain informed the writer that the destination was Hamburg.

The insincerity of the claim that church property was needed for conversion into funds to combat the famine in the Volga district was conclusively demonstrated from another quarter. In May, 1922, the Vatican proposed to the Soviet Government that the chalices and sacred objects of a liturgical character then being requisitioned in Petrograd should be left in the possession of the churches in consideration of an equivalent sum in cash to be paid by the Holy See. The text of the proposal follows:

THE VATICAN
SECRETARIAT OF STATE OF HIS HOLINESS

May 14, 1922 (No. 3605)

To HIS EXCELLENCY, M. CHICHERIN,
　　Russian Delegation, Genoa

EXCELLENCY,

. . . In this connection, I have the honour to inform you that, according to a telegram from Mgr. Cieplak to the Holy Father, the State authorities of Petrograd in-

variously from $250,000,000 to $1,000,000,000. No effort was made to sell them for famine relief.

sist on the surrender of the sacred and valuable articles of worship in order that the money from the sale of them may be devoted to famine relief.

On this subject I hasten to inform Your Excellency that the Holy Father is ready to buy these sacred and valuable objects, and to deposit them with Archbishop Cieplak. The price agreed on will be immediately paid to Your Excellency or to any other person whom the government may nominate.

I beg Your Excellency kindly to favour me with a reply to this request as soon as possible, and to be good enough to transmit the necessary orders to Petrograd.

Accept, Excellency, the assurance of my very high esteem.

(*Signed*) JOSEPH PIZZARDO

(*For the Secretary of State of His Holiness*)

The Soviet Commissar of Foreign Affairs replied, under date of May 17, from the Genoa Conference:

SANTA MARGHERITA

May 17

. . . In what concerns the very interesting proposal contained in the second part of your letter, they were immediately transmitted by me to Moscow, where they will certainly be examined with all the good-will such proposals deserve.

No answer was vouchsafed by the Kremlin. Again on June 7, 1922, a telegram was sent directly to Lenin by the Cardinal Secretary of State:

HIS EXCELLENCY, M. LENIN, Moscow

. . . Besides, I should be very grateful to know what reception has been accorded to the proposal of the Holy

See to buy the valuables conformably with the letter addressed to M. Chicherin on May 14.

(*Signed*) CARDINAL GASPARRI
The Vatican, *June* 7, 1922.

I suppose that some clear mind at Moscow saw the impasse. If the offer were to be accepted, the vessels of the altar would be saved and money would still be guaranteed for famine relief. Obviously that would nullify the very purpose of the confiscation, which was not famine relief, but destruction. On the other hand, the offer could not be explicitly refused at a moment when the Soviet Government was desperately in need of funds and had authorized Maxim Gorky to make his famous appeal to the world. Formal refusal would let the cat out of the bag and reveal the true purpose of the confiscation. Hence the offer was ignored; no answer was ever returned. But none was needed. The patent conclusion is on record for all time.

Arrested in March, 1923, together with fourteen of his clergy, the Catholic Archbishop of Petrograd was put on trial for his life and condemned to death, as was Monsignor Budkiewicz, Vicar of St. Catherine's on the Nevsky Prospekt. The indignation of an outraged Christendom saved the life of Archbishop Cieplak, but was unable to effect the slightest modification of the Soviet purpose to execute Monsignor Budkiewicz. That distinguished and respected prelate paid for his constancy by having his brains blown out on the night between Good Friday and Holy Saturday, March 30-31. The author of this

report was present in the courtroom during the five
days of that historic trial and can testify that the
only crime proved against the victims was their in-
ability to accept the alternative proposed by Mr.
Krylenko, the Public Prosecutor.   The question was
put in my own hearing:

"Will you stop teaching the Christian religion?"

"We cannot," came the uniform answer.   "It is the
law of God."

"That law does not exist on Soviet territory," replied Krylenko.   "You must choose. . . . As for
your religion, I spit on it, as I spit on all religions."

The basic issue of the religious "problem" in Russia was thus publicly defined by the Soviet State:
clear-cut alternative and clear-cut acceptance of the
penalty.   Those who survived that trial went unflinching to prison or to exile with the same fortitude
their successors are manifesting in 1931.

Some historians of Bolshevism prefer to combine
the first two phases of this warfare on the Church
into one general period, ending with 1923, and desig-
nate it as the time of direct persecution.   They are
substantially correct, and our further division of the
same period is intended merely to mark a discernible
change of tactics within that broad division.   The
latter part was characterized by attempts to legalize
the persecution by resorting to the fiction of court
sentences, whereas the earlier practice was one of
unmitigated and unrelieved extermination. The complete catalogue of victims has been put at 8,100 up
to 1924—a figure which refers to members of the

Orthodox clergy alone and church servants, but does not include the laity.

The third phase, from 1924 to 1928, has been described as the period of comparative quiescence. If less spectacular and less sanguinary, it proved equally effective through its calculated programme of slow attrition that achieved the gradual disappearance of religious persons without possibility of replacement. Joseph Bielogolovy, forty-six years of age, a brilliant professor of the Ecclesiastical Academy at Petrograd, was early signaled out by the Bolshevik authorities—and rightly so—as a priest of true episcopal timber. Urged to accept "consecration" at their hands as bishop of an anti-Catholic sect which would enjoy their subsidized favor in order to labor at the undermining of faith in general, he calmly spurned the insidious offer and paid for his loyalty to conscience with his life. He was shot in 1928. Dominik Ivanov, about the same age, former Vicar of St. Catherine's, Petrograd, banished to the unspeakable horror of Solovetsky Island in the White Sea, succumbed in the freezing darkness of that island prison during the same year. It was from this new Siberia that eighteen prisoners, worn to skeletons, escaped, as if by a miracle, two years ago and reached the shores of Finland. "Kill us here," they begged the astonished Finnish guards between Martukule and Kiolaarvi, "but don't send us back where they will kill us by inches."

There still remain on Solovetsky Island, undergoing the agony of slow execution, the following

Catholic clergymen: Monsignor Boleslav Sloskan, Apostolic Administrator of Mohilev and of Minsk, who was arrested in August, 1927, and, after the worst form of physical and moral torture, deported to the Island and sentenced to hard labor (it is of this confessor of the faith that the Sovereign Pontiff made mention in his letter of February 2, 1930); Paul Chomicz, thirty-six years of age; Vincent Dejnis, forty-nine years of age; Adolphe Filip, forty-four years of age; Vincent Ilgin, forty-three years of age; Joseph Iuzwik, fifty-six years of age; Casimir Siwicki, forty-five years of age; Miecislas Szawdinis, thirty-four years of age; John Troigo, forty-nine years of age; John Versocki, forty-one years of age; the two theologians Tysowski and Woronko. All belong to the diocese of Mohilev. The list continues: Nicolas Alexandrov, Potapi Emilianov, and that intrepid hero Leonid Feodorov, Exarch of Russian Catholics of the Oriental Rite, and Bishop Frison.

And still the list goes on: Cesar Feodorovitch, Victor Kriventchouk, Basil Styslo, Paul Ascheberg, Joseph Kolch, and John Furch, the last of whom was sent into exile for the crime of having warned his parishioners against certain immoral moving-picture films then being shown at the local cinema.

The last name we have is that of Father Shchepaniouk, a priest of the Oriental Rite from Kiev. The complete roster of those undergoing a similar agony for conscience's sake in distant points, such as Siberia, Turkestan, and the Caucasus, is known only to God. But among them stand out the venerable

Apostolic Administrator of Kiev, Monsignor Theophile Skalski, fifty-two years of age, and Father John Deubner; the former has been imprisoned for three and one-half years, the latter for more than eight years. Canon Anton Vassilevsky sealed his faith with his life during the first week of October, 1929, dying in South Caucasus, in absolute isolation.

This list is but partial; it was correct in the summer of 1930, but new additions and the merciful hand of death have doubtless impaired its strict accuracy at the present writing. (See Appendix II.) Many of these martyrs and confessors of the common faith of Christendom I knew personally. I also know their crime. They believed in God, taught His revelation, and the moral law as God gave to each the light to see His truth and justice. Confronted by an atheist government demanding surrender of religious liberties, they refused to abdicate an inalienable right as familiar to Americans as the air we breathe. We accept the atmosphere about us as matter of course; we only know how precious it is when the hands of a strangler close about our throat. The memory of Mr. Krylenko's gleaming bayonets around those doomed men and the farewell touch of an unfaltering hand in the heavily guarded corridors of the Butyrki Prison served to illumine the meaning of human liberty and enhance its value forever. It was worth a lifetime of theory to the present writer.

The latest period, 1928-1933 (it is planned to

abolish religion by the final year of the Five-Year
Plan), may be described as the closing phase of
legalized extermination. December 31, 1933, is
fixed as the date for the "liquidation" of churches,
chapels and other "prayer houses." Under the latest
decree twenty churches will remain in the Soviet
Union for the needs of approximately two million
Catholics. Simultaneously with the adoption of the
Plan, legislation was prepared for a more comprehensive attack on the religious front. Identifica-
tion of this objective with the political and economic
purposes of the Plan is common in Soviet literature and in the pronouncements of public officials. Not only is membership in the Communist
Party, with the privileges it confers, reserved for
those who profess atheism, but entrance into the col-
lectives becomes practically impossible for practising
believers. Naturally, both these statements have
been denied, but the evidence is abundant and con-
clusive. Soviet reports on party membership from
the beginning record the number of members expelled
for religious "superstition." [5] Refugees to Germany
during the mass flights of 1930 testified that they
were willing to accept collectivization but unwilling
to submit to obligatory atheism. The Regional Committee of the Party in Samara "cleaned" the Middle
Volga section by expelling 453 persons for "fulfilling
religious rites." [6] *Bezbozhnik* frequently carries

[5] *Trud,* July 3, 7, 1930; *Bezbozhnik,* August 20, 1930.
[6] *Bezbozhnik,* August 20, 1930.

full-page illustrations to the same effect—the Five-
Year Plan crushing three grotesque figures labeled
Jehovah, God and Allah, with the explanation: "The
Five-Year Plan—this is a practical plan for annihilation in the fight against religion. Long live the Five-
Year Plan!" [7] Or a workman, flanked by two
enormous new factories, is sweeping Almighty God
into the ash heap. Another workman, against a background of chimneys and new construction, is dump-
ing Christ from a wheelbarrow into the refuse pile.
A Communist boy, about five years of age, bears a
banner inscribed, "I am going over to the continuous
working week," and kicks over a church in his way.
A grotesque angel, trumpet in hand, stationed outside a stable suggesting Bethlehem—the Virgin, with
an ox and an ass, is seen inside—interrogates a disappointed Saint Joseph: "Well, can I blow? Has he
been born?" Joseph answers that there will be no
birth—the five-day week has destroyed all that.

But it is the legislation of April, 1929, adopted
simultaneously with the Plan, that provides the full
key to the situation by outlining the administrative
methods to be employed for the complete liquidation
of religion. On three successive days, April 26, 27,
and 28, 1929, *Izvestia* reproduced the text of the new
decree, dated April 8.[8] The general tenor of these
ordinances reveals a programme whose ultimate purpose is gradual suppression of external worship in
order thus to achieve eventual disappearance of re-

[7] November 22, 1929.
[8] See Appendix I.

ligion as a fact. This is a favorite Bolshevik device. First reduce an institution or a person to impotence by throwing a network of obstacles around it; then, in due time, proceed to its physical destruction as something "no longer useful or needed." Article 13 of the Constitution of July, 1918, and Article 4 of the law of May 11, 1925, made ambiguous mention of freedom of conscience and provided equal authorization for "religious propaganda of all cults and anti-religious propaganda." This was at least a semblance of religious toleration. I say "semblance" because as early as 1926 the Commissariat of Justice interpreted what Soviet jurisprudence meant by liberty of conscience. It was explained that the law secured freedom of belief in the subjective but not in the *objective sense*. With characteristic cynicism, and with complete superfluity, officials conceded that the Soviet Government does not hinder any individual from believing whatever he likes, or from not believing in anything at all, so long as his external actions are in conformity with the existing law of the land. But even that last shred of protective legality disappeared in 1929.

The new decree—which also abrogates four other ordinances published between 1921 and 1923— makes no mention of liberty of conscience, of worship, or of religious propaganda. The only guarantee accorded in this field is to anti-religious activities, which alone enjoy governmental favor and unlimited scope. Believers are mentioned only as subjects of penalties, persons to be controlled, limited, segregated by social discrimination, and punished for the slightest infraction of the multitudinous prohibitions leveled against religious practices. The decree registers their existence as a necessary statement of fact. There is no bill of rights for them, but only a catalogue of anticipated crimes. The original, organic law of the land already deprives of all civic rights priests and nuns; the new text includes in that disenfranchisement all lay folk as well who identify themselves with the exercise of religion—such as beadles, charwomen and sweepers of sacred edifices, sextons, choir singers, and deacons.

The document requires some six thousand words to weave its suffocating net around those of its prospective victims who persist in religious "superstitions." It prescribes rules governing every phase of the existence of religious organizations, the method of listing and handling free-will offerings, and the repair of buildings used for religious purposes.[9]

Even the hiring of janitors, the acquisition of wood for fuel, and the repairs of the "prayer building" are covered in the decree. The rules are so drastic as to limit the clergy and teachers to conducting their offices in the territory in which they reside permanently "and which belongs to the particular religious association."[10]

[9] Paragraphs 10, 11, 25, 26, 28, 29, 30, 31, 32, 33, 34, 35, etc. No such hampering restrictions are imposed on atheist propaganda, which is protected, subsidized, and developed by the government.
[10] Paragraph 19. Anti-religious propagandists, trained under State auspices, are permitted and encouraged to range over the entire territory of the Union. But a Catholic clergyman, residing

Providing that every citizen may become a member of only one religious-cultural association, the decree defines a religious association as "a local association of believing citizens who have reached the age of eighteen years, of one and the same religion, conviction, or sect, to the number of not less than twenty persons who have associated themselves for the joint satisfaction of their religious needs." [11]

At the outset the decree says flatly that "religious societies and groups of believers do not enjoy the rights of juridical bodies." Thus, being deprived of legal existence, the religious associations are hedged about in the provisions of the decree to the extent of sixty-eight paragraphs.[12]

Religious instruction to anyone under eighteen years of age had already been forbidden, no matter where given. The spirit of the April decree will punish parents who teach their children to recite prayers even in the privacy of the family.

Religious associations are forbidden to create mutual-aid banks, coöperatives, industrial associations, "and generally to use any property in their control for any other purpose except the satisfaction of their religious needs." They are forbidden, more-

in Moscow, for instance, could not serve the Catholics of Leningrad. Nor could a bishop govern outlying parishes. The purpose of this provision is to localize each religious faith, cut off the individual groups from the parent stem, and thus gradually destroy unity.

[11] Paragraph 8. The obligatory registration of names furnishes a self-supplied roster of "counter-revolutionaries" to the G. P. U. Obviously those who dare to register are exactly the persons the Secret Police are most anxious to detect.

[12] This means that they are subject to all the penalties of the law, with none of its protections.

over "to assist their fellow members by giving them material support," or to hold "special meetings for children, youths, and women for prayer purposes and generally Biblical, literary, needlework, and other meetings for the teaching of religion, etc." They also are forbidden to arrange "excursions and children's playgrounds, to found libraries and reading rooms, to organize sanitaria and medical assistance." [13]

In buildings used for prayer, "only such books may be kept which are required in connection with the particular cult."

Religious societies and "groups of believers," as the phraseology of the decree reads, may not function until after they have registered with the proper administrative department, meaning the local executive committee or the city soviet or the executive committee of the volost or other higher body. Declaration of registration must be filed on a special form prescribed by the government. After registration, believers may receive "by contract" from the local government the free use of special houses of prayer and objects especially designated for cult purposes.[14]

While executive officers of religious bodies may enter into arrangements dealing with repairs of buildings, the hiring of janitors, and the purchase of

[13] Paragraph 17. Works of mercy and charity are thus forbidden to religious groups. As members unable to work can expect neither State nor Communist assistance so long as they believe in God, the alternatives are apostasy or else starvation, poverty, and death.

[14] Paragraphs 10, 64. "May receive"—*i.e.*, within the discretion of a local Commissar who is under oath to execute a governmental policy aimed at the abolition of all religion.

fuel, they may not rent candle factories or establish printing shops for the publication of "religious and moral books."

Executive and auditing agencies of religious associations may meet without permission of the governing authorities, but they may not organize nationwide associations except by special permission of governmental bodies. Permission for congresses and conferences in the territories of the autonomous republics is granted by the People's Commissariat for Internal Affairs or the administrative agent corresponding to this body in the autonomous republic.

While national or federated religious congresses may form executive bodies to carry out their decrees, lists of the executives, together with the minutes and proceedings of the congress in duplicate, are to be provided to the government body which granted permission for the gathering, on governmental blanks furnished for that purpose.

"Religious congresses and the executive organs by it selected do not enjoy the rights of juridical bodies," the decree says, "and besides this they are not enabled to: (1) establish any kind of central treasury for the collection of voluntary contributions; (2) establish any compulsory assessments of any kind; (3) own any property of the cult or obtain any such property under contract, or become possessed of such property by way of purchase, or rent any premises for religious gatherings; (4) enter into any kind of contract or form any kind of enterprise.

"Property required for the carrying on of the cult,

such as was surrendered to the believers forming the religious society, under contract, and such other property as was acquired by them or donated to them for the necessities of the cult, are considered nationalized and are charged on the accounts of corresponding city soviets, of the regional executive committee, or the executive committee of the volost, as in use by the believers."

While church property is nationalized in the decree, it is turned over "by contract" for "the use of believers." Under the contract those who use the property obligate themselves to care for it as they would for government property entrusted to them and to pay all expenses, including heating, insurance, taxes, and local assessments. The cults must possess inventories of the property, together with all other property acquired by gift, purchase, or otherwise. The sects are also required to admit without hindrance at all times, except when religious services are going on, authorized government agents for the examination of the property.[15]

Elaborate rules are contained in the decree regarding "liquidation" of churches and church property. In cases where no persons are to be found who will take over church property, notice to that effect is to

[15] Paragraphs 29, 33, 64. The arbitrary, unilateral contract contains terms impossible of fulfillment, such as crushing taxes, local levies collected from churches considered in the same category as theatres, extortionate insurance, forced tribute to local Communist agencies, and fantastic penalties for the disappearance of even so much as one candle. Local Communists have frequently destroyed certain articles, broken the windows during the night, or robbed the church, and then demanded liquidation of the edifice because of "breach of contract."

be affixed to the doors, and if nobody desires to take over the property within a week of such notice, the Central Executive Committee may dispose of it. Within two weeks of the posting of notice that the "prayer house" is to be liquidated, the believers may appeal to the Presidium of the All-Russian Central Executive Committee.[16]

"Contracts having as their object the renting of premises by nationalized, municipalized, or private houses for the needs of religious associations may be dissolved even before the expiration of the term of the contract, by ordinary judicial processes," the decree continues.[17]

"In the liquidation of a prayer building the property of the cult is disposed of in the following manner: (a) all objects made of gold, platinum, silver, and of brocade, as well as of precious stones, are taken up on the roster of the governmental funds and are turned over to the disposition of the local fiscal organs or to the disposition of the organs of the People's Commissariat for Public Education, if these objects were on their roster; (b) all objects of a historical, artistic, or museum value are turned over to the organs of the People's Commissariat for Education; (c) the other objects, such as ikons, vestments, banners, etc., which possess a special significance in the performance of the cult, are turned over

---

[16] Antecedent terrorism often prevents even the bravest souls from accepting the responsibility.

[17] Paragraph 38. The ordinary judicial process consists in declaring the church "a nest of counter-revolutionaries." The Department of Justice has now been abolished in Soviet Russia.

to believers for installation into other prayer buildings of the same cult; these objects are entered upon the register of the property of the cult in the usual manner; (*d*) articles of common use, bells, furniture, rugs, candelabras, etc., are to be entered on the roster of the governmental funds and are turned over to the disposition of the local fiscal organs or to the disposition of the organs of People's Education, if they are listed on their roster; (*e*) so-called transitional property, money, incense, candles, wax, wine, wood, and coal, which fulfill a definite purpose either for the carrying out of the conditions of the contract or for the performance of the religious rites of the cult, are not subject to seizure, should the society continue its existence after the liquidation of the prayer building." [18]

In case of default of the religious associations as to the terms of the contract, or upon failure to carry out any orders issued by the governmental bodies, the contract may be voided. In case of appeal to the Presidium of the All-Russian Central Executive Committee, the building cannot be replevined until after a final decision by the Executive Committee.

Under the decree, new "prayer buildings" may be

[18] Paragraph 40. American newspapers during 1930 published an abundance of pictures showing the burning of religious equipment and the destruction of sacred objects under governmental auspices. In December, 1931, the finest church in Moscow, that of the Holy Redeemer, erected by the Russian people in thanksgiving after the defeat of Napoleon, was demolished. In November, 1932, news was received that another historic edifice, the Church of St. Isaac in Leningrad, is to be converted into a museum. The other outstanding edifice, the Kazan Cathedral on the Nevsky Prospect, has suffered a similar fate.

constructed upon petition of the religious societies under rules laid down for the erection of buildings and also of "special regulations promulgated by the People's Commissariat for Internal Affairs."

Procedure under which a technical commission may order a church to be demolished is given in some detail. The decree provides that the funds for the demolition of church property are to be obtained "from the sale of the building materials recovered in the course of the demolition of the buildings," and "any surplus moneys, after paying expenses, are to be turned over to the government and classed as government income."

Church members may effect collections and accept voluntary contributions in or outside of the church, but solely among members of the particular religion and solely for the purposes connected with the religion.

"Any and all compulsory collections for the use of religious associations are subject to criminal prosecutions in accordance with criminal statutes of the U. S. S. R.," the document says. "Free-will donations in money by the believers are to be accounted for by the treasurer of the religious association in a book showing income and expenditures."

Prayer meetings are allowed in buildings not adapted for that purpose only after notice to the village, city, or governmental authorities, and the performance of any kind of religious ceremony is not permitted in any governmental, social, coöperative, "and private establishment and undertaking." This prohibition, however, does not extend to religious rites performed at the request of the dying or seriously ill confined in hospitals and in places of detention, "in a place apart, as well as the performance of religious rites in cemeteries and crematoriums." [19]

Two weeks' notice is required before permits can be issued for religious processions. All religious associations, under the decree, are required to register within a year, and those not complying will be closed.

The order is signed by M. Kalinin, Chairman of the All-Russian Central Executive Committee; A Smirnov, Deputy President of the Soviet of People's Commissaries of the U. S. S. R.; and A. Dossov, for the secretary of the All-Russian Central Executive Committee. The document is dated Moscow, Kremlin, April 8, 1929.

A groundwork of legality having been thus copiously supplied by the government, complete extermination of religion should then be merely a matter of time—by 1933. The decree was duly signed by M. Kalinin, President of the Union. A short time later, the kindly old gentleman stepped over to the Association of the Godless and pointed out to its general assembly the practical steps to be taken for the achievement of the evident purposes of the decree. *Izvestia* of Wednesday, June 19, 1929, reported the address of the head of the Soviet State. His general

---

[19] Paragraph 58. "In a place apart." A Catholic is dying and asks for the last rites of his church. To receive the sacraments, he must submit to be transported, in a dying condition, to a *specially isolated* room which will be designated at the whim of the authorities.

theme was: "Warfare on religion is a necessary and a highly efficacious means to prepare the way for Communism."

"Comrades," he concluded, "it seems to me that our work of propaganda on the anti-religious front is relatively weak. We must spread the idea of atheism and the Association of the Godless in the factories, the workshops, and in the country places. . . . But with prudence, however, for the conflict against religion must not only use external means. It is a philosophy as well—it erects materialism above idealism. Consequently, the government cannot do everything, if the ground is not prepared. . . . Let us suppose that tomorrow Easter is coming round again. Without doubt, from the point of view of a simple atheist, one should simply exterminate those, all those, who observe this foolish feast of nothingness. . . . But, Comrades, if to you who are the executors of the atheist programme the activity of the government seems insufficient, remember this: in order that the government may not have to limit itself to external measures of repression against religion, it will be necessary to augment and develop the centers of atheist activity."

With the President of the Union thus clearly tracing the campaign, no competent student of Russian affairs can doubt what the Bolsheviks are the first to admit. The Commissars frankly and cheerfully propose as their ideal what Gladstone so well described in his succinct phrase: "The negation of God erected into a system of government."

The customary denial of religious persecution has periodically been cabled from Moscow and complete liberty of conscience vindicated, provided, of course, it be exercised within existing legislation. This interpretation, which seems to satisfy certain timid souls in America and elsewhere, is to be expected, as denial and countercharge have formed the order of the day in every attack on religion. The Roman Neros first set that fashion by outlawing Christianity and then massacring Christians, not precisely because of their religion, but for illegally refusing to offer a few grains of incense to the pagan deities.

The Soviet government fears no famine today, but from its own statistical records the destruction of church edifices—Catholic, Orthodox, Protestant, Jewish, and Moslem—by demolition, by dynamiting, by conversion into clubs, cinemas, museums, warehouses, and circuses still goes on. A dispatch from Soviet sources dated February 22, 1930, puts the number of churches closed or destroyed during the past year at 1,370. They were "needed for public purposes" or confiscated "on demand of the local peasants and workers" or for non-payment of taxes (sometimes 50 per cent per annum of the total value) or "liquidated" to furnish a playhouse for Communist children. A church is requisitioned for a Communist club because the parishioners did not repair the leaking roof—permission to do so having been carefully refused by the local commissar. The classical example, worthy of a high place in the annals of cynical hypocrisy, is that of the local soviet which

had heard rumors to the effect that the foundations
of the parish church had subsided, making the edifice
dangerous for the good parishioners. To verify this
report it was obviously necessary to inspect the
foundations; to do this the church was torn down
instanter. To the great relief of the commissars they
found the foundations to be as solid as the Kremlin
wall. Various pretexts appear, but the churches in-
variably disappear. *Plus ça change plus c'est la
même chose.*

Violation of the law forbidding religious instruction to groups under eighteen years of age, whether
in public or in private, is constantly invoked whenever a demonstration of Communist purity is deemed
advisable.[20]

In the case of a church which may happen to be
open and functioning, it is the simplest of simple matters to assign some zealous young Communist of sixteen or seventeen years to the welcome task of slipping
in among the congregation and furnishing evidence.
Reading the Gospel of Jesus Christ would be sufficient. Next morning the offending priest is on his
way to Siberia or lost among the host of forgotten
prisoners in the cells of the G. P. U. He may even
be executed in virtue of the unique provision of the
penal code which provides that, if a court imposes the
maximum penalty for a given offense, then the Central Executive Committee has the legal power to
commute that penalty into death by shooting. Hence

[20] By the decree of January 23, 1918, reaffirmed by the circular
to every parish on January 3, 1922.

the Revolutionary Court may impose a purely correctional and disciplinary penalty of one year in prison. But, if that period is the maximum sentence allowed under the statute invoked, the prisoner runs afoul of a supplemental paragraph, number 33, and may be eliminated at the pleasure of the Central Executive Committee.

With reason the Soviet Government last year announced the abolition of its Department of Justice and the substitution of a Commissariat for the Preservation of Revolutionary Order.

A mother in her home, with her children at her knee, is teaching her offspring the faith of their forefathers. She is denounced and may be faced with a dread possibility—of going to prison or paying a heavy fine, or suffering the moral torture of seeing her child torn from her bosom and placed in the Communist school, where it will be taught the militant atheism of the State at the expense of the parent. To be sure, this is all quite legal, if by "legal" one means in accord with Soviet law.

And yet the Premier of Soviet Russia, Mr. Alexis Rykov, in an interview reported by the United Press, assured the world in 1930 that nobody had been executed, exiled, imprisoned, or starved to death for religious beliefs, but only for "counter-revolutionary activity." In this, he claims to be technically correct. Having publicly proclaimed Almighty God its enemy, the Soviet State cynically considers as treasonable all aid, comfort, and consolation given to the cause of God. The full might of the government, its

army, its police, its legislation, its control of food, of
lodging, and of education, its subsidized terrorism
and espionage—in a word, the State itself is mobi-
lized to extirpate religion in the concrete by direct
and indirect attack. The helpless victims, for their
part, are bound hand and foot by a network of dis-
criminatory legislation and the ever-present menace
of the G. P. U. Possessing neither power nor influence, nor representation, nor financial resources, nor
printing presses, nor means to avert starvation when
their food cards are withdrawn, they are guaranteed,
nevertheless, full freedom of conscience and equal
liberty of religious belief and practice!

If this be not persecution, words have lost their
meaning.

The Protestant religions have not escaped the common fury. No journalist in Europe or America is
better qualified to analyze the Soviet persecution
than Paul Scheffer, whose long residence through
many years in Moscow has enabled him to penetrate
to the heart of the Russian problem. In an article
published in *The Commonweal* on April 23, 1930,
dealing more particularly with the fate of Evangelical pastors, Mr. Scheffer wrote:

It will serve to give an idea of the way in which the
campaign against the clergy has been conducted to state
that during the year 1929 the following ecclesiastics active
in congregations of German origin along the Volga and in
the Ukraine met such fates as these: Pastors Eberlein
and Waniger were sentenced to five years in prison,
Pastor Brungard to two years, Pastor Keusche to eight

years. Pastor Rosenbach disappeared without trace. . . . A Protestant dignitary in Kharkov was jailed and then set free under the provision that he was to labor to frustrate the efforts of German settlers to leave Russia. In these little German communities all excepting a very few Protestant and Catholic churches have been closed. Here is a small specifically documented excerpt from the whole miserable story, and even it is incomplete.

Commenting on the general anti-religious programme as he had observed it since 1922, Mr. Scheffer adds:

It is therefore not correct to hold that persecution of religion in Russia is of recent origin. It has been systematically and purposefully carried on since the creation of the Bolshevik State, even though with varying degrees of severity. . . . The dozens upon dozens of stipulations imposed upon the religious life of Russia by this April (1929) decree acted like a net in which faith could be strangled without too vociferous a struggle. The decree is indeed a very interesting illustration of the 'systematic revolution on a scientific basis' which is the essential characteristic of the Soviet régime.

The Jewish religion is assailed with the same persistency and with equal hatred. In an authoritative report delivered before the American Jewish Congress held on December 8, 1929, at the Hotel Pennsylvania, New York, Mr. Leo Glassman presented the results of ten months of investigation into the fate of his co-religionists in Soviet Russia. Facts, dates, places, names, and circumstances are freely cited in substantiation of his indictment of the Soviet

government's manoeuvres to abolish belief in God.
And the Chief Rabbi of England, Dr. J. H. Hertz,
in a letter to the *London Times* on February 14,
1930, protests against "the strangulation of religious
instruction" in Russia, and labels Rykov's assur-
ances of complete religious liberty "a cruel jest."
Appealing to right-minded Englishmen, the Chief
Rabbi continued:

Let them voice their indignation and horror at this
spiritual pogrom. For what is trampled under foot under
Soviet rule today is conscience, religious liberty, and
everything that is most divine in the human spirit.

From the followers of Mohammed, the following
energetic protest was forwarded to the Holy See in
early 1930.   In alluding to this telegram, Mon-
seigneur d'Herbigny, President of the Pontifical
Commission for Russia and a Vatican official, assumes responsibility for its authenticity, omitting for
prudential reasons the place of origin:

We Mussulmans . . . take the liberty of bringing to
the attention of Your Holiness, as chief representative of
Christianity, the fact that our co-religionists, the Tartars
of the Volga regions and in the Crimea, are being bitterly
persecuted by the Soviet authorities along with the Christians.   Our mosques are being closed by thousands, our
priests are being cast in prison, deported, or executed
because of their faith and their loyalty to the religion
of our ancestors.   The Bolsheviks make no distinction
between Christian and Mussulman, since the Moscow
Government seeks to destroy all religious belief and so
is at war with God.   As the religious persecution in Rus-

sia menaces both faith in general and the high moral standards based upon that faith, we earnestly hope that Your Holiness will raise your voice in defense of the religion of Islam before public opinion and before the conscience of believing Christians throughout the entire world.[21]

And from Constantinople itself—where, it may safely be assumed, nothing appears in the public prints that is not acceptable to the present Turkish Government—comes a remarkable specimen of plain speech addressed to Moscow. In the newspaper *La République* of May 14, 1930, is found an article over the signature of M. Mouharrem Feyzi and bearing the significant title, "Turkish Unity and World Politics" (*L'unité turque et la politique mondiale*).

After disclaiming any intent to interfere in the internal affairs of the Soviet Government, which would be as inadmissible as unwarranted interference in the internal affairs of Turkey, the author notes that the oppression of twenty-five million Moslems residing on Soviet territory fully justifies his protest. After specifying the measures of persecution—including death sentences, deportation, arrests, confiscation of mosques, and so forth—the author adds these weighty comments:

Turkey has been of enormous assistance to Russia in the establishment of her influence and in enabling it to continue. This was done because Soviet Russia promised to leave Turks masters of their own destiny. When the

[21] The Papal letter of February 2, 1930, had already included an appeal for "the other victims who retain their belief in God."

Soviet régime was faced with all kinds of difficulties and was even in serious danger, it was Turks who held out the hand of friendship and saved them from shipwreck. Not a Turk of the Crimea would serve in the armies of Wrangel and Denikin. These superhuman efforts saved the Soviet régime. These two examples which we have just given suffice to demonstrate the value of Turkish friendship. We consider it to be, for us, the clear duty of friendship to recall to Soviet memory these pages of history.

It would be erroneous to conclude that Mr. Stalin's decree in March, 1930, calling a halt on "physical warfare" against God, meant any relaxation of the governmental campaign for the extirpation of religion by 1933. It was a counsel of prudence, not of wisdom. The emphasis has merely been shifted from one sector of the front to another—to that occupied by the Association of the Militant Godless. Already supreme arbiter of education, systematically inculcating atheism in the schools, master of life and death by the terrorism of the G. P. U., sole proprietor of printing presses, landlord of all lodgings, and autocrat distributor of ration cards, the Soviet Government sponsored and set on its way in 1925 the league of atheists which was to function so zealously in the latter phase of the campaign. From 87,033 members in 1926, it has reached approximately 3,000,000 at the present writing. It has over 25,000 "cells" spread through factories, shops, villages, schools, universities, public institutions, trade unions, the army, the navy, and workmen's clubs. The Association claims it will have 17,000,000 members by the last year of the Five-Year Plan. Its printed output has been enormous, reaching into every nook and corner of the Union where mails or couriers could penetrate.

Notoriously blasphemous periodicals such as the *Atheist* and the *Anti-Religious* have been poured into home, school, and kindergarten by the millions. Other miscellaneous printed propaganda in the form of pamphlets and brochures reached the grand total of 34,000,000 copies in 1929. Anti-religious literature counted 180 separate book titles in the same year, and boasted over 5,500 professionally trained atheist journalists (*Bezbozhkor*), who had been graduated from training schools conducted under State supervision. Special universities have been created by the State to provide higher education for propagandists on the anti-religious front and empowered to grant appropriate degrees. Stage, radio, and lecture platforms have been organized; three full anti-religious operas, four operettas, eleven revues, thirteen musical comedies, twenty vaudeville sketches, and twelve children's plays lampooning religion were announced as the programme in that sector for the next two years. It is hoped that the anti-religious stage will rival the Moscow Art Theater.

One of the favorite farces is entitled *The Judgment against God*. In it the Deity is summoned before a Soviet tribunal and there charged with incompetency in the creation of the world and indicted for all the evils of mankind. As the Divinity does not appear to defend Himself, He is condemned for contumacy, amid ribald and blasphemous hilarity directed against His own sacred person and those who believe in Him.

Aviation has not been neglected as a means of pushing the attack skywards. On June 19, 1929, the Association of the Godless contributed to the government a new aëroplane which was named "The Atheist." Its special function was described in the deed of gift—"to make war on heaven." It dramatizes the situation by cruising over Moscow on the lookout for God.

In June , 1930, the Sixteenth Congress of the Communist Party expressed its satisfaction with the results obtained. The following resolution was adopted and transmitted to all regional headquarters for execution:

The party should consolidate and develop the important successes obtained in the action for the liberation of the masses from the reactionary influence of religion.

In reproducing this resolution in its illustrated edition of July, 1930, *Bezbozhnik* interpreted it as follows:

To consolidate and develop the success means to reenforce, deepen, and develop our labor, our fight against the religious opium.

In the resolution of the Central Committee concerning the Trade-Union Congress it is also stated that the unions must give a regular organization to the anti-religious propaganda and intensify it. Thus we have perfectly clear directions from the Sixteenth Congress of the party concerning anti-religious work. The Union of the Militant Godless will apply itself with all its strength to put into practice the decision of the Sixteenth Congress.

The directions are now in process of execution. Contact has been established with foreign atheist associations and a "World Congress" is not far off. It will suffice in this respect to cite without comment an Associated Press dispatch from Berlin:

Alarm has been expressed here at the report that the Russian 'Godless Internationale' intends to conduct an intensive anti-religious campaign outside the Soviet Union by transferring its headquarters from Moscow to Berlin.

The Economic Party in the Reichstag has listed an interpellation to Chancellor Bruening urging that the Federal Government take all possible measures to prevent the organization of any of its branches from obtaining a foothold on German soil and that all States be instructed to bar such groups.[22]

An international Encyclopædia of militant atheism is contemplated, in several languages. One tangible by-product of the party's directions was revealed in the anti-Christmas pageant staged in a New York theater under Communist auspices on Christmas Day, 1930. The wholly un-American character of that inspired innovation was evident.

The devastating results of these years of militant atheism are now apparent and easy of verification.

[22] *New York Times,* Jan. 30, 1931.

It is among the young that the programme has achieved its most appalling results. Russia has developed a vast multitude of semi-illiterate, corrupt, immoral, uncontrolled and uncontrollable young men and women whose highest ideal is to satisfy the cravings of licentious appetite. How could it be otherwise? The atmosphere of crass materialism and positive atheism which envelops the official school system has released the growing generation from obedience to parents or to conscience. When a State deliberately breaks down the barrier of parental and spiritual authority provided by the home and the church, it is opening a floodgate which no other human power can control. Add to this the influence of Madame Kollontai, with her doctrines of free love, free marriage, and jungle promiscuity, and the demoralizing circle is completed. How corruptive her influence has been may be judged from her novel, *Red Love*. The progress of immorality in the schools is her outstanding achievement. A decent respect for the common opinion of mankind prevents me from quoting the circumstantial portions of her various reports and recommendations.

Small wonder, too, that a cablegram from Moscow, dated February 2, 1930, containing the results of a questionnaire distributed by the Moscow Communistic Academy, should reveal the inevitable degradation to which human relations may descend, when

> Religion, blushing, veils her sacred fires,
> And unawares Morality expires.

Circulated among factory workers in the Moscow area, the questionnaire sought information as to their marrying practices. Numerous Communist girls replied that, divorce being obtained for the asking, they had changed their husbands four or five times a year. One aspiring Messallina replied that she had married sixteen times in three and a half years—an average of a new husband every twelve weeks.

The Kremlin has been obliged to take cognizance of the growing danger to public morals consequent on the general relaxation of restraining influences. On January 23, 1931, Mr. Duranty reported the increasing immorality as "causing some anxiety in high circles." The present state is summarized by the correspondent of the *New York Times* in the issue of January 25, in the following words: "It is a shocking and unexpected, though from a purely cold-blooded scientific point of view a quite comprehensible, phenomenon, but that does not make the problem any easier to solve."

It was against this profanation of the sanctities of life and the perversion of helpless childhood that Pius XI raised his voice in protest to the nations and bowed his head in prayer. In a key sentence of his historic letter of February 2, 1930, the Sovereign Pontiff wrote:

The authors of these impieties wish to destroy religion and God Himself: what they effect is rather the ruin of intelligence and even of nature itself.

In thus appealing to the common instincts of mankind, the Pontiff was but continuing that uniform defense of religious liberties and religious rights in Russia which he initiated eight years before, when the Great Powers first met Bolshevik Russia in conference at Genoa. On that occasion he dispatched his Assistant Secretary of State, Monsignor Pizzardo, to the conference for the purpose of pleading with the Allies for the oppressed of all beliefs in Russia—Orthodox, Catholic, and Jew—and to petition for religious guarantees as a *condicio sine qua non* of recognition.

The text of the papal letter ran, in part, as follows:

At the historic moment when there is question of re-admission of Russia into the consortium of civil nations, the Holy See desires that the interests of religion, which form the basis of all true civilization, shall be safeguarded in Russia. In consequence, the Holy See asks that, in the agreement to be concluded between the Powers represented at Genoa, the three following clauses shall in some manner, but a most explicit manner, be inserted:

1. Complete liberty of conscience for all, whether citizens of Russia or strangers, is guaranteed in Russia.

2. The private and public exercise of religion and of worship is also guaranteed. (This second clause is in conformity with the declarations made at Genoa by the Russian delegate, M. Tchicherin.)

3. The immovable property which belonged or still belongs to any religious body whatever shall be restored to it and respected.

Owing principally to the preponderant influence of one European Power, these humane proposals were politely shelved as a possible embarrassment in the development of trade relations with the Bolsheviks. During the intervening years, Pius XI has never ceased his protests on behalf of the Russian people; he even offered the Soviet government, as we have seen, during the famine to redeem at his own expense the sacred vessels they were then confiscating under pretense of famine relief. The same communication contained an appeal for the release of the Orthodox Patriarch Tikhon, and other prelates of the Russian Church. The letter, as has been stated, was ignored.

Nothing daunted, the Sovereign Pontiff, in 1922, dispatched the Papal Relief Mission to Russia where, supported by the charitable contributions of the Catholic world, it sustained and fed 160,000 starving Russians during the critical period of the famine. In all, it is estimated that the Holy See expended in the neighborhood of $1,500,000 in this act of Christian charity and friendship to the Russian people, then passing through the most critical period in their long and stormy history.

Again, in 1924, in the Consistorial Allocation of December 18, Pius XI renewed his protest against the Soviet attack on the individual, the family, religion, and on the authority of the State: "After having tried for such a long time with all our mind and all our heart to relieve the sufferings of the Russian people, we feel it our duty, imposed on us by the universal paternal mission which God has entrusted to us, to warn most earnestly and exhort all men and especially all heads of governments in the name of our Redeemer that all those who love peace and the public welfare and all those who believe in the sanctity of the family and in human dignity may unite to avert from themselves and their fellows the grave dangers and inevitable injuries of socialism and communism."

The papal letter of February 2, 1930, which gave pause to Mr. Stalin, was not unwarranted interference in the internal affairs of the Russian people, nor an incitement to political action. It was a defense of one of the most fundamental, universal, and inalienable human rights against an unjust aggressor. Within its own sphere, which is the spiritual and the supernatural, it in nowise differed from his previous acts of protest. The Soviet government, by its deliberate choice, has transferred its belligerency to every hearth and home, and enlarged a domestic policy into an international menace which strikes at the very foundations of Christian civilization. It is intellectual suicide for a man, whether he be a prime minister, a senator, or a paid propagandist, to avert his eyes from the evidence now so abundant and keep repeating stale platitudes about "keeping hands off a purely internal question." In the face of established facts it becomes moral cowardice to remain silent.

The present generation of Soviet youth, taken by and large, must be considered not merely as lost to religion but gained in substantial numbers to militant atheism. The widespread Bolshevization of the young is one of the most significant facts emerging from the Revolution. It is Moscow's most practical and most enduring achievement. In the case of the relatively small percentage of Catholic children (the total Catholic population today is somewhere between 1,500,000 and 2,000,000 out of Russia's 160,-000,000) the spiritual debacle is less notable. Resistance has been firmer and support more active from the Universal Church outside Russia. No institution save the Papacy could have organized that world-wide act of supplication on March 19, 1930, which so enheartened Christian Russia in chains. Other elements concur. The influence of the home is still sacred in Catholic circles. The ancestral Faith has become more precious precisely because of persecution which drives men always nearer God.

More tangible results, however, are discernible in another field where the Bolsheviks count on the truth of the ancient warning: Strike the Shepherd and the flock will be dispersed. A brief comparison between the status of the Church before 1917 and subsequent to the November Revolution will illustrate the direction of Bolshevik strategy.

Persecution is no new experience for the Catholic Church in Russia. Considered as an alien sect by the Orthodox Tzars, its history records a long series of oppressive enactments, autocratic suppression of dioceses and religious establishments, frequent imprisonment and exile both of clergy and laity, even

violent periods during which martyrdom was not in-
frequent. But despite all the human obstacles
thrown in its way by a bureaucracy which had inherited the historic resentments of Byzantium the
Faith held fast. In point of fact, during the two
short years of Second Spring following the granting
of religious toleration in the Constitution of 1905,
the inherent vitality of the Catholic principle manifested itself in the astonishing phenomenon of 500,-
000 converts from Orthodoxy.[23] The list of converts
among educated and cultured Russians is long and
distinguished: Madame Narishkin, Princess Baria-
tinski, Princess Volkonski, Prince Gagarin, Prince
Galitzin, Count Shuvalov, Countess Nesselrode,
Miss Ushakova and numerous others. In the reign
of Alexander I, neophytes were often hard put to it
in order to practise their new beliefs. It is related
of Madame Swetchine that she made both her profession of faith and her general confession while
walking up and down her drawing-room engaged,
to all intents and purposes, in a prolonged conversa-
tion with her son's tutor. This was a favorite device
to escape the attention of the secret police and evade
the penalties and illegalities associated with practising the Catholic faith. Merejkovsky records that
brilliant court parties frequently afforded the only
opportunity for converts to receive the sacraments,

[23] Including over 300,000 Uniate Catholics who had been forced
into Orthodoxy by the Tzar. Among them were 100,200 "ob-
stinates" (uporstvujushchie) who had abstained from the sacraments for thirty years in order not to be enrolled as Orthodox
in the census.

as their homes were under the close surveillance of the Holy Synod.

Before 1917 there were considerably more than 13,000,000 Roman Catholics in the Russian Empire, served by 4,600 priests. In that specific territory, which may for convenience be described as Muscovite Russia, exclusive of the Kingdom of Poland, there were one archdiocese and six suffragan sees. Moghileff, the seat of the metropolitan, exercised jurisdiction over the largest ecclesiastical province in the world, embracing three-fourths of European and the whole of Asiatic Russia—5,450,400 square miles. Two of its archbishops I had the honor to know personally. The first, Von Ropp, had been imprisoned by the Bolsheviks and then driven into exile. The second was the heroic Cieplak, whom I saw stand unflinching in a circle of bayonets before the Revolutionary Tribunal and deliver his *"non possumus"* to the new Caesars. Sentenced to death at midnight of Palm Sunday, 1923, he turned and raised his hand in a last episcopal blessing to certain friends hidden in the throng of jeering Communists who had flocked to the court to enjoy the Neronian spectacle. For the condemnation had been predetermined, the hour deliberately chosen for its awe-inspiring value and admission was by ticket. As Macaulay says, of the State trials under Henry VIII, it was "murder preceded by mummery." Justice was caricatured to make a Soviet holiday. Saved by the indignant protests of civilized nations from the tragic fate which befell Monsignor Budkiewicz on Good

Friday night, 1923, Archbishop Cieplak was imprisoned in Moscow where it was my further unforgettable privilege to visit him more than once and communicate messages of support and encouragement from the present Sovereign Pontiff to the last Catholic bishop in Russia.   Later several new bishops were consecrated.

But to return to our comparative tables.   Within the territorial limits now controlled by the Soviet power, there were, in 1917, the year of the Bolshevik Revolution, 614 Catholic churches in operation; today 182 remain.   In addition, there were 581 chapels; today not one remains.   There were 896 priests; today 110 are at liberty while 200 languish in Bolshevik prisons.   The remainder have perished from privation and starvation or have been exiled and executed.   In 1917 there were 7 seminaries; today not one remains.   There were eight bishops; today, of the new hierarchy since created, two are at liberty and three in prison at forced labor.

These sombre actualities are sometimes obscured by tourists returning from Moscow and reporting that they visited churches and found religious services being conducted as usual. But it must be remembered that Moscow, Leningrad and the larger cities to which visitors commonly confine their visits are but a small fraction of the vast territory under Soviet control.   And even in those centers of population, the visitor, however open-minded, could only have visited the churches that still exist or are open.   What of the thousands that have been closed or destroyed?

And why were they closed? Let him not forget that the Orthodox or Catholic priests whom he may have seen at the altar are those who are still alive and at liberty. Did the visitor have an opportunity to inspect Solovetsky Island, or the cells of the G. P. U. or the prison camps where so many are confined under conditions of actual slavery? And what guarantee is given that the ministers of religion whom he then saw are at liberty now? They are disappearing daily. And the lay members of all churches who remain loyal to their faith do so at peril of their lives, their liberty, and their happiness.

Conclusions based on fragmentary evidence or on the selected facts which the Soviet guides permit the foreigner to see are worthless. Above all, let the casual visitor to Moscow not forget that the Soviet attitude is to be judged, not by what remains of religious liberty but what has been destroyed, and by the character of the counteragencies and laws sanctioned by the government to annihilate what does remain.

Nor does it contribute to clarity to hear the explanation that the Soviet government is acting with strict legality and only forcing religion "to obey existing laws as every government requires."

Exactly so. It is precisely the content of those laws as much as the manner of their enforcement which constitutes the very essence of persecution. The Soviet State has set up a new definition of legality which is not admitted by other civilized nations or by international law. No self-respecting nation, for example, has admitted the validity of the Soviet laws which confiscated without compensation the property of all foreigners, or the decrees repudiating all foreign debts.

In addition to the competency of the legislator and the necessity or utility of the legislation, law implies justice and right reason should promote the common good and contain no invasion of a higher right. The opposite theory is the very soul of tyrannous absolutism and the breath of its nostrils. If all laws, decrees and ukases, however arbitrary and oppressive, are to be meekly obeyed simply and solely because they have been promulgated by the party in control, then Christianity would have perished in the Coliseum, Magna Charta would never have been written in defense of English liberties, Belgium would not today be an independent nation, the United States of America would still be an insignificant colony of Great Britain and there would have been no Russian Revolution at all.

Serenely confident of the outcome of this conflict between light and darkness, the Church continues in prayer and hope and suffering. She has nineteen centuries behind her and all the future before her. Hence, she is not pressed for time, as the Bolshevik is, nor haunted by undue fear. But eternal vigilance is the price of liberty and defense of the supernatural a solemn duty inseparable from her mission. Before the Soviet government's continued invasion of the most sacred human heritage, before its calculated degradation of the soul for the deification of the flesh and in the face of its conspiracy to extend that attack to the entire world, the Catholic Church will not recoil, nor retreat nor compromise. She must perish first—if that were possible.

Pius XI possesses neither political nor economic nor any other form of material sanction applicable to the enemies of Christianity. He is the most defenseless sovereign in the smallest state ever acknowledged by international usage. His appeal is to God and the moral instincts of mankind. With no sword in hand save only the two-edged blade of Truth and Justice He has dared to take a stand on the altar of His City of Souls and proclaim an ancient verity: No state on earth is placed so high as to be beyond the reach of the natural and the divine law. So Christianity replied from the catacombs to the Caesars on their thrones. They passed to return no more, and their seven hills became earth's central shrine where reigns an immutable form in Peter's chair. So she answered Julian the Apostate as he cast his own blood skywards and confessed: "Thou hast conquered, Galilean." So have the Hildebrands replied and the Leos, the Gregories, the Ambroses and the Piuses throughout the centuries. So has the latest Pius replied to the latest avatars of irreligion who have contrived the most formidable synthesis of negations ever assembled by the mind of erring man.

It will be the province of future historians to record the manner in which issue was finally joined between followers of the Word made flesh and those who made the flesh their Logos. Into that warfare of mind with matter all men are born.   Now it is Russia's appointed hour.   Complete resolution of that age-long controversy will only be revealed when the promised Angel of the Judgment shall cleave the firmament, bid time cease and unveil the substance and the splendor of imperishable truth.

APPENDIX I

PRESENT LEGISLATION ON RELIGION IN FORCE IN THE UNION OF SOVIET SOCIALIST REPUBLICS (U.S.S.R.)

Translation of the Decree Dated April 8, 1929 [1]

Decree of the All-Russian Central Executive Committee and the Council of People's Commissars respecting Religious Associations.

No. 353. April 8, 1929.

("Collection of Laws and Ordinances of the Russian Socialist Federal Soviet Republic," No. 35, May 18, 1929, Part I, page 474.)

The All-Russian Central Executive Committee and the Council of People's Commissars of the R.S.F.S.R. decree as follows:

1. Churches, religious groups, doctrines, religious movements and other religious (cult) associations of all kinds are subject to the Decree of the Council of People's Commissars of the R.S.F.S.R., dated the 23rd January, 1918 (Collection of Laws of 1918, No. 18, Law No. 263), regarding the separation of the Church from the State and the separation of schools from the Church.

2. A religious association of believers of any cult shall be registered as a religious society or group of believers.

A citizen may only belong to one religious (cult) association (society or group).

[1] State paper, Russia No. 1, 1930. His Majesty's Stationery Office, London.

3. A religious society is a local association of believers, having attained the age of eighteen years, of one and the same cult, belief, conviction and doctrine, and numbering not less than twenty persons, who have combined for the purpose of making provision for their requirements in the matter of religion. Those believers who, owing to lack of numbers, are unable to form a religious society, may form a group of believers. Religious societies and groups of believers have no juridical rights.

4. A religious society or group of believers may only carry on its activities after registration at the competent department of the local Executive Committee or Town Soviet, at the Sub-District (Volost) Executive Committee or at a Town Soviet which is not the administrative centre of a Region (Rayon) or District (Uyezd).

5. In order to effect the registration of a religious society, the organisers, who must number not less than twenty persons, shall lodge a petition for registration with one of the administrative bodies mentioned in Article 4, in accordance with the form sanctioned by the People's Commissariat for Internal Affairs of the R.S.F.S.R.

6. In order to effect the registration of a religious group, the representative of the group (Article 13) shall lodge a petition for registration with one of the administrative bodies, mentioned in Article 4, of the area in which the group is established, in the form sanctioned by the People's Commissariat for Internal Affairs of the R.S.F.S.R.

7. The administrative bodies mentioned in Article 4 shall, within one month from the date of the receipt of this petition, either register the society or group of believers or else inform them that registration has been refused.

8. A list of the persons comprising the religious society or group of believers, their executive and audit bodies and their ministers of religion shall be communicated to the administrative body charged with the registration of the religious association in question, within the period, and in the form, sanctioned by the Commissariat for Internal Affairs of the R.S.F.S.R.

9. Lists of members of religious societies or groups may only contain the names of those believers who have agreed that their names shall be included in the list.

10. Believers belonging to a religious society with the object of making provision for their requirements in the matter of religion may lease under contract, free of charge, from the Sub-District (Volost) or Regional (Rayon) Executive Committee or from the Town Soviet, special buildings for the purpose of worship and objects intended exclusively for the purposes of their cult.

Furthermore, believers who have formed a religious society or group of believers may use for religious meetings other buildings which have been placed at their disposal by private persons or by local Soviets and Executive Committees. All the provisions of the present Decree regarding buildings used for religious worship shall apply to these buildings. Contracts for the use of such buildings shall be concluded by individual believers who will be held responsible [for their execution]. In addition, these buildings must comply with the sanitary and technical building regulations.

Each religious society or group of believers may only use one building for religious worship.

11. Arrangements for the administration and use of religious property, such as contracts for the engagement of watchmen, for the supply of fuel, for repairs to

the place of worship and other religious property, for the acquisition of supplies and property necessary for the performance of religious services and ceremonies and for similar matters closely and directly connected with the observations and services of their cult, and for the renting of premises, may be made by citizens who are members of the executive bodies of religious societies or are representatives of groups of believers.

No contract embodying such arrangements may contain in its text any reference to commercial or industrial transactions, even if these are of a kind directly connected with the affairs of the cult, such as the renting of a candle factory or of a printing works for the purpose of printing religious books, &c.

12. General meetings of religious societies or groups of believers may only be held if special permission has been obtained: in villages from the Sub-District (Volost) Executive Committee or from the Regional (Rayon) administrative department; in towns from the administrative department.

13. For the proper administration and use of religious property (Article 11) as well as for representative purposes, religious associations may elect executive bodies by open vote from among their members at general meetings of believers, numbering in the case of religious societies three members and in the case of groups of believers one member.

14. The registering body may exclude any individual member from the administrative body of a religious society or group of believers.

15. For the proper control of religious property and of funds received by voluntary contribution, religious associations may elect at general meetings of believers

an audit committee of not more than three members.

16. Meetings of the executive and audit bodies of religious societies and groups of believers may take place without notification being given to, or permission received from, the authorities.

17. Religious associations may not (*a*) create mutual credit societies, cooperatives or commercial undertakings, or in general use the property at their disposal for other than religious purposes; (*b*) give material assistance to their members; (*c*) organise for children, young people and women special prayer or other meetings, or, generally, meetings, groups, circles or departments for biblical or literary study, sewing, working or the teaching of religion, &c., or organise excursions, children's playgrounds, public libraries or reading rooms, or organise sanatoria and medical assistance.

Only books necessary for the purposes of the cult may be kept in the buildings and premises used for worship.

18. The teaching of any form of religious belief in State, public and private teaching and educational establishments is prohibited. Such teaching is permitted exclusively at special theological courses organised by citizens of the U.S.S.R. by special permission of the Commissariat for Internal Affairs of the R.S.F.S.R. and, in the territories of the Autonomous Republics, by permission of the Central Executive Committee of the Autonomous Republic concerned.

19. The work of ministers of religion, religious preachers and instructors, &c., shall be restricted to the area in which the members of their religious association reside, and to the place where the premises used for worship are situated.

The work of ministers of religion, religious preachers

and instructors, who regularly serve two or more religious associations, shall be restricted to the area in which the believers who are members of those religious associations permanently reside.

20. Religious societies and groups of believers may organise local, All-Russian and All-Union religious congresses and conferences, but they must obtain permission on each occasion from:

(a) The People's Commissariat for Internal Affairs of the R.S.F.S.R. if they desire to organise an All-Russian or All-Union Congress on the territory of the R.S.F.S.R. or if the congress covers the territory of two or more Areas (Kray), Provinces (Oblast) or Governments (Gubernia).

(b) The corresponding Area (Kray), Province (Oblast), Government (Gubernia) or Circuit (Okrug) administrative department if the congress is to be local.

Permission for the organisation of a congress or conference in an Autonomous Republic shall be obtained from the People's Commissariat for Internal Affairs or their representative in the said Republic.

21. Local, All-Russian and All-Union religious congresses and conferences may elect from amongst their participants executive bodies for the purpose of putting into effect the resolutions of the congress. Lists of the members of the executive bodies elected at a religious congress and the records of the congress in duplicate shall, in the form sanctioned by the People's Commissariat for Internal Affairs of the R.S.F.S.R., be furnished to the administrative body which gave permission for the congress to be held.

22. Religious congresses and the executive bodies

elected by them do not possess the rights of a juridical person and, in addition, may not—

(a) form any kind of central fund for the collection of voluntary gifts from believers;

(b) make any form of enforced collection;

(c) own religious property, receive the same on contract, obtain the same by purchase or hire premises for religious meetings;

(d) conclude any form of contract or deal.

23. The executive body of a religious society or group or of a religious congress may use stamps, seals, and forms bearing its name, but solely for religious purposes. These stamps, seals and forms may not bear emblems or legends in use by the institutions or administrative bodies of the Soviet authorities.

24. The initiators and organisers of religious congresses, meetings and conferences may be either religious societies and groups of believers or their executive bodies or the executive bodies of religious congresses.

25. Property necessary for the observance of the cult, whether handed over under contract to the believers forming the religious society or newly acquired by them or given to them for the purposes of the cult, is nationalised and shall be borne on the charge of the competent Town Soviet, Regional (Rayon) or Sub-District (Volost) Executive Committee for the use of the believers.

26. Premises used specially as living quarters for watchmen situated within the confines (fence) of the place of worship or in its neighbourhood shall, in the same manner as other religious property, be handed over under contract for the use of the believers free of charge.

27. The place of worship and religious property shall be handed over for the use of the believers forming a

religious society under a contract concluded in the name of the competent Regional (Rayon) Executive Committee or Town Soviet by the competent administrative department or branch, or directly by the Sub-District (Volost) Executive Committee.

28. A building to be used for religious purposes and the property therein shall be taken over under contract from the representative of the Sub-District (Volost) or Regional (Rayon) Executive Committee or Town Soviet by not less than twenty members of a religious society, who shall place the said property at the disposal of all the believers.

29. In the contract concluded by the believers with the Town Soviet, Sub-District (Volost) or Regional (Rayon) Executive Committee, the persons taking delivery of a building to be used for religious purposes and other property for the use of the believers (Article 28) shall bind themselves:

(a) To keep and protect it as State property entrusted to them.

(b) To undertake any necessary repairs to the building used for the cult and to bear any expenses connected with the maintenance and use of the property such as heating, insurance, protection, payment of rates and taxes, &c.

(c) To use the property exclusively for their requirements in the matter of religion.

(d) To refund any loss caused to the State by damage to, or loss of, the property.

(e) To keep an inventory of all religious property and to enter therein all property newly acquired (whether by purchase or gift or from another religious building, &c.) which is not the personal property of individual citizens, and to write off the inventory, with the knowledge and consent of the Executive Committee or

Soviet with which the contract has been concluded, such articles as have become worn out.

(*f*) To allow the authorised representatives of the
Town Soviet or Sub-District (Volost) or Regional (Rayon) Executive Committee or Town
Soviet to enter without hindrance at all times,
with the exception of such times as religious
services are being held, for the periodical verification and inspection of the property.

30. Places of worship having a historical, artistic, or
archæological value, on the list of the People's Commissariat for Education, shall be handed over in a similar
manner and on a similar basis, with the proviso that the
regulations laid down for the care of monuments of art
and antiquity on the list of the Commissariat shall be
observed.

31. Any local inhabitant of a corresponding belief,
conviction and doctrine may sign the contract regulating
the use of the building and religious property and acquire
thereby, even after the religious property has been
handed over (to the believers), the right to take part in
the administration of the property on equal terms with
those persons who first signed the contract.

32. Any person who has signed the contract may have
his signature removed from the said contract on giving
the necessary notification to the administrative bodies
mentioned in Article 4, but this shall not relieve him of
responsibility for loss or damage to the property at any
period antecedent to the said notification.

33. Buildings used for religious purposes must be insured against fire, at the expense of the persons signing
the contract, in favour of (in the name of) the Executive
Committee or Town Soviet. In case of fire, the insurance money received may be spent either on the restora-

tion of the place of worship which has been burnt down or, at the discretion of the competent Executive Committee, on the general cultural needs of the area, in strict accordance with the terms of the Decree of the Presidium of the All-Russian Central Executive Committee of the 24th August, 1925, concerning the use of insurance money received for places of worship which have been burnt down (Collection of Laws of 1925, No. 58; Law No. 470).

34. Should there be no persons desirous of taking over for religious purposes any building or religious property on the terms stipulated in Articles 27-33, the Town Soviet or Sub-District (Volost) or Regional (Rayon) Executive Committee shall place on the doors of the religious building a notification to this effect.

35. If on the expiry of one week from the date of the publication of this notification, no notification has been received of a desire [on the part of any person] to take over the building and property on the prescribed conditions, the Town Soviet or Sub-District (Volost) or Regional (Rayon) Executive Committee shall so inform the higher Executive Committee. In this communication the administrative body concerned shall indicate the date of the erection of the place of worship, its condition and the objects for which it is proposed to use the building and shall give their observations on this proposal. The Central Executive Committee of an Autonomous Republic not possessing Circuit (Okrug) branches, or the Provincial (Oblast), Government (Gubernia) or Circuit (Okrug) Executive Committee shall determine the further fate of the said building and all property therein, in accordance with Articles 40-42.

36. The disposal for other purposes of a religious building in use by believers (*i.e.*, the liquidation of a

place of worship) shall only take place, on the authority of a specific Decree of the Central Executive Committee of an Autonomous Republic, or of an Area (Kray), Provincial (Oblast) or Government (Gubernia) Executive Committee, if the building is essential for State or public use. The believers forming the religious society shall be informed of this Decree.

37. If the believers forming this religious society shall, within two weeks from the notification to them of the Decree liquidating their place of worship, appeal against this Decree to the Presidium of the All-Russian Central Executive Committee, the whole question of the liquidation of the place of worship shall be submitted to the Presidium of the All-Russian Central Executive Committee. In this case the contract with the believers shall only lose its force and the building used for the cult shall only be taken out of the hands of the believers, if a resolution confirming this decision is passed by the Presidium of the All-Russian Central Executive Committee.

38. A contract for the renting of premises which have been nationalised or taken over by a municipality, or for the renting of private houses, for the requirements of a religious association (Article 10, section 2), may be rescinded before the expiration of the term of the contract by ordinary judicial procedure.

39. The liquidation of a place of worship in such a case shall be conducted by the administrative department or section upon the instructions of the competent District (Uyezd) or Regional (Rayon) Executive Committee or Town Soviet, in the presence of representatives of the local finance department and other departments, in cases where they are interested, and of a representative of the religious association concerned.

40. Upon the liquidation of a place of worship religious property shall be disposed of as follows:

(a) All articles of platinum, gold or silver, or cloth of gold or silver, and precious stones shall be placed to the credit of the funds of the State and shall be handed over to the local financial body or administrative body of the People's Commissariat for Education, if these articles are on their list, for disposal at their discretion.

(b) All articles of historical, artistic or museum value shall be handed over to the administrative body of the Commissariat for Education.

(c) Other articles (icons, robes, banners, covers, &c.) having special significance in the observance of the cult, shall be handed over to the believers for transfer to another place of worship of the same cult: these articles shall be entered in the inventory of religious property under the general rules.

(d) Articles in general use (bells, furniture, carpets, chandeliers, &c.) shall be placed to the credit of the funds of the State and handed over to the local financial body or administrative body of the educational authorities, if these articles are on their list, for disposal at their discretion.

(e) Cash and consumable property such as incense, candles, oil, wine, wax, wood, and coal, which are necessary for the execution of the contract or for the performance of religious services, shall not, if the society continues to exist after the liquidation of the place of worship, be subject to appropriation.

41. Places of worship and their watchmen's quarters which are subjected to liquidation may, if they are entered on the list of the local special section dealing with the funds of the State, be handed over by the latter, free of charge, for the use of the Executive Committee or

Town Soviet concerned, on condition that the buildings in question shall continue to be regarded as nationalised property and that their demolition or use for any other purpose than that specified shall not take place without the knowledge and consent of the People's Commissariat of Finance of the R.S.F.S.R.

42. Local special sections dealing with the funds of the State shall only enter on their list those buildings formerly used for worship which are not on the list or in the care of the Department of Science of the People's Commissariat for Education as architectural monuments, and which cannot be used by the Executive Committee or Town Soviets as centres of cultural enlightenment (schools, clubs, reading rooms, &c.) or as dwellings.

43. In case of the nonfulfilment by any religious association of the conditions of its contract or in case of the non-observance by the association of orders issued by an administrative body (concerning re-registration, repairs, &c.) the contract may be cancelled. The right of cancelling a contract shall be reserved to the Central Executive Committee of an Autonomous Republic, or to an Area (Kray), Provincial (Oblast) or Government (Gubernia) Executive Committee, upon the recommendation of subordinate Executive Committees and Soviets.

44. If an appeal against the decision of an administrative body mentioned in the preceding Article (43) is lodged with the Presidium of the All-Russian Central Executive Committee within a period of two weeks, the actual sequestration of a place of worship or of religious property shall only take place when a final decision has been given by the Presidium of the All-Russian Central Executive Committee.

45. The construction of new places of worship may

take place at the desire of religious societies provided that the usual technical building regulations and the special regulations laid down by the People's Commissariat for Internal Affairs are observed.

46. If a place of worship is, on account of its age, in danger of complete or partial collapse, the administrative body of the Regional (Rayon) or Sub-District (Volost) Executive Committee or Village Soviet may recommend the executive body of the religious association or the representative of the group of believers to suspend religious services and meetings of believers until such time as the building has been examined by a special technical commission.

47. Immediately upon a recommendation for the closing of a place of worship being made, the officials making the recommendation shall communicate with the Department of Building Control and inform them that the technical inspection of the building is urgently necessary. A copy of this communication shall also be sent for their information to the administrative body which has made the contract granting to the believers the use of the religious building and property.

If the building is on the list of the People's Commissariat of Education, a copy of the said communication shall be sent to the Provincial (Oblast), Government (Gubernia), or Circuit (Okrug) education department.

48. The technical commission (Article 46) which has been appointed by the Department of the Building Control or by the engineer, shall include with a consultative vote:

(a) A representative of the local education department, if the religious building is on the list of the People's Commissariat of Education.

(*b*) A representative of the competent administrative department, Regional (Rayon) administrative department or Sub-District (Volost) militia or Town Soviet of a town which is not the administrative centre of a Region (Rayon) or District (Uyezd).

(*c*) A representative of the religious association.

49. The findings of the technical commission shall be set forth in a memorandum recording the inspection, and these shall be binding and must be carried out.

50. If the technical commission find that the building is in danger of collapse, the memorandum must state whether the building should be demolished or whether it will be sufficient to carry out repairs. In the latter case the memorandum must state exactly what repairs are necessary and the period required to carry them out. Religious associations may not allow meetings for worship or any other purpose to take place in such a building until the repairs have been completed.

51. If the believers refuse to carry out the repairs set forth in the memorandum, the contract made with them for the use of the religious building and property is subject to cancellation by a decision of the Central Executive Committee of an Autonomous Republic, or of an Area (Kray), Provincial (Oblast) or Government (Gubernia) Executive Committee.

52. If the technical commission find that it is necessary to demolish the building, the contract made with the believers for the use of the building shall be cancelled by a decision of the Presidium of the Central Executive Committee of an Autonomous Republic or of an Area (Kray), Provincial (Oblast) or Government (Gubernia) Executive Committee.

53. On the cancellation of a contract and the conclu-

sion of an agreement for the demolition of a building with the local education department and the local finance department, the provisions of the memorandum of the technical commission regarding the demolition of the place of worship shall be carried out by the Sub-District (Volost) or Regional (Rayon) Executive Committee or Town Soviet and paid for out of the sums realised by the sale of the building materials obtained from the demolition of the building. The sums remaining after meeting the expenses of demolishing the building shall be placed to the credit of the State.

54. Members of groups of believers and religious societies may raise subscriptions among themselves and collect voluntary offerings, both in the place of worship itself and outside it, but only amongst the members of the religious association concerned and only for purposes connected with the upkeep of the place of worship and the religious property, for the engagement of ministers of religion and for the expenses of their executive body.

Any form of forced contribution in aid of religious associations is punishable under the Criminal Code of the R.S.F.S.R.

55. All religious property, whether received as an offering or acquired out of voluntary offerings, must be entered in the inventory of religious property.

Voluntary gifts (offerings) for the decoration of a place of worship or of religious objects must be entered in the inventory of religious property in use, free of charge, by the religious society.

Voluntary offerings in kind made with any other object than the above, and monetary offerings for the needs of the religious society or for the maintenance (repair, heating, &c.) of the place of worship, or for the use of ministers of religion need not be entered in the inventory of religious property.

Voluntary monetary offerings by believers shall be entered by the treasurer of the religious association in an account book.

56. Members of the executive body of a religious society or representatives of a group of believers may expend monetary offerings, as may be required, for the management of the place of worship and religious property.

57. Meetings held for the purpose of worship by believers combined in groups or societies may take place, without notification being given to, or permission obtained from, the authorities, in places of worship or in specially adapted premises which comply with the technical building and sanitary regulations.

In premises not specially adapted, religious meetings of believers may take place after notification has been made—in village settlements to the Village Soviet and in town settlements to the Militia department, or, if the latter does not exist, to the administrative department.

58. No religious service or ceremony may take place in any State, public, co-operative or private institution, nor may any religious object be placed within such institutions.

This prohibition shall not apply to the performance, at the request of a person who is dying or seriously ill in a hospital or prison, of a religious service in a place apart or to the performance of religious services at cemeteries or crematoria.

59. Religious processions and religious services and ceremonies may only take place in the open if a special permit is obtained on each occasion—in towns which are

the administrative centres [of a territorial division] not smaller than a Region (Rayon) from the competent administrative department or section, in towns which are not administrative centres and in workers' colonies or health resorts from the Presidium of the Town Soviet or Soviet of the health resort and in villages either from the administrative department of the Regional (Rayon) Executive Committee or the Sub-District (Volost) Executive Committee. Application for a permit must be made not less than two weeks before the date of the proposed ceremony. No special permit is required for religious services in connexion with funerals.

60. In the case of religious processions around religious buildings which form an integral part of a religious service, no special permit or notification to the authorities is necessary, either in towns or villages, provided that the said processions do not interfere with the normal traffic of the streets.

61. Religious processions and religious services and ceremonies may only be held beyond the area (of residence) of the religious association concerned if a special permit is obtained on each occasion from the administrative body which has sanctioned the use of their religious property. Such a permit may only be given if the consent of the Executive Committee of the Region (Rayon) in which it is proposed to hold the procession, service or ceremony has first been obtained.

62. A record of the religious societies and groups of believers in their area shall be kept by those administrative bodies which register religious associations.

63. Administrative bodies which register religious associations (Article 6) shall supply statistics regarding

them in the form prescribed by, and on the dates fixed by, the People's Commissariat of Internal Affairs of the R.S.F.S.R., to District (Uyezd) and Circuit (Okrug) administrative departments, to the People's Commissariats for Internal Affairs of Autonomous Republics and to Area (Kray), Provincial (Oblast) and Government (Gubernia) administrative departments, which shall, in their turn, summarise these statistics and send them to the People's Commissariat for Internal Affairs of the R.S.F.S.R.

64. Supervision of the activities of religious associations and of the safety of buildings and religious property leased to them under contract shall be exercised by the registering administrative body, and in villages such supervision shall also be exercised by the Village Soviet.

65. All religious associations already in existence within the territory of the R.S.F.S.R. at the time of the publication of this decree must, within a period of one year, register at the place in which they are established, in the manner laid down in and with the administrative body indicated in this Decree.

66. Religious associations which do not comply with the requirements of the preceding article shall be considered to be dissolved and the procedure contemplated in such cases by this Decree shall take effect.

67. With the publication of this Decree the following Decrees of the R.S.F.S.R. cease to remain in force:

(1) The Decree of the All-Russian Central Executive Committee dated the 27th December, 1921, regarding valuables in churches and monasteries (Collection of Laws of 1922, No. 19: Law No. 215).

(2) Decree of the Presidium of the All-Russian Cen-

tral Executive Committee dated the 30th July,
1923, respecting the transfer of the ten days
of rest granted to citizens of the Orthodox faith
(see Article 112 of the Labour Code, 1922
issue) from the old style to the new style
(Collection of Laws for 1923, No. 70: Law No.
678).

(3) The Decree of the All-Russian Central Executive
Committee dated the 14th August, 1923, explaining the procedure for the transfer of the
ten days of rest to the new style (Collection of
Laws for 1923, No. 72: Law No. 707).

(4) The Decree of the Council of People's Commissars dated the 19th September, 1923, regarding the disposal of church property in general
use (Collection of Laws of 1923, No. 79: Law
No. 762).

68. The People's Commissariat of the R.S.F.S.R.
shall, within a period of one month, withdraw all departmental circulars, explanations and orders, which contain
provisions contrary to the present Decree and shall publish a list of those departmental acts which remain valid.

(Signed)   President of the All-Russian Central Executive Committee,

M. KALININ.

Deputy President of the Council of
People's Commissars,

A. SMIRNOV.

Deputy Secretary of the All-Russian
Central Executive Committee,

A. DOSOV.

April 8, 1929.

APPENDIX II

Since preparing the foregoing report the author has learned that John Deubner has regained his freedom, and despatches from Warsaw in the early days of November, 1932, reported that 39 Polish prisoners had just arrived from Soviet Russia, having been exchanged for Soviet prisoners held in Poland. Among them were 18 priests, all but two of whom were Roman Catholics. The scene of the transfer was the frontier town of Stolpce. The prisoners were described as "living ghosts" as they tumbled from two filthy boxcars. Their luggage was a few wooden boxes and paper bags. In contrast, the Russians exchanged by Poland arrived in a Pullman train. All were neatly dressed and laden with luggage. The men puffed contentedly at cigars.

Among the priests was the Rt. Rev. Theophilus Skalsky, Apostolic Administrator of the Diocese of Zhytomir, who had been held prisoner by the Bolshevists since June 20, 1926, first in the prison at Jaroslav and then in the famous Butyrky prison at Moscow.

Most of the prisoners had been condemned to penal servitude in the north of Russia. They reached the frontier in a state of utter exhaustion. Until the last moment they did not know they were to be liberated. Their joy at seeing their native land knew no bounds. The release was due to the efforts of the Red Cross, whose representative on the Soviet side is Mme. Pieszkov, wife of the famous Russian, Maxim Gorky.

The Papal Nuncio to Poland, His Excellency, the Most Rev. Francesco Marmaggi, communicated to the returned prisoners a special blessing sent them by His Holiness, Pope Pius XI. The Holy Father, in blessing the prisoners and their relatives, expressed his hope that the blessing would help them to forget their past woes. God's special favor, by which they obtained their release, should help them, he said, in the work which is awaiting them in their native land. Another blessing was sent by His Holiness to those who, despite great difficulties, obtained the return of the prisoners to Poland.

The prisoners' accounts of their suffering in Russia brought tears to the eyes of their fellow countrymen. Msgr. Skalsky, after he crossed the border, knelt and made the Sign of the Cross toward Russia.

The Rev. John Swidersky told of his arrest during church services at Ploskirov. "The G. P. U. agents beat me until I became unconscious," he said. "I was kept without bread and water for three days and then beaten again. For two years I remained in prison without trial."

The Rev. Casimir Naskrocky, also seized during church services, was held for four years without trial. "My food," he said, "consisted of stale bread, horseflesh and soup made from dirty water and stale potatoes."

The Rev. Father Liliewsky told of having conducted his parish at Winnica for twenty-eight years. Prior to his arrest in January, 1930, he was often the victim of atheistic attacks. Taken to prison, he was brought to trial in March of that year with eleven other priests and twenty-one Poles.

"The court," Father Liliewsky said, "consisted of members of the G. P. U. We were refused counsel. Twenty-seven of our number were condemned to death and the sentences were carried out. I was sentenced to hard labor at a prison camp near Archangel. The guards, composed of members of the Communist party expelled to the camp for criminal offenses, are inhuman in their treatment of the prisoners. My scant belongings were stolen. They took my shoes and I had to go barefooted until I made a pair of wooden shoes. Each morning at five we had to arise—the ailing prisoners included—or be beaten."

Father Czeslaw, another priest, told of the prohibitive prices charged for food in Russia. "One egg costs $2.50 in the Ukraine," he said. "One loaf of stale bread sells for $4. A shirt is priced at $25." One priest, the Rev. Francis Andruszkiewicz, said he had been in prison for five years and that both his hands had been broken by G. P. U. agents.

IX

THE CHURCH IN CONTEMPORARY SPAIN

Marie R. Madden

To preface this essay with the statement that Spain is not a Catholic society today and has not been one for nearly two hundred years, may surprise many. If one considers what constitutes a Catholic society and then reviews the events in Spain from the reign of Philip V, one appreciates the truth and significance of this statement. As the tree is known by its fruits, and the individual Catholic by the Catholic virtues which adorn his life, so too the character of a society is known by its fruits, its social institutions. We judge institutions by their principles, by their organization and by the results of their functioning. Judged by this criterion we can only give the title of Catholic to an institution when its principles, its organization, its results are informed by the Catholic view of life. By such a standard Spain is not a Catholic society.

Be it noted here that while a society is undoubtedly made up of individuals, it is not a mere mass in which numbers are significant. A society may possess a majority of believing Catholics and yet not be Catholic. For a society is that mysterious entity, an organized network of institutions which catch up and integrate the manifold life of man, guiding his instincts, satisfying his interests, supporting his aims, at once receiving his action and moulding his choices. The term Catholic, of course, includes not only the implications of the natural law, but more essentially the fuller and richer interpretation which is the function of the Catholic Church to make more clear and to expound.

I

Relations of Church and State

Tradition reverently informs us that when St. James the Apostle was about to set out on his travels, Our Lady told him she would meet him in Spain, and devotion to Our Lady of the Pilar reminds us that the Church in Spain was practically contemporaneous with the Church in the world.[1] Circumstances, however, did not present the favorable moment for applying the teachings of the Church to the organization of society as a deliberate choice of the will of the people until the Third Council of Toledo. From then on we may watch the slow growth of social institutions moulded on Catholic principles and the norms gradually crystallizing for the relations between Church and monarchy.[2] Politically the Span-

[1] Villada, Zacarias, *Historia Eclesiástica de España,* I, Madrid, 1929.

[2] In this article we take the stand that monarchy in the medieval sense has been superseded by the state in the modern *practice,* though not in the terminology of the usually accepted political theorists. That is we hold that what the people expect today of what they call the state as an institution, the medieval people

ish people set up a Catholic *república* in which the twin directing agencies were the ecclesiastical and the secular (civil) authorities.[3] The first was represented by the episcopate, the second by the King and on the administrative side by the *municipios*, *señorios* and other similar institutions. Each authority had its own special field of work but the complex nature of man frequently demanded that the ecclesiastical should advise the secular, and the secular support and defend the ecclesiastical. We see this concretely worked out in the mutual coöperation of each as specified in the codes and *fueros*.[4] The important coöperation which the ecclesiastical authorities lent because of the special events in Spanish history, gave a unique position to the Church in Spanish society. This is why we find individual ecclesiastics participating in the function of government, as members of the King's Councils, as *oidores* of *Audiencias* and as holders of *señorios*. That is why we have the recognition of canon law on a legal equality with that of the civil law and the interpenetrations of the latter with the principles borrowed from the canon. The

expected of the monarchy as an institution, though with this difference: Owing to a return to pagan principles, the state in modern practice is expected to do the work done by many other institutions, including the Church, of the medieval society and thus it tends to become not only all absorbing but coterminous with society. (For an interesting discussion of modern theories of the state, see Emerson, *State and Sovereignty in Modern Germany*, Yale University Press, 1928.)

[3] De Vitoria, *Relecciónes Teológicas* (Madrid, 1917), II, 127.

[4] Cf. the *Forum Iudiciorum, Las Siete Partidas;* Ziegler, A., *Church and State in Visigothic Spain*, Catholic University, 1930; Madden, M. R., *Political Theory and Law in Medieval Spain*, Fordham University, 1930.

reason why Spain had ecclesiastical *fueros* and representation of the clergy in the Cortes derived directly from this situation, but indirectly from the
Catholic theory of social organization, which considers the spiritual interests of man as worthy of
recognition, and so important as to have this recognition publicly proclaimed in the proper institution
—the Cortes—which represented the various necessary interests of man. That is why also we have the
diezmo in Spain. As the interrelations produced by
the above situation were gradually organized and
settled into the framework of Spanish life, the Spanish people did indeed possess a Catholic society.

Nothing, however, is perfect in this imperfect
world, nor did Spanish society escape this rule. Owing to the generally sympathetic coöperation between
the ecclesiastical and secular authorities, a certain
institution was allowed to grow up, arising rather
naturally out of the conditions of the Reconquest,
and of the intimate relations between the Church and
the monarchy. This was the institution of the *Real
Patronato,* correct enough in theory but capable of
much abuse when those managing it forgot or confused the theory behind it.[5] It was not until the

[5] The right of patronage was a favor granted by the Holy See
more or less frequently from the fifth century to various of the
faithful in order to encourage them to found and endow churches
and benefices. It consisted in the power to present a cleric for
a vacant benefice (cf. St. Thomas, *Summa* 2: 2. q. 100, art. 4).
It was conceded as a reward and a favor, to ecclesiastics or the
laity (cf. *Las Siete Partidas, Partida* I, *Tit.,* xv, *ley* xv). It is
called a right because out of the favor granted resulted permanent
and legal consequences such as certain rights and duties. Cf.
Gómez Zamora, *Regio Patronato* (Madrid, 1897), c. v, 163-221.
Cf. Lafuente, Vicente de, *Historica eclesiástica de España,* 2nd.

discussion on the authority and power of the King
in the terms of the definitions of the Justinian code
began at first insensibly, then consciously, to influence the Spanish monarchs to take an attitude towards the rights of the patronage which opened up
the long dispute on the *Regalia* between the popes
and the kings.   Upon the advice of jurists more
versed in the Roman than the canon law, the kings
began to assume that what was granted originally as
a favor owing to the particular circumstances of the
time, was really a natural right and therefore inalienable. The confusion of thought by which this conclusion was reached is well illustrated in the
celebrated book by Rivadeneira [6] which has so influenced the modern anti-clerical theorists.   From
considering the patronage as a right *de iure,* it was
but a step for the Roman lawyers to assume it a lay
function and thence in a further short step to secularize the whole institution, including the *diezmo.*
The whole function of the patronage was then assumed to be inherent in the royal sovereignty and
by so much a "royal, a lay, a secular" power, to use
the words of Rivadeneira, which should have jurisdiction over ecclesiastical persons and property.[7]

ed., Madrid, 1875. Interesting references are to be found in
Ballesteros y Beretta, A. de, *Historia de España,* VI, pp. 373-4,
Barcelona, 1932. Gonzales-Albern, J. Escobedo, *Las Relaciones
entre la Iglesia y el Estado en la historia, doctrina y los canones,*
Madrid, 1927.
 [6] Rivadeneira, D. Antonio Joaquín de, *Manual Compendio del
Regio Patronato,* c. iv, c. vi.
 [7] Ballesteros, VI, pp. 229-35. Morales, A. de, *Patronato
eclesiástica de los Reyes de España* in *Revista general de Legisla-
ción y jurisprudencia,* Madrid, XL. Portillo, Enrique, *Estudios
críticos de historia eclesiástica española durante la primera mitad*

The acceptance of these ideas was so rapid after
the reigns of the Catholic kings and abuses under
them both in Spain and elsewhere so alarming that
the necessary reforms were instituted in the Council
of Trent. Many of the disciplinary reforms of this
same Council were not well received by the Spanish
sovereigns. As a consequence of the evils resulting
from this policy and the dangers from the extrava-
gant interpretation of the *Patronato* adopted by the
Bourbon Philip V, the papal court adopted a new
policy. It aimed as diplomatically as possible to
emancipate the Church in Spain from the shackles
with which these false ideas on the *Patronato* had
gradually hampered her liberty of action. Since
many of the abuses had become rooted in custom
this was not easy to initiate or to accomplish, but it
has remained the keynote of the Vatican policy to
the present day.

The first open challenge to the authority of the
Pope came in the attempt to restrict the powers of
the papal nuncio. At the request of Charles I in
1537, a nuncio was appointed to the Spanish court.
Certain special functions were assigned to him, jurisdiction over certain cases formerly heard in Rome,
the granting of certain papal benefices and the collection of certain revenues of ecclesiastical prebends
and the *expolios* of deceased archbishops and bishops
and the income of vacant benefices. Between the
attempts of the kings to control the Church through

del siglo xviii in *Razón y Fé*, vol. 17 (1907), and *Diferencias entre
la Iglesia y el Estado con motivo del real patronato en el siglo
xviii* in *Razón y Fé*, vol. 20 (1908).

this nunciature and various abuses which arose in connection with the lawsuits, there was considerable criticism in the Cortes (1713) and the Royal Council. The applications of the *pase regio* [8] and the objections of the nuncio to these frequently brought very strained relations between the Vatican and the Spanish sovereigns. Philip V had even gone so far as to close the nunciature in 1709. A committee was formed from the Council of State and Castile to arrange the question. Among the regalists were D. Franciso de Solís, Bishop of Cordova and Viceroy of Aragon, who drew up the list of complaints against the Roman Curia in a report on the *regalias* of the king and the jurisdiction of the bishops. Opposed to regalism was D. Luis Belluga, Bishop of Cartagena. In his memorial he countered all the statements of the regalists and had with him the Archbishop of Santiago and the Bishops of Toledo, Seville and Granada. Macanaz, of the pro-French party, presented his memorial of the Fifty-five Points to the Council of Castile. Negotiations were entered into

[8] The *pase regio* was a right claimed by the kings to promulgate or refuse to promulgate the papal bulls and pontifical decrees. Without this royal authorization, they would not be legally binding in the Spanish possessions. Such a privilege had been granted by Pope Urban VI under special circumstances, and the idea was eagerly seized upon by rulers ambitious to control the Pope. Alexander VI permitted the nuncio at the Spanish court and also the chief chaplains of the Catholic kings to examine or revise the bulls of indulgence in order to establish their authenticity. This was taken as a pretext by which the kings assumed the authority to order that all the rescripts and papal documents should first pass the Royal Council (*Novísima Recopilación, Lib.* II, *Tít.* III, *ley* 9). The *pase regio* as a royal right has been emphatically condemned by various popes, including Leo X, Clement VII, Clement XI, Benedict XIV and Pius IX.

also in regard to the abuses connected with the non-enforcement of certain of the disciplinary decrees of Trent. All these complaints led to the Bull *Apostolici Ministerii* issued by Innocent XIII on the advice of Cardinal Belluga y Moncada. The points dealt with related to the conditions for ordination, obligations of pastors, suppression of benefices and chaplaincies without endowments, the cloister of nuns, duties of the regular clergy, procedure of the tribunals of the nunciature and other ecclesiastical courts.

The last two raised the delicate question of the *Patronato*. The Marqués de Mejorada y de la Braña, secretary of the *Patronato* under Philip V, in a letter to Don Santiago Riol, one of the under secretaries, attempted to prove with documents that the *Real Patronato* was "the most precious stone which adorns the Crown of Castile." It comprises all the rights of the *Patronato* (*soberana regalia*) whether obtained by papal donation or originating in the superiority of the Crown over the Pope. These last were inalienable.

Such statements could not be ignored by the Pope and negotiations were initiated by the Pope between the two courts in order to clear up the difficulties. A Concordat (September 26, 1737) was drawn up between Clement XIII and Philip V arranging many of the minor points at issue but the vital question of the right of the *Patronato* was not squarely faced. Article 23 diplomatically postponed for future discussion the principles at stake, leaving the question of the vacant benefices and the *expolios* as it had been.   Though in the interests of peace the concordat was ratified by both parties, neither was pleased and the royal jurists immediately raised loud outcry that the authority of the King had been placed under that of the Pope.   Under the impact of the arguments of the leading Spanish jurists, particularly Don Gregorio Mayans y Ciscan, fifteen years of controversy ensued.   Again in the Concordat of June 11, 1753, arranged between Benedict XIV and Ferdinand VI, the direct statement of the issue was avoided, the Pope considering the time inopportune for more than the statement of the facts of the *Patronato* as conceded by the popes to the Spanish sovereigns.[9]   The Holy See upheld the principle at issue by reserving directly from the *Patronato* fifty-two ecclesiastical benefices in Spain.   It was made clear that the rights of nomination did not confer any jurisdiction over either ecclesiastical persons or churches.[10]

As a result of negotiations in regard to ecclesiastical court procedure, the King agreed to deposit at Rome a sufficient endowment (1,143,333 Roman *escudos* at 3 per cent and a promise of 5,000 for the

[9] Lafuente, Modesto de, *Historia General de España*, XIX, pp. 317-18.
[10] This was stated in the Bull of Adrian VI to Charles I: "cuyo derecho de Patronato así confirmado y concedido, sea de la misma naturaleza, vigor, fuerza y privilegio, *que el que compete a los Reyes*," quoted in Gómez Zamora, *Regio Patronato español e indiano*, Madrid, 1897, p. 249.

support of the nunciature at Madrid) to compensate for the fees resigned by the papal court.[11] The income from the *Cruzada* was assigned to the Crown.

The papacy perceived that the temper of the Spanish court was in nowise favorable to any other settlement and with that patience and vision so characteristic of its divine mission was content to await a more favorable time to secure its main point, the entire freedom of the Church in Spain. But the long argument had prepared the minds of the leaders for the decidedly anti-papal and anti-clerical policies of Charles III and his ministers.[12] Another factor was that Catholic opposition had lost vigor as a result of the decay of the study of Scholastic philosophy in the seventeenth century. Spanish philosophical thought became much influenced by Cartesian and empiricist theories. The Abbé Juan Andrés and the ex-Jesuit Arteaga spread such opinions and though Scholastic thought was not unrepresented, it had a small audience.

These new ideas were working also for a reorientation of social classes which the rise of a commercialized middle class was to force in the nineteenth century. The nobility and clergy were to lose to

[11] For the text of the Concordat of 1753 see *Colección de los Concordatos*, Madrid, 1848; Lafuente, Modesto, *Historia General*, XIX, pp. 311-22.

[12] For a summary of the policy of Charles III, see Ballesteros, V, p. 173; VI, pp. 233 sq., and references. Cf. also the work of the encyclopedists Feijóo, Torres Villaroel, Mayans y Ciscan, Campomanes, Capmany and Jovellanos.

it their functions of leadership.[13]   Though the principles of the Protestant revolt foreshadowed this condition even in Spain, the momentum produced in Spanish society by the brilliant reigns of Charles I and Philip II appeared to hold the old classes in being even into the formalism of the eighteenth century.   No one in Spain could then appreciate that the face of society was to be so changed, for no one could imagine a different hierarchy of classes or different institutions.

Nevertheless this is exactly what was happening. Old classes were dying, new institutions were being prepared.   The leaders of this social action were visioning the secular state and secular society but they did not immediately perceive that this meant new institutions.   To them at that time it simply meant the displacing of certain of the old institutions not from society but from a position of leadership.

The first social institution attacked was the Church; the family was not seen to be an obstacle until later days.   By a series of royal decrees the Spanish Church was more and more subjected to

[13] Note these statistics quoted in Chapman, *History of Spain,* New York, 1930, p. 459:

	1787	1797
Ecclesiastics	182,425	168,248
Nobles	480,589	402,059
Civil Employees (government)	41,014	31,981
Soldiery	77,884	149,340
Students	50,994	29,812
Farmers and farm laborers	1,871,768	1,677,172
Manufacturers and artisans	310,739	533,769
Servants	280,092	......
Merchants	No figures	25,685

the King's authority: in case of conflict of laws between the civil and ecclesiastical courts, the preference was given to the former; a law of 1766 required the bishops to supervise the priests lest they should criticize the government; the right of asylum and the personal immunities of ecclesiastics were limited by a law of 1774. During the reigns of Charles III and Charles IV the Inquisition was much restricted. The attitude towards the Society of Jesus and the confiscation of so many of the ecclesiastical and charitable endowments during the latter part of the eighteenth century, are further examples of this spirit. The dislocation of education produced by these events had of course important consequences, for the new teachers were already imbued with encyclopedist ideas, for which many of the clergy had been prepared by an enthusiasm for the ways of Jansenism.

When the Cortes of 1812 assembled at Cádiz there were already two generations of leaders almost completely de-Catholicized, but the masses of the people, if indifferent to religious interests, had not thoroughly assimilated the new ideas. Hence, although the Constitution of 1812 really served notice on those of the Spanish people who had eyes to read it aright that the old Catholic society was dead, its curious mixture of the old and the new won a sufficient support for the policy of the leaders. The old monarchy was killed outright, sovereignty was declared in the people, and hence eventually to be administered as a secular thing, but the religion of Spain was officially declared to be the religion of the people and the exercise of none other tolerated. How empty was this formula was to be revealed in the immediate restrictions placed upon the action of the Church in practically every sphere of life, even in the forum of individual conscience, for an attempt was made to limit the number of Religious communities and even of vocations. Even with all this it was not possible to erect the secular state and secular society right away, but every generation since then has seen the effort made to make them a fact and a reality.

What was the Church to do in this new orientation of the social life of the people? Unfortunately few of the ecclesiastical leaders appreciated the seriousness of the changes and the true nature of the developments in the social classes. The nuncio protested and was exiled for his pains. Most of the hierarchy considered that the crucial point of attack was the monarch and not the principles of the monarchy as an institution, and so rallied to the defense of Ferdinand VII who was to prove indeed a broken reed. The Bishop of Orense, Don Pedro de Quevedo y Quintano, is thought to have saved at least the outward forms of the monarchy. In the secret sessions of the Cortes held on March 9, 1812, a long and bitter debate was held over the meaning of *guardar y obedecer* in the constitutional oath and over the interpretation of the phrase *residir la soberanía en la nación*. Could this latter be considered as apart from that of the King? If so, the oath could not be taken was one argument. Another held that the deputies having sworn to the King as their sovereign, the State was then constituted and therefore sovereignty of the people could not mean any right taken from the King. The debate over this was inconclusive, and finally in order to come to a prompt decision, the minority overrode the majority by unscrupulous methods and decreed exile and confiscation of property for any deputy who should take a stand against the constitutional oath. The Cortes then formally swore to the Constitution on March 19, 1812.[14] Despite the continued protests of the Bishop of Orense no one took the hint.

The reasons for this are not far to seek. Considering the insidious way in which the new propaganda had been spread in Spain and the general attacks on the rights of the Church and the Religious Orders, it was perhaps not possible for those generations to grasp how widespread the new principles were. The clergy and the majority of the people also could hardly imagine the possibility of a Spain not Catholic and neither appreciated the reorientation of institutions which had actually taken place as a result of the success of the Reformation and the economic ideas of the Industrial Revolution.[15] These had in fact reshuffled the old social classes and in the new alignment the so-called middle class

[14] Risco, A., *Las Cortes de Cádiz y el obispo de Orense* in *Razón y Fé*, vol. 75 (1926); Lafuente, M., *Historia General*, XXVII.

[15] The Spanish economists had been discussing this for some time, but the point of the debate had been missed.

occupied a strategic position, and therefore it should
have been held to the Church, if the society was to
remain Catholic. This the hierarchy failed to see,
partly because of the war on the Church which
proved an effective smoke-screen and was serious
enough to prevent all effective effort of defense.
It was not until the Syllabus of Pius IX cleared the
way that a Pope, like Leo XIII, could call attention
to the necessity of new institutions, even now despite the great Encyclicals of Pius XI a very new
idea. Meantime the middle class was lost to the
Church.

In such a situation the Church was left little choice
of action. There was the duty and the necessity
of teaching society once more the old Catholic principles and so to prepare the way for the reforms, but
the Church could not take the first steps towards
this desideratum. First, the secular State decided to
monopolize education [16] and secondly, to hold fast
to the *Patronato*. Thorough-going secularists might

[16] The first law organizing public education was passed by the
Cortes of 1821. Education was to be supported by the State, and
free. Private free education was permitted, but must be super-
vised through examinations before a tribunal composed of professors from the public establishments. Primary, secondary and
university education was provided for, one primary school for
every fifty inhabitants, and provincial universities (fifty-two provinces were created by the Cortes of 1821). Charitable agencies
were to be directed by the *Juntas municipales de beneficia,* one in
each town. This program was not carried out in detail but the
aim was made clear of secularizing all the work formerly maintained by the ecclesiastical agencies. How this was carried out
later may be seen by consulting the law of Don Claudio Moyano,
September 9, 1857; the law of 1859 which gave the monopoly to
the State; royal decrees of July 20, 1900, of August 21, 1900, of
October 23, 1913, of October 25, 1914, of May 25, 1915, municipal
statute of March 8, 1924, and the decree of March 15, 1924.

be expected to welcome the complete break with the Church which the abandonment of the *Patronato* implied, but where are thorough-going secularists to be found? The Spanish variety, at least, saw in the *Patronato* too good an opportunity to shackle the Church to consent to abandon it and besides was not powerful enough to ignore the Church so completely. The association and coöperation of Church and State were too old, too thoroughly accepted by the whole people, and real piety was ingrained in enough of the people for this to be possible. But there was no effective opposition to despoiling the Church of her property.[17]

The Vatican saw the situation, its advantages and disadvantages, very clearly and after the events of 1820 [18] adopted the policy of conciliating the gov-

[17] The handling of the *diezmo* illustrates this. It was reduced to one-half of the amount paid in and devoted exclusively to the endowment of the clergy and the upkeep of the churches. The State renounced the *novena*, the *excusado*, the *tercias reales* in Castile, the *cencio diezmo* in Aragón, etc. This meant also that those of the laity who had earlier obtained possession of these funds were now left without them. To indemnify these, all the rural and urban landed property, the *censos foras,* rents and rights possessed by the clergy and the church buildings, except the rectories, palaces of the bishops and their gardens and orchards, were confiscated. All this was put at the disposal of the National Commission on the Public Debt. Diocesan commissions were set up to make the distinctions between the direct endowments of the clergy and that for the upkeep of the churches and the necessary ceremonials. The total of the *diezmo* was fixed at 30,000,000 *reales*.

[18] During 1816-17 Granada and Madrid were centers of Masonic efforts to restore the constitution of 1812 and these groups engineered the revolution of 1820. Clubs similar to those of the French Revolution were organized in the Cortes. These new Liberals broke with those of 1812 and following the principles of Marat became the ancestors of the Radicals of today such as Blasco Ibánez, Lerroux, Soriano, etc. Cf. Lafuente, M., XXX; Albornoz, Alvaro de, *El Partido republicano,* Madrid, 1918;

ernment as far as possible on the question of the *Patronato* while endeavoring to secure the liberty of the Church and awaiting the favorable opportunity to awaken the Catholic conscience of Spain. The stormy days of 1837 and 1845 incident upon the attempts to establish further the secular State left few opportunities to come to an arrangement of the questions pending between Church and State. For many years bishops were not nominated, sacred orders were not conferred, and the life of the Church was almost at a standstill. Sentiment in Spain was not favorable to these conditions and the violent outbreaks forced the secularists to conclude a truce in the Concordat of 1851 signed on March 15 of that year by the representatives of Pius IX and Doña Isabel II. The status of the Church was determined by this and the convention held in 1859 until the fall of 1931.

A study of the forty-six clauses makes clear the advantages gained by the Church and the strength of the old Catholic tradition. The Catholic religion with all its rights and prerogatives according to the law of God and the sacred canons was recognized as the official and only religion of the Spanish nation and forever to be conserved (Article 1).[19] Education

Morayta, *Masonería Española, Páginas de su historia,* Madrid, 1915.

[19] This is not quite as strongly put as a similar clause in the Constitution of 1812: La religión de la nación española es y será perpetuamente la Católica apostólica Romana, única verdadera; la nación la protege por leyes sabias y justas y prohibe el ejercicio de cualquiera otra. Cf. also Article 11, par. 1 of the Constitution of 1876 and Article 11 of the Constitution of 1845.

The jurists considered *nación* and *estado* at least in this usage in whatever branch, public or private, was to be in conformity with the doctrines of the Catholic religion and to ensure this the bishops and other prelates were to be allowed to watch over (*velar*) "the purity of the doctrine of Faith, of the customs and above all of the religious education of the youth" . . . even in the public schools (Article 2).[20]

Articles 3 and 4 of the Concordat reaffirmed the rights of the clergy to fulfill the duties of their calling without any molestation or interference and the Queen's government bound itself to lend aid and support in all such matters when requested. The *real órden* of November 8, 1890, further recognized that the government held that Article 11 of the Constitution "recognized the incontrovertible right of the Church to be respected in its laws." All this was one thing. To carry it out loyally and

as synonymous. Cf. Villada, *Reclamaciones legales,* ca. iv, p. 1; Minteguizaga, *El Artículo 11 de la constitución;* Lopez Peláez, *El derecho español,* p. 28.

On the other hand, clauses 2 and 3 of Article 11 of the Constitution of 1876 open a loophole whereby this important article of the Concordat might be nullified and Pope Pius IX so protested to the Archbishop of Toledo and the hierarchy of Spain. The Liberals of course in this constitution were attempting a compromise between the principles of secularism and the principles of Catholicism and tried one of their favorite dodges of the issues. They explained clauses 2 and 3 to mean that no public toleration of any cult contrary to the Catholic religion would be allowed, but private toleration was quite different. This is the sense of the *real órden* signed by Cánovas del Castillo, President of the Council of Ministers, October 23, 1876, and the same idea was repeated in the Cortes by the Minister Martín de Herrera in 1876 and by Calderón Collantes in 1878. Anti-Catholic propaganda was prohibited in the sessions of the Cortes of June 7, 1876. These equivocations forced the Church to constant protests and gave the Liberals time to work on public opinion so that it would neither understand nor support the position of the Church.

[20] Cf. canons 1373, 1374, 1375, 1381 of the Revised Code of 1918.

sincerely was apparently beyond either the will or the power of the government.[21]   Articles 5-27 arranged the details of organization of the dioceses and similar matters; Articles 20, 26 specifically required the recognition of the Council of Trent in regard to vacant Sees and parishes.   There were signs during the dictatorship that the government was moving towards a more cordial coöperation in regard to the *Patronato* with the Holy See.   For example, the royal decree of March 10, 1924, created an ecclesiastical *junta,* to discuss the vacancies for the prebends, as a subcommittee of the *Patronato.* The membership was almost entirely ecclesiastical.

Article 28 dealt with the establishment of seminaries under ecclesiastical direction and in Articles 29, 30, 35 the government agreed to preserve the Religious Orders devoted to contemplation, education and other pious works, also the *Colegio de Misiones para Ultramar,* the Congregations of St. Vincent de Paul, of St. Philip Neri, Daughters of Charity of St. Vincent de Paul and others approved by the Holy See.   Articles 31, 35 arranged the salaries of the clergy and the expenses for the upkeep of the churches and ceremonies.   These clauses were made necessary by the various confiscations of ecclesiastical properties during the century, particularly those of 1845.   While the Church might secure

[21] Cf. the debate on education which raged during 1922 apropos of the reform of the *Consejo de Instrucción pública,* and the case of the Lerida professor who in the Normal School was propagating false ideas on marriage.   When the bishop intervened, as of legal right, he received no support from the government.

fresh revenues from new donations, justice demanded some reparation at least for these confiscations but Article 35 made clear that the Vatican insisted only on what was reasonably possible with reference to 1845. Much of the property originally confiscated by the government had passed into other hands (Article 42). Articles 40 and 41 expressly recognized the right of the Church to hold and administer property and to acquire it by the usually admitted just titles and the regulations of the Council of Trent.[22] Article 44 confirmed the earlier Concordat of 1753. Article 45 established the perpetual nature of the Concordat and provided that it could not be abrogated unilaterally, not even in a constituent Cortes. (Concordat is the term applied to a solemn treaty arranged between the ecclesiastical and civil powers officially, if personally between the sovereigns it is called a concordium.) As such it was the law of the land and in fact the Concordat was proclaimed as law on October 17, 1851.[23]

The royal decree of May 19, 1919, recognized the

[22] These clauses were not carried out in the changes in government that followed 1851. A law of May 1, 1855, allowed fresh confiscations and so upset the fulfillment of the Concordat that it was necessary to enter into negotiations as a result of which the *Convenio* of 1859 was concluded as an integral part of the Concordat. It more specifically and in detail arranged the question of the ecclesiastical endowments rendered necessary by all the confiscations, again with great consideration on the part of the Vatican.

[23] Cf. *Razón y Fé*, vol. 63, p. 87. According to the royal decree of October 13, 1856, "The Concordat of 1851 ... is both a most important law of the State and an Act with all the force of an international treaty. Under this last concept its dispositions cannot validly be set aside nor altered without the agreement and consent of the high contracting parties." This royal decree was signed by all in the Council of Ministers.

new Code of Canon Law, on petition of the Archbishop of Toledo to the Council of State. The question was then raised, does this give it force as civil
law? The tone of the debates in an earlier Cortes
on this point seemed to consider that ecclesiastical
law had the force of civil law,[24] but, on the other
hand, there is some doubt that canon law was recognized as ecclesiastical law only, which is not quite
the same thing.[25]

Thus the theory. It will be perceived that the
practice turns on the point of whether the society
in which such laws are operating is Catholic or not.
The practice is very clear that Spanish society is
not Catholic.

The status of the Religious Orders turns upon
the same point. In a secular society, Religious Orders are considered merely corporations whose
juridical existence depends upon the good pleasure
of the State. Hence the law must prescribe the
terms of their existence as it does for any corporation. This view finds support in the Roman law
which having recognized corporations determines
also the rights and duties they may enjoy. But
Religious Orders in the Catholic theory are not mere
corporations and in Catholic Spain it never occurred
to anyone to doubt their true nature, or to imagine
that the State could initiate or dissolve them.

The pretensions of the sovereigns and the lawyers
on the *Patronato* and the *regalia*, however, paved the

[24] Cf. *Razón y Fé,* vol. 11, pp. 413 sq.
[25] Cf. *Razón y Fé,* vol. 58, pp. 409 sq.

way for a new view on the Religious Orders and with Charles III the first attempts at the supremacy of the authority of the State were made with the exile of the Society of Jesus.

The government during the years 1820-23 assumed the same authority, but the most drastic expression of this was the law of July 22-29, 1837, Article 1 of which suppressed all the monasteries, convents, schools, congregations and houses of the Religious of both sexes. Public opinion was not quite prepared to accept all this and an exception was made of the missions for Asia established in Valladolid, Ocaña and Monteagudo, though under strict regulations of the government in regard to rules and the admission of novices (Article 2). Practical necessity decreed the restoration of the teaching and hospital Orders though only provisionally while they were fulfilling the conditions of secularization. The teaching Orders permitted were not to be considered as Religious communities but as establishments of public instruction dependent upon the government (Article 3). Similar rules were laid down for the Hospital Brothers and the Sisters of Charity of St. Vincent de Paul (Articles 4-8). Cloistered nuns were dispensed from their vows irrespective of ecclesiastical canons (Articles 12, 13). All the real property, income and capital, of all the houses of Religious of both sexes, suppressed or permitted, were taken over by the *Caja de Amortización* to be applied to the public debt (Article 20). These laws were unequally enforced, depending upon whether the moderate or radical Liberals were in power, but the radicals were in power often enough to make impossible the proper development of the monastic life, with all the social consequences this implies.

During the Revolution of 1868 the laws of October 12, 15, 18, decreed new suppressions starting with the Jesuits and adding all monasteries, convents, schools and congregations which may have been founded since 1837. The Constitution of 1876 permitted liberty of association and under this law Religious Orders began to come back, though the Orders of Sisters permitted to exist in 1837 did not flourish owing to the restrictions. The Sisters of the Poor, Religious of the Sacred Heart, Carmelites of Charity, Adoration, Oblates, Servants of Mary, Servants of Jesus, Slaves of the Sacred Heart, Sisters of Hope, were among the new foundations. The older Orders of men permitted included Augustinians, Franciscans, Observants, Discalced Carmelites, Capuchins, Dominicans, Carmelites, Trinitarians, Jesuits, Passionists, Redemptorists, Brothers of St. John of God, Brothers of the Christian Schools, Salesian Fathers, Fathers of the Heart of Mary. Carthusians and Trappists were also founded.

Despite the growth the status of the Orders was very precarious. The royal decree of December 24, 1851, proclaimed that in virtue of the Articles 43 and 45 of the Concordat, Articles 12, 13 of the law of 1837 were abrogated, repeated again in the royal order of September 19, 1867, but the agitations of 1868-69 swept these safeguards aside. The attempts to bring the Religious Orders back under the clause of liberty of association in the Constitution of 1869 was one of the events which wrecked the government of Don Amadeo of Savoy. The Constitution of 1876 in Article 13 declared the right of every Spaniard to form associations "for the ends of human life." The laws of 1837 and 1868 were not abrogated but the interpretation of the government was that they were incompatible with the Constitution of 1876 and with the law of associations of June 30, 1887, which recognized the liberty of association, even religious. Article 2 excepted the Religious Orders mentioned in the Concordat. The law of May 26, 1889, recognized the right of Religious Orders to obtain and hold property.[26]

While it is true that Religious Orders under these interpretations of the Constitution of 1876 could exist and flourish, it is also true that the terminology of the Constitutional clauses is capable of two interpretations. To recognize a right may imply that the right is prior, it may also imply in the interpretation of the secularist a granted right. This is Liberal doctrine and the Liberals have not changed their stripes or their principles. When the test of interpretation comes, the liberal Liberals who have governed Spain since 1876 can always be trusted to revert to their true colors.

A Catholic society would hold ecclesiastical laws to be the law of the land and the State should aid

[26] Buitrago, J., *Las Ordenes religiosas, su existencia legal y capacidad civil en España,* Madrid, 1889.

in enforcing them; in case of conflict the spiritual interest as the superior law would prevail. But this was the whole question at issue between the Church and State. The Church was saying Spain had been a Catholic society and hence the State had been Catholic, and though now neither was so, both should and would be so again. The State was saying no. Catholic Spain lies in the past; Spain now, society and State, is secular. This deadlock lies behind the contradictions of the Constitution of 1876 and is largely responsible for the collapse of the government in 1932.[27] That the dictatorship failed to resolve the difficulty was due to the general neutrality of Spanish society in this long debate. Why this was so will be more evident when we discuss the second part of our theme, Catholic Action.

[27] Though not completely, for the inefficient ordering of the parliamentary institutions (in the elections of 1923, 23 parties were represented), and the neglect of a proper municipal reform had important influences. The uprisings of Granada in 1919 and the long debate over Señor Maura's reform bill for the *municipios* of 1907 and the law of July 16, 1918, are significant. This question of the *municipio* is a good illustration of what we mean by the necessity of a reorientation of institutions since the Protestant revolt. Since the Constitution of 1812 the *municipio* has been a field of experimentation in which it was assumed that following the ideology of the French Revolution the *municipio* was a *personna natural* (es municipio la asociación natural reconocida por la ley de personas y bienes, determinada por necessarias relaciónes de vecindad dentro del termino a que alance la jurisdicción de un ayuntamiento) under the government which could transform it at will according to the ideas of the ruling party. The Cortes of Cádiz considered it merely one of the wheels of the machinery of state and upon this basis all the reforms since proposed have been attempted.

II

CATHOLIC ACTION

Before taking up this question we must say a few words about secular action,[28] for Catholic Action has been obliged to act against this background.

Since the constituent Cortes of Cádiz of 1812 first presented the avowed plan of making Spain a secular state, secularist or lay action has concentrated on three main lines of attack, politically for a republic, educationally for the lay control of education, socially for an articulate public opinion opposed to Catholic tradition.

Republican (in the post-French revolutionary sense of the term) sentiment existed in Spain in the late eighteenth century. French ideas were propagated through Don José Marchena and Don Andrés María Guzman, the friend of Marat. Masonic lodges were founded by the Italian adventurer José Balsamo, agents for propagating the new ideas as early as 1795. There were some advocates for a republic in the Cortes of Cádiz in 1807. The newspaper *El Robespierre Español* was their organ and by 1820 the *Exaltados* appeared as a republican party. This revolution, however, saw the Republicans definitely divided into two groups, a cleavage which remains to this day in Liberal circles. In 1821 at Cádiz a newspaper, *El Eco de Padilla*, defi-

[28] González Blanco, Edmundo, "El Problema religiosa en España," in *La España Moderna*, vol. 157, Jan., 1902: "the eighteenth century secularized morality, the nineteenth religion, the twentieth will secularize the whole of the exterior life of society in a thoroughly concrete way."

nitely favored a socialistic republic and a conspiracy
to establish this was uncovered in Malaga. The
second group hesitated before these principles and
as moderate Liberals returned to the eighteenth-
century program, popular during the reign of Charles
III. Their aim was to leave institutions pretty much
as they were, abstracting from them any religious
or distinctively Catholic characteristic. As time went
on some of these saw the futility of the monarchy
under such a régime and so came out for a republic,
though not a radical one. The republican socialists
gained many adherents in the south and were particularly active between 1835-38. In the following
year the Madrid republicans started *La Legalidad*
and *La Revolución* organs for their propaganda,
while in 1840 Rodríguez Solís drew up a party program. It included suppression of the throne, government of the nation by a central *junta* composed
of representatives from provinces, an irremovable
judiciary, the establishment of the *jurado,* free, compulsory primary education, religious liberty, liberty
of the press, of assembly, of association and the
division of the state lands among the workers. After
1858 a group appeared with definite socialistic ideas
and *La Aracción,* founded by Fernando Garrido, and
La Fraternidad were frankly communistic. Many
of these ideas have reappeared in the Constituent
Cortes of 1931.

Republican opinion continued sharply divided over
these various principles so that the party was never
more than a party of factions. This partly explains

the failure of 1873. After this the party split again on two points, the first on the essence of the republic, liberal or socialist; the second on the form, federal or centralist. Now one leader, now another came to the fore, Pí y Margall, Figiueras, Salmerón, Menendez Pallares, Roberto Castrovido, Soly y Ortega, Melquiades Alvarez, Lerroux, Soriano, Indalecio Prieto, Fernando de los Rios, representing all shades of opinion. At the turn of the century the interminable debates at least made this much clear, the Liberal principles were too thin to carry the weight of institutions. Spanish realism woke up, and whatever Romanones, Sagasta, the Mauras, Alcalá Zamora, or Sanchez Guerra might be privately, they were of no value publicly save as camouflage. Behind them the influential leaders concentrated on essentials and worked for a Socialist republic.[29]

Contemporary Socialists are divided into two groups: the so-called moderate group represented by the *Unión general de Trabajadores* of Madrid; the *Confederación nacional de Trabajo* of Barcelona representing the syndicalist movement. Between 1881-1888 the *Federación de Trabajadores de la Región Española,* an anarchist group, held a series of Congresses at Barcelona, Madrid, Seville and Valencia. The Congress of Barcelona presented the following: the working class in the possession of

[29] *El Partido Republicano;* Ballesteros, V, ch. iii; Bailey, W. Diffie, The Socialist Movement in Spain, *Current History,* August, 1931; Mora, Francisco, *Historia del socialismo obrero,* Madrid, 1902; *La Abolición del salariado,* Severino Aznar Embid, read on reception into *Real Academia de Ciencias morales y políticas,* Madrid, 1921.

public power, collective ownership, organization of society on collective work. Though as an organization it ceased to exist after 1888, the anarchist group flourished, particularly in Cataluña and Valencia. Syndicalism in Cataluña began to favor the *Sindicato único,* an idea which gained favor rapidly after the World War. It secured the support of the *Federación nacional de Agricultores* organized at Córdoba in 1913. Violence generally marked its propaganda.

In contrast the *Unión general de Trabajadores* of Madrid aimed at securing its program through political action. The chief leader here was Pablo Iglesias. The liberal Liberals and the conservative Liberals joined forces to prevent the election of a Socialist but Iglesias finally secured election in 1909 to the Cortes. By 1918 nine radicals and six Socialists were elected to the Cortes. In 1922 five of the seven members representing Madrid were Socialists. The Socialists are well organized and disciplined and though affiliated with the Second International, have not disdained the Third. Communists have appeared in their ranks, they have received support from university professors who have intellectualized the movement as it were. Thanks to these various features the Socialists controlled the Constituent Cortes of 1931.

The propaganda for lay education has been directed by the Liberals up to the summer of 1931. Article 11 of the Constitution of 1876 and Articles 1-4 of the Concordat provided for religious instruction in the schools, but the national schools have never been professedly Catholic. During the revolution of 1868 all the debates of the Cortes reveal a decided propaganda for atheism and secularism which has constantly increased. Protestant schools were permitted in 1868 in the newer quarters of Madrid. By 1924 there were 54 such schools, with 11,478 pupils (5,927 boys). Avila also had a small school with 72 pupils.

Up to last spring, theoretically the law of Public Instruction of September 9, 1857, was still in force. Article 2 provided that primary instruction should include first Christian doctrine and ideas of sacred history accommodated to the child mind. Article 4 provided for the same studies on a more advanced scale for the higher classes. Articles 13, 14, 15, required the same in the secondary schools. Articles 68, 69, 70, 71, required that a teacher of a primary grade should be prepared to teach these subjects. Article 87 required that Christian doctrine be taught from catechisms approved by the bishop. Article 92 required episcopal approval for textbooks. Article 93 required all books selected by the government to be submitted to ecclesiastical supervision. Article 170 held sufficient cause for removal of a teacher to be that he imparted pernicious doctrines. Article 295 required that the civil and academic authorities should place no obstacle in the way of episcopal supervision. Article 296 permitted any diocesan prelate who found pernicious doctrines in books or explications of the teachers to give a report to the government, which would then take the necessary steps.

Nevertheless, despite these laws, they were not always observed [30] and of late contrary laws were passed. The royal decree of August 17, 1901, practically suppressed religious instruction in secondary schools by leaving it optional. The decree of April 25, 1913, was contradictory. Article 1 made it obligatory in primary schools in accordance with the law of 1857, but Article 2 excepted the children of those parents who professed a religion other than Catholic.[31]

Constant debate was kept up on liberty of instruction and the degree of intervention permitted the State. The Conde de Ramonones while Minister of Instruction in 1902 gave the liberal interpretation of Article 12 of the Constitution of 1876: "Liberty of instruction in order to form the national soul . . . in a form so definite that afterwards all other liberties would be useless." He always considered it necessary for the State to take on the office of guarding liberty of conscience, since the children of parents who professed various religions would attend the public schools and hence in order to avoid the difficulties of a mixed school, public instruction would have to be lay.[32]

These views were vigorously opposed by the hier-

[30] Decrees of July 20, 1900; August 21, 1900; October 23, 1913; October 15, 1914; May 25, 1915; Municipal Statute, March 8, 1924; decree of March 15, 1924, all emphasizing governmental control.

[31] Noguer, N., *El Artículo 11 de la Constitución de 1876 y et proyecta de código Penal* in *Razón y Fé* and also *Los delitos contra la religión en el proyecto de código penal, ibid.*, vol. 82 (1928).

[32] The liberal interpretation of Article 12 was also upheld in the Cortes of 1901, sessions 8, 9, 14, 18, 19, 21 of April by Señor Labra, Sánchez de Toca, Marqués de Pidal, Portuondo y Azcárate.

archy, which maintained such a policy was a denial of true liberty.[33]   There was no possibility of reconciling the two views, as the Liberals stood for the secular State.   Simultaneously the propaganda to win public opinion for the lay schools was carried on by such leaders as Manuel Cossio, Don Francisco Giner de los Rios, Pérez Galdos, Castilleja and others in the *Junta para amplicación de Estudio*.[34]   The *Institución Libre de Enseñanza* had its headquarters in Madrid and endeavored to popularize principles of coeducation, neutrality in religious matters, and education for life in the terminology of the exponents of the new education abroad.   Dependent centers were established throughout Spain.

Considering all these tendencies it can readily be seen that the government could not be too enthusiastic about fostering public education, for that would mean either Catholic education or dangerous arguments.   This throws a great light on why illiteracy was so high in Spain during the nineteenth century and why Catholics were not sufficiently well educated to rally to the intelligent and political defense of their religion as they should have.

The third secularist propaganda for an articulate public opinion unfavorable to Catholic Spanish tradition was even less creditable, but even more effective.   The aim here was to convince the people that

[33] *Exposición de los prelados españoles* to the Sovereigns in the Catholic Congresses of Saragossa, 1890, Tarragona, 1895, Lugo, 1896, Compostela, 1902.

[34] For the ideas of Giner de los Rios, cf. *Boletín de la Instrucción Libre de Enseñanza*, August, 1882.

Catholic Spain of the old tradition was all that *la leyenda negra* of the foreign propagandist had pictured her. Castelar took up this theme; so did Salmerón and even Don Juan de Valera and the sharptongued Azorín. Ganivet [35] and Ortega y Gasset in his *España invertebrada* showed the same spirit of carping censure. Blasco Ibáñez, Soriano, Unamuno and others less famous joined in the chorus. The keynotes struck were always anti-Spanish and anti-Catholic. According to *El Siglo Futuro* an anti-Spanish campaign was fomented in Europe and America in 1909. Don Manuel Bueno in *El Imparcial* noted an offensive started by Herriot in France against the Church which was copied in Spain. Even the great daily *ABC* frequently printed articles consistently defaming Spain and belittling Spanish genius and action.[36] The effect of all this may be imagined upon a people with such a poor system of education. But a languid interest was taken by the government until lately in the rich treasures of the national archives. Foreign students often commented upon the carelessness with which these were guarded. Many of the collections had been taken from different ecclesiastical libraries dur-

[35] Cf. *Angel Ganivet, Vida y obra,* Melchor Fernandez Almagro, Valencia, s. a.

[36] Ercilla, Ugarte de, *Campañia de difamación antiespañol* in *Razón y Fé,* vol. 72. Even in the nineteenth century effort had been made to revive the true story of Spanish greatness notably by Pérez Pujol and Hinojosa y Naveros. Following these the twentieth century saw a great interest in the study of medieval institutions, notably Galo Sánchez, Claudio Sánchez Albornoz, Salcedo and others of their school, but while some of these were Catholic, they were not Catholic in spirit and interpretation. The Catholic traditions were nowhere thoroughly taught in Spain.

ing the turmoils of the century. Though the government did publish some of the great collections of the Acts of the Cortes and similar documents historical and constitutional, and notable scholars here and there pursued their lonely if fruitful way through the archives, very few of the valuable conclusions which could have been drawn from their studies reached the general public.

In view of all the above circumstances Catholic action as such was not noticeable until the Revolution of 1868. It was difficult for the leaders to realize that the traditions of Catholic action had practically gone from the minds of the people. Institutional forms remained, it is true, but the spirit had fled. To restore Catholic Spain was the task, but the means were not easily evident. The Faith was not dead, but the Catholics were living retired lives and had lost the sense of social action. They were looking upon religion as a private thing, a matter of personal interior life alone, and forgetting that the Church is a social institution.

At first, action was confused and abortive. Various associations of Catholics were formed. Academies of Catholic youth arose and disappeared. Through the efforts of the Marqués de Viluma of Madrid an association of lay Catholics was formed in 1868 aimed to unite their efforts in a legal and vigorous resistance to the attacks of the secularists. Branches were formed throughout Spain. It received the approval of Pius IX in the following year who especially commended its abstention from politics.

Other groups, however, considered political action more efficacious and the Catholic *monarquía* was founded drawing many members from the earlier associations. The government eventually dissolved both groups.

Some good was accomplished. Apologetical works were produced; missions were encouraged; schools for adults opened (1870-71). Signed petitions in favor of religious unity were presented to the Cortes of 1869, one with 3,448,396 signatures. At the same time the Catholic Ladies' Association of Madrid was maintaining 33 schools for boys and girls, and their *Junta provincial* supported 23 parochial schools. In 1888 Don Andrés Manjón founded his first school for the poor of Granada. This later developed into the famous Ave María schools, noted for the then novel theory of integrated education. These schools have been very successful and are much admired by foreigners. In general the people were apathetic and after twenty years of effort the work all but died. As early as 1865 Father Antonio Vicent, S.J., had founded at Manresa a *Círculo católico de obreros* and in 1867 the *Asociación protectora de artesanos jóvenes* was founded for apprentices at Madrid. Father Pablo Paslets founded a similar *círculo* in Valencia in 1872. In 1880 ten *círculos* were founded in the Diocese of Tortosa.

Under the stimulus of Leo XIII the next attempt to revive Catholic action was made on May 3, 1889, with the calling of a national Catholic Congress which declared its aims to be (1) the defense of the truth

in Spain, that is, the social reign of Jesus Christ, (2)
to work for Catholic unity. A *junta central* under
the direction of the Bishop of Madrid-Alcalá was
organized and diocesan committees were recommended. Other congresses were held [37] and a tenta-
tive constitution approved. The Primate was made
honorary president.

The scanty results of all these efforts were gradually making clear that Catholic action was not yet
on the right track, but the key was not found until
the *Rerum Novarum* of Leo XIII, which appeared
in 1891. This far-seeing Pope grasped the cause of
all the difficulties, but so thoroughly had the great
majority of modern Catholics lost the knowledge of
their traditions that only the few saw his point. In
his encyclical Leo XIII hinted at the necessity of
creating new institutions. Thus only could channels
be formed for the coördination of activities and
media be created for the reforms or for the proper
reshaping of society.[38] He warned that this was
absolutely essential and laid down as the first condition of a just society the spirit of peace and harmony
that only the religious spirit can give. He went
further than general principles and proposed as the
first new institution the *opificum collegia*. The discussion over the form these should take shows how
thoroughly de-Catholicized intellectually Spain was.
The choice of terminology *opificum collegia* was

[37] Saragossa, 1890, Sevilla, 1892, Taragona, 1894, Burgos, 1899,
Santiago, 1902.
[38] The Pontiff made the reasons for this more evident in many
other of his encyclicals too familiar now to quote.

beautifully calculated to suggest the sociological values of the group integrated into an institution, but unfortunately so little did that generation appreciate the condensed philosophy of the Latin concept when imbued with Christian principles, that the *opificum collegium* was translated into *sindicato*.

As a result the distinction between social work and social institution was lost and Catholic action was divided, one action favoring group activity, another institutional activity. A time-consuming debate began on what should be the aim of the *sindicato,* and of the action generally. Was it to be moral or cultural, economic or professional, or in the vocabulary of the secularist, religious or lay? Over and over again the pontiffs and hierarchy emphatically stated that Catholic action must be unmistakably Catholic, which to many people meant only singing hymns and offering up prayers. If from one point of view valuable time was lost in arguing over the pure or mixed *sindicatos,* from another, the long interminable argument was an effective way, and really quick in the long run, of educating public opinion. It must be admitted Spanish genius was quicker to catch on to these distinctions than in some other countries.

Again the pontiffs had to come to the rescue and clarify the issues. In the Encyclical Letter to the Bishops of Italy, July 28, 1906, Pius X condemned nationalism as it led to laicism and emancipation from ecclesiastical authority in social action. The word Catholic and not Christian (as it included heretics) was to be used. He maintained further that to

restore all things in Christ, action was demanded but
"an action directed in every thing to the integral and
scrupulous fulfillment of the Divine Law and the
precepts of the Church, to the profession frank and
resolved of religion." In his encyclical to the hierarchy of Brazil, December 18, 1910, he further defined Catholic action to mean Catholic civilization in
the totality of every and each element constituting it
(*i. e.*, civilization).[39]

At any rate the education of Spanish Catholic public opinion had profited sufficiently for Cardinal
Aguirre to publish his norms of Catholic action,[40]
Cardinal Reig y Casanova [41] to organize more definitely than heretofore the action and Cardinal Segura
y Saenz [42] to add further integrating activities, such as
the publication of a *Boletín oficial*, which printed its
first issue in January, 1929, the central secretariate,
the foundation in the most important diocesan centers
of *juntas perceptuadas* and the collection of statistics
of all the institutions and work of Catholic action.

Cardinal Reig y Casanova defined Catholic action
to mean the application and generosity of the faithful in the creation and support of works which with
distinct, specific ends have the general aim of improving the condition spiritual and moral of the people in order to secure their eternal destiny. Social

[39] Cf. the *Singulari quadam,* and articles by Narciso Noguer on
various points raised in the discussion, *Razón y Fé,* vol. 63 (1922).
[40] *Normas de acción social católica,* Toledo, 1910; *Reglas sobre
la Federación de obras católicas sociales,* May 4, 1912.
[41] Pastoral Letter of February, 1924; *Principios y bases de re-
organización de la acción católica española,* Toledo, 1926.
[42] Pastoral letter of December 25, 1928.

action in its different aspects, cultural, beneficial, political, feminine, agrarian, labor and even purely economic, have to have as the common denominator, Catholic action which gives to it solidity and unity not only for homogeneous works for their specific ends but also for the heterogeneous ones. He goes on to say: "There is a unity which is mechanical, *i.e.*, the juxtaposition of individuals or entities, a mathematical thing, often as in a parade or congresses. This is not organic unity, the kind to be desired, which consists not in juxtaposition but in penetration of the spirit, in the union of souls, in the common religious basis, in the reciprocity and purity of sentiment, all of which results when Catholic action is truly Catholic." [43]

Cardinal Aguirre had already proposed the new coördination of Catholic forces, aiming to unify the action of existing institutions, to safeguard religion and to aid by spiritual and temporal works the nation as well as individuals. The point was to include Catholic action in the framework of the ecclesiastical hierarchy, forming parochial and diocesan centers so as to secure unity of action, cohesion, solidarity and coördination in the technique of institutions. The representative element prevails over the elective.[44] It organized a corporate apostolate, lay and ecclesiastical, an idea dear to the Spanish mind.

The question was raised, was Catholic action to be

[43] Pastoral Letter of February 26, 1924.
[44] Spanish Catholic action more nearly approached to the Dutch and Italian plans than to the German *Volksverein* or national conference idea of the United States.

political? The answer here was most clear, decisive and precise. No, if by Catholic political action is meant participation in the struggles of party factions. To quote the forceful Spanish, *no debe estar enfeudada á un partido político determinado*. This of course is not the same thing as prescinding from political action. That is impossible, granting the position of man in the twin societies, civil and ecclesiastical. One thing the Popes never do is to confuse politics and political parties. Neither has the Spanish hierarchy. Completely aware of the vast distinction between principles of politics and the modern party factions of parliamentary government, between the idea of an institution and its organization, between ultimate principles and technical principles, the Primate laid down the following points for the duties of Catholic action in regard to politics:

1. To prepare the individual for political life.
2. To promote the union of all Catholics.
3. To arrange a fundamental program in regard to all "mixed" matters, deferring to the directions of the Holy See.
4. To recall other groups to Catholic principles.
5. To prepare the solutions for numerous matters in which the State touches the laws of conscience, even indirectly, and to know thoroughly such solutions.[45]

[45] To assist in this work of education, the Spanish episcopate in 1922 inaugurated a great campaign for the creation of a social university to train young people in political science, administrative and social; to increase Catholic primary schools, to systematize and harmonize Catholic action in the *sindicatos obreros*. The Liberal press raised a great outcry against this campaign. Cf.

The structure of Catholic action is planned [46] from the point of view of integrating the various groups working out the solutions of problems and is aimed directly to teach the groups how to function, and to be the daily object lesson of how the solution of one problem is closely related to the solution of others. In this way the public mind and the public conscience will be prepared for the reconstruction of Catholic civilization and the establishment of the new institutions visioned by the Popes.

Hence at the center of all Catholic action is the *Junta nacional* and the *Secretariado central* under the direction of the Primate, hierarchy and diocesan advisors. In general it is charged with the duty of examining the general problems and assessing the value of the proposed solutions; specifically it defends the right of the Church as a social institution. Individual Catholics participate in the work of this *junta* through their individual membership in various local or national societies, organizations and institutes, which are represented in the parish, diocesan and central *juntas*. The *Juntas centrales* integrate the whole nation, through the *Junta central de acción Católica femenina* and the *Junta central de cabelleros*. The parish and diocesan *juntas* are mixed, that is, consist of representatives of both the men's and the women's organizations.

The *Juntas parroquiales* direct and encourage the various parish activities on consultation with the

La Acción católica y la Política in the pastoral letter of Cardinal Segura, February 27, 1930, in *Razón y Fé,* vol. 90 (1930).
[46] *La Acción Católica* in *Razón y Fé,* vols. 77 and 78.

pastors, in the spiritual, charitable and social order. They see that the objectives of the diocesan *junta* are carried out in the parish. The membership consists of the presidents of the associations, institutions, Catholic works of both men and women of the parish, together with those of the leading parishioners who in the judgment of the pastor would be of value. The *junta* elects its own officials and its president is the parish representative in the diocesan *junta*. It makes its own budget and is supported by an annual collection and private donations.[47]

The diocesan *junta* is the integrating organization of the diocese. It directs the Catholic action in regard to all public manifestations of the family, of the school, of public morality, observance of holy days, etc. It carries out the objectives of the *Juntas centrales*, supervises the constitutions of the *Juntas parroquiales*. It is composed of officers appointed by the bishop and the presidents of the parish *juntas*. It reports annually to the bishop and *Junta central*. There is a diocesan assembly in which the members of the *Juntas diocesanas*, the presidents and counsellors of the parish *juntas* and the counsellors of the diocesan assist. The executive department is the *secretariado diocesano*, which forms also an information bureau, a central guide for the propaganda and the permanent link of the whole diocesan action.

The *Junta central Femenina* is identical with the

[47] *Las Juntas parroquiales de acción católica, carta pastoral del Excmo. Señor obispo de Barcelona,* Barcelona, 1919. These were organized in 1909 to review the state of the parish from the point of view of religion and of the rechristianization of the people, and to prove the need of lay coöperation.

Junta Central de la acción católica de la Mujer. It
has a resident secretariate in Toledo under the administration of a director general, a prelate assisted
by a sufficient number of priests, regular and secular.
It supervises the *Acción de la Mujer* throughout the
country, coördinates its work with the diocesan sec-
retariates, publishes various pamphlets and bulletins,
plans congresses and social weeks and aids the national organization affiliated to the *Acción católica
española* and directs the propaganda.[48]

La Acción Católica de la Mujer was organized
March 24, 1919, by Cardinal Guisasola with the following aims: the study and solution of feminine
problems, the education of women, to defend and
protect women in industry, to assist them in securing
a just wage, to protect the interests of women before
the public and the government, to guard the observance of all laws in favor of women and children
before the Chambers of Commerce and industry and
the *Instituto de Reformas sociales,* to impose respect
for women and children particularly in the streets, in
shops and in factories, to organize campaigns against
social vice. It maintains relations with the *círculos
de estudios, la Escuela social femenina* and publishes
a monthly bulletin. Several dioceses publish similar
bulletins, Barcelona *La Unión católica femenina,*

[48] Sixty-five reviews were directed by the Catholics, among the
most important forming Catholic opinion were: *La Ilustratión del
Clero* of the Fathers of the Heart of Mary; *Estudios franciscanos*
of the Franciscans; *La Ciudad de Dios* of the Augustinians;
España America, La Ciencia Tomista of the Dominicans; *Razón y
Fé* and *Sal Terra* of the Jesuits; the *Revista Católica de Ciencias
sociales,* etc.

Salamanca *El Mensajero social*, Bilbao *La acción católica femenina*, Murcia, *Luz y Amor*, Valencia *La Mujer Católica*, El Ferrol *Luz y Aurora*, Córdoba *Acción católica de la Mujer*, Avilés *Fé y acción*.

The *Junta central* is resident at Madrid and there are diocesan and parish *juntas*. The *Junta central* is divided into sections *Enseñanza, Religión, Moralidad, Hispanoamericana, Prensa, Obrera, Beneficencia, Missional, Municipalista*.

There are also various federated national associations of women's activities: The *Unión de Damas Españolas del Sagrado Corazón de Jesús* was founded in 1908 by the Marquesa de Unzá del Valle. It supports many pious and charitable works. The *Confederacción nacional de Obreras Católicas* was founded in 1909 through the Children of Mary. It was known at first as the *Sindicato obrera Femenina de la Imaculada*. Branches of this in the various trades grew rapidly and in 1918 it was federated, and in 1924 reorganized as the *Confederación nacional* by Cardinal Reíg y Casanova. In 1929 there were 176 institutes with 35,280 members. It has celebrated five regional assemblies (between 1920-27) and has secured many important improvements in working conditions, hours of labor and wages, and has reduced considerably the influence of Socialists and syndicalists.

The *Instituto de la Mujer que trabaja* was founded in 1900 by R. Cayetano Soler. It provides old-age pensions, sick benefits, maternity aid. The Apostolate of Ladies for the Improvement of Working-women was founded in 1901 by the *Instituto de Damas Catequistas* (organized 1880). Its membership is drawn from distinguished families and it has fostered trade schools in Madrid (1916), Bilbao and Valencia, besides catechetical work. It looks after the spiritual interests of the working-women by fostering retreats and missions.

The *Institución Teresiana,* organized in 1911 and approved by Pius XI, is an association of ladies holding degrees as normal-school teachers, inspectors or superior teachers, who devote themselves to the cultural and religious education of women. It has also received support from the Minister of Public Instruction.

The *Institución Católica de Protección post-carcelaria de la Mujer* was started in 1921 and organized in 1924 under the presidency of the Bishop of Madrid-Alcalá and approved by the Primate in 1928. It maintains a *Casa de Trabajo* to train the women for useful work, a *Granja agrícola* for those who prefer country work, and a *Casa de Familia,* houses of correction. It coöperates with the various laws from 1908-1928 aiding this class of women.

There are also several associations of young women. The *Juventud Católica femenina* was founded in 1924 by Cardinal Reig y Casanova to develop in the young girls of all classes a proper Catholic spirit, a loyalty to the Church and Holy See. It has organized *círculos de estudios,* conferences, evening classes for working girls, catechetical classes, retreats, visiting the poor, libraries and various devotional works. It is organized into diocesan and parish groups with various classes of membership, aspirants, 12-18, *números* 18-35, and honorary members who subscribe 250 pesetas. In 1929 it had a membership of three hundred. It has sent representatives to the International Association of Catholic Youth, meeting in 1926 in Luxemburg, in 1928 in Holland.

There is also the recently formed *Confederación de Estudiantes Católicas* which has opened a *Casa social* in Madrid. Many of the professors of the State schools serve on the organizing committee.

The *Acción Católica de Caballeros* has a similar organization to that of the women with the additional duties of creating a better spirit between employers and employees, and of developing a program of economics in agriculture, industry and commerce. According to its constitution, the *Junta central* devotes itself to defend the rights of Catholics in private and public life, to stimulate and foster Catholic unity of culture and institutions of learning and education, to guard the family as an institution, to protect and foster young men's associations, to promote the spirit of charity, to organize social weeks and national assemblies, to defend and orientate Catholic social action everywhere in Spain. The executive committee is divided into cultural, corporate education, defense, charity and *vigilancia*. It is supported by collections made in the parishes on the Feast of Christ the King, the patron of Catholic action.

The various organizations of men constituting the

Catholic action are: Society of St. Vincent de Paul, organized in 1833; the *Confederación nacional Católica Agraria,* proposed in 1912, organized in 1914, and confederated in 1916. In 1929 it had 50 federated groups, 2,276 *sindicatos,* representing 199,788 families and a membership of 988,940. It conducts five dailies, 20 reviews and bulletins, 14 *casas sociales.* Up to 1928 it had spent 200,000,000 pesetas in aid, 300,000,000 in loans, 20,000,000 for coöperative undertakings, had 50,000 *hectares* under lease and 38,000,000 invested in insurance against fire and hail. It has a broad program, financial, insurance, ordering of the economic life. It has held regional assemblies of the *sindicatos* frequently, has fostered rural banks, consumers' coöperatives, warehouses, producers' coöperatives. The soul of the movement is Don Luis Diez del Corral.

The *Confederación nacional de Sindicatos Católicos de Obreros* resulted from a conference held at Madrid in 1919 of sociologists and representatives of the working-men. A committee was appointed consisting of delegates from the *Sindicatos obreros, sindicatos católicos libres sociadades maritimas* of Cádiz, *sindicatos femeninas* and the *Federación de Sindicatos* of Madrid. It was legally erected on July 22, 1919. Its official organ is the *El Eco del pueblo* of Madrid. It has held four national congresses, two plenary ones, and a national pilgrimage to Loyola.

Agrarian federations, agricultural associations, agricultural *sindicatos,* rural banks were not new in

Spain. They had been discussed by the *Sociedades económicas de amigos del Pais* of the eighteenth century.[49] *Camaras agrícolas* were instituted by royal decree of November 14, 1890, and *communidades de labradores* by the law of July 8, 1898. Social agrarian action took a new impetus from the law of January 28, 1906, creating agricultural *sindicatos,* the rules for which came out on January 16, 1908. The Catholic *sindicatos* are influential.[50]

The *Asociación Española de San Rafael,* for the protection of emigrants, was organized in 1913 and reorganized in 1929. The *Confederación Católica de Padres de Familia,* organized in 1913, maintains a monthly bulletin and publishes also *La pública Inmoralidad.* The *Junta nacional de Prensa Católica* dates from 1926. It maintains an information bureau. A press association had been founded in 1908 in Saragossa, operating under the *Comisión de Custodia y Administración.* Subcommittees were organized in each diocese. The *Asociación Católica nacional de Propagandistas,* founded in 1909, has for its object the Catholic propaganda in the social and political order. Among the spiritual regulations are monthly Communion, the rosary is said before each conference and all the members make a yearly three-day retreat. It works through *círculos de estudios* and propagates its ideas directly in the various organs of Catholic action and in its monthly

[49] Cf. *Cédula,* November 9, 1775, *Novíssima Recopilación,* Lib. VIII, *tít.* xxl, *ley* 1.

[50] Muñiz, D. Lorenzo, *La Acción social agraria en España,* Madrid, 1924.

bulletin. It has held several regional assemblies of late years: 1928 Aragon, 1927 Andalusia, 1928 Asturias, 1927 Castile and León, 1927 Valencia, 1927 Vascongadas and Navarre. The most noteworthy of its activities are the foundation of the great daily *El Debate,* the campaign against Canalejas in 1910, against Romanones and his effort to eliminate religious instruction in the schools in 1911.

Parochial organization of the young men was founded in 1924 and in the National Congress of 1927. Diocesan unions also exist. The *Juventudes Antonianas,* originating in Portugal in 1896 through the efforts of the Franciscan Juan de la Santísima, had the first Spanish foundation in Santiago in 1905. The Holy See approved it in 1911. Its aims include piety, instruction, morality, charity and social work. Some of the centers maintain evening schools for poor children where reading, writing, arithmetic, design and music are taught. Libraries and study groups are also fostered. *El Porvenir Antoniano* is the official organ in Spain. In 1929 there were 35,700 members of both sexes, 102 centers.

The *Confederación de estudiantes católicos de España* has a similar organization to that of the women. It dates from March 7, 1920, and aims to improve the quality of education, to organize conferences and *ateneos* and study groups. It holds general assemblies and congresses and maintains a bulletin. It is divided according to careers: law, medicine, sciences, etc. The first national assembly was held in January, 1923, at the University of

Saragossa. Regional assemblies were held in 1924-25. The following statistics are from the fifth assembly held in the University of Granada, 1926-27: 28 federations, 84 associations, 19,700 members.

The *Junta nacional de Peregrinaciones*, organized in 1925 during the Holy Year celebrations, is under the direction of the Bishop of Madrid-Alcalá. During 1926, 1927 and 1928, it directed the Franciscan pilgrimage to the East on the occasion of the canonization of the Martyrs of Damascus and one to the Italian Franciscan shrines. The *Acción de la Mujer* organized a pilgrimage to Our Lady of the Pilar in Saragossa, to Lisieux in 1926, Paray-le-Monial in 1926, Lourdes in 1927. Two national pilgrimages have been made to the monument of the Sacred Heart and altogether some 30,000 have gone on pilgrimage under the influence of this organization.

One of the interesting organs of Catholic action is the *Legión católica Española*, a secular organization to defend and promote the interests of Jesus Christ. It was founded on April 29, 1924, by Father José Conejos, S.J. It maintains circulating libraries, catechetical work, social conferences, founds schools, fosters retreats, aids the press, has a national and diocesan organization. There are 87 branches, 56 of these are in Valencia and there were 17,000 members in 1929, seventeen times the number in 1924.

Though no attempt has been made to form federations of *Asociaciones católicas Patronales*, this movement began to flourish in Valencia in 1928. The aim was to spread Catholic ideas among this group and to establish *sindicatos* of Catholic employers in industry and commerce. It has held some small conferences and supports a monthly bulletin, *Boletín social Patronal*.

Leagues against public immorality have been formed since 1925 and in 1927 a general secretariate was established. The *Institución del Divino Maestro* was organized in 1926 under the Bishop of Madrid to include pupils of normal schools. It was approved by the government in 1927 and has founded a practice school on the ideas of Manjón. A federation of Catholic teachers was organized in 1912 to defend Catholic relations and the interests of teachers in general. It includes all teachers whether public or private and has an organ *La Enseñanza Católica*.

The *Banco Popular de León XIII*, organized in 1904 at Madrid by the Marqués de Comillas with a capital of 100,000 pesetas to furnish loans at moderate interest to agricultural and industrial *sindicatos* has had a very useful career. Many other social works are fostered by the various Religious Orders, but they are too numerous to mention here. Of particular interest are some of the activities of the Jesuits. The *Fomento social*, established in 1926, has for its objective "to serve all the works and institutions dedicated to social and religious action, fostering the study of social questions and the accompanying social action." It does not aim to form a school of theory but to offer an opportunity to discuss and study various theories in the light of the social doctrine of the Church. It aims to serve the reviews and dailies with articles, books and pamphlets, and to develop for schools an information service, to prepare study courses, and in general to be a kind of consulting laboratory of theory and practice. It has developed steadily. In 1929, it served 102 dailies and reviews, and 64 groups subscribed to its study course service.

The *Centro escolar y Mercantil* is another interesting activity. Founded in 1912, it has directed its attention to the middle class, aiming to instruct them in the duties of public life, the Cortes, the *municipios*, the judiciary, army, business and public finance, in order to form not only a pious and Catholic group, but men who would be active and influential in their various circles, especially in the field of public opinion. The *Centro* has academies of jurisprudence, letters, history, medicine, commerce and industry. It has opened a *Casa Social*, which began to be very active during 1928-29. A commercial university was opened at Deusto in 1916.

The *Instituto Católico de Artes y Industrias*, organized in 1908 as a school of mechanics and electricity under the auspices of the Marqués de Vallejo and the Duke of Pastrana, has been most successful. Free instruction was provided and by 1923 it was greatly overcrowded. A course in engineering was added. The equipment was very fine and its fame attracted students from South America and elsewhere. It made a study of the electrification of Spain and started a review, *Annales del Instituto católico de artes y industrias,* in 1922, which is learned and technical. Unfortunately this was one of the first objects of attack on the part of the revolutionary mobs.

The Daughters of Mary Immaculate, to instruct girls for domestic service, was organized by Doña Vicenta María López de Vicuña in 1876, approved by Leo XIII in 1899, and the constitutions were approved in 1904. In 1912 it also received royal approbation and has been a most useful institute in preparing girls for this kind of work.

The first national Congress of Catholic action was held in 1929. Forty bishops and four cardinals assisted.

This rather brief survey reveals that although works of charity and piety were not wanting in Spain since 1868, all Catholic action made very decided and remarkable progress once Catholic action was officially organized. It will be noted that all the specific activities converged on the one great problem of first restoring the Catholic faith in knowledge and practice to the people of Spain. Spain had a very small proportion of Catholics, and until this restorative work should be done, the educational, political and economic reconstruction could not be accomplished. Such a task was too tremendous to have reached very large proportions by 1931, but results were very encouraging and very apparent in a new spiritual awakening of which the consecration on May 30, 1919, of the whole nation to the Sacred Heart on the *Cerro de Angeles,* the geographical center of Spain, the retreat movement, the devotion to Christ the King, the catechetical congresses in 1913 and 1926, and the Marian Congress of Covadonga in 1926, are the main features.[51]

The weakest points were in the field of political and economic action, as might be expected.[52] This was not alone because the spirit had to be recreated and time was necessary for this, but because as the ferment of Catholic action began to penetrate the intellectual leaders, the magnitude of the problem was appreciated. It was realized that the leaders would have to digest many facts and erect sound theories before reforms could be established.[53]

The foreign student who notes the character of the books published by Catholics in Spain during the last twenty years, who turns over the pages of the influential reviews and scans the articles on sociological topics and notes the tone of debate on such questions as the suffrage, feminism, the municipal organization, the social uses of property, the eco-

[51] The retreat movement had begun in 1882 in Catuluña. There are fifteen retreat houses in Spain. Parish retreats were started in Castile. Between 1923-25, 3,700 made retreats: 441 intellectuals, 1222 agriculturists, 1484 industrialists, 553 merchants. Cf. *Razón y Fé*, vol. 74 (1926).

[52] *El Debate* (February 20, 1929) remarked that what Spain needed was an organization of the civil element in order to offer the monarchy an instrument. The mistake of the dictatorship was that it frequently tried to govern with Catholic ideas but not with Catholics (cf. Fourth Congress of *Confederación nacional de sindicatos de obreros*, *Razón y Fé*, vol. 85, 1928, also, vol. 87, article *Partidos políticos*).

[53] Cf. the social conferences organized by *El Debate* in 1920. Topics discussed ranged from politics to social action, from the functions of the state to the function of the family, Socialism and Catholicism contrasted, the *Rerum Novarum*, property as a social function, political parties, government, individual rights, all opening up the whole argument on the relations of Church and State as they have been defined since 1789.

nomic régime and particularly the nature of Catholic action, the pure and mixed *sindicatos,* and the obligatory organization of workers cannot fail to be impressed.[54] It might be said that the Spanish Catholic mind was just awakening to the great social problems of the modern age. Now that the existing organization of modern societies, inherited from the near past of three hundred years, is here slowly, and there rapidly and violently, being transformed into a lay Socialistic society with a centralized and increasingly autocratic state, Catholic thought is at the crossroads of doubt. Shall it attempt to re-impregnate existing institutions with Catholic principles, or shall it seek to create new institutions from the ground up?

Spain has already seen this done in her society twice (thrice if we count Spanish America). The writer of this article is rash enough to venture the opinion that she is preparing to do it again. The detailed and widespread organization of her Catholic action, its sweep and range of ideas even in ten years, has spread a network of integrated group activity over the whole of Spanish society. In 1931 it was apparent that the meshes were beginning to pull and tighten into a pattern. Spanish genius is capable of enormous and sustained energy when aroused, and knowing this perhaps explains why the secularists

[54] The *Instituto de Reformas sociales* at Madrid in 1921 discussed a report on the project of obligatory association (apropos of the royal order of January 16, 1919). Don Severino Aznar attempted to uphold the idea of "free association in an obligatory coöperation"; a long debate followed, but the report was killed.

struck just when they did. Later might be too late.[55]

In the crash of the monarchy, of the *Patronato,* of the nobility, of parliamentarianism, many ruins are being swept aside. As matters now stand in the proposed new constitution, the issue so befogged in the nineteenth century by these old ruins is clearly and unmistakably joined. The curtain is rung down on the old fantastic Liberal compromise, and the secularist state unadorned appears. The new Constitution approved by the Cortes in the fall of 1931 establishes the supremacy of the State in the three main social institutions, the Church, the family and education; though it does this frequently in the vocabulary of the old Liberals, the enacting laws to be passed can be easily organized into a thorough Socialist society. It was this Liberal vocabulary which won support for the constituent Cortes among a large number of Catholics who had escaped or ignored the educating influences of Catholic action.

Article 3 declares the State has no religion. Article 24 grants the power to the government of dissolving all Religious Orders and confiscating their property. Appropriation of funds for religious purposes is forbidden; the religious budget is to be closed in two years. Religious Orders regularly owing obedience to authority other than that of the

[55] It is of great interest to note that at the Ninth Congress for the Advancement of Science held in 1923 at Salamanca, it was proposed to admit theology as a science. The Bishops approved and the proposition was graciously received by the central congress of the Spanish Association for the Advancement of Science. But the committee could not see its way clear to admitting it as a separate section, but it was admitted under philosophy, section vi.

State are immediately suppressed and their goods confiscated. Other Religious Orders are to be dissolved if the interests of the State require it. The Ministry of Justice is to regulate the Orders, their property is to be limited and they are forbidden to engage in industry, commerce or education. The Orders are to be subject to all revenue laws and they must make an annual report to the State of all financial operations.

Article 25 provides liberty of conscience and freedom of worship. Article 41 legally destroys the family by legalizing free love, allowing divorce by mutual consent or even the mere will of the woman, though the husband must present a just cause. All children, however born, are legitimate.

Articles 42 and 45 tolerate private property temporarily, but for the social good the State is to socialize eventually all property. Article 46 provides for the State monopoly of education with instruction entirely lay. Work is to be the central feature of its method and it is to be inspired by ideals of human solidarity. The churches may teach their respective doctrines subject to inspection by the State, in their own establishments. Article 47 gives the State the right to grant professional degrees for the whole country. Teachers are public functionaries. A law is to be enacted later embodying these principles. As the Catholics' protest made no objection to the claim that the State should supervise education, the issue was not sharply brought out, and hence the educational clauses represent a compromise between the liberal Socialists and the radical Socialists. As the education is to be lay, the aims of both will be accomplished.[56]

The enforcement of almost any one of these clauses can precipitate a civil war, for no compromise adjustment seems possible under them as under the old Constitution of 1876. Whether the government will enforce them or whether it can enforce them under the kind of political institutions this constitution provides is the question. The institution of the *jurado* (discarded before in Spanish history as a nuisance and source of confusion),[57] the single chamber Parliament, the regulations in regard to a vote of censure, the restoration of the Permanent Commission, the executive powers of Articles 92, 93, 94, the provisions for regional autonomy and the supremacy of the State in all circumstances (Article 20), are all nicely calculated to produce a balance of forces in true Latin stoic style, but which will produce a confusion wherein action will be impossible. The leaders of the constituent Cortes recognize their own feeble grasp on the realities of politics, for in Article 60 the Cortes in session may authorize the government to decree legislation. Though this authority must be given separately for each piece of legislation, it will not be difficult for the group in power to engineer the elections and votes of confidence.

[56] Cf. articles on the constitution in *Razón y Fé*, vol. 96, August-September, 1931. *The Nation*, October 28, 1931; articles by Mr. Montavon of the N.C.W.C. News Service published in the *Brooklyn Tablet* during November and December, 1931.

[57] Izaga, L. *El Jurado institución para la administración de Justicia, Razón y Fé*, vol. 60 (1921).

INDEX

INDEX

Jesuits, 14
Jews, in Belgium, 10
Jews, in Russia, 250

Kelley, Francis C., 173
Kenney, Dr. James F., *Catholic Church in Ireland*, 140-166
Kirchliches Handbuch, 109
Knox, Father Ronald, 51
Kolping, Father Adolph, 120
Kulaks, 221
Kulturkampf, 106
Kurth, Godfrey, 18, 34

Labor Party, in England, 56
Language question, Belgium, 3
Lateran Treaty (1929), 182
Lavigerie, Cardinal, 81
Law of Guarantees, 182
League for Large Families, 41-42
Legion of Mary (Ireland), 163
Legislation on religion (U.S.S.R.), 281-289
Lenin, 213-227
Leningrad, Catholics in, 237
Leopold II, 2
Leo Society (*Leogesellschaft*), 118
Leo XIII, 55, 81, 108, 171, 328
Library, Louvain, 6
Liége, University of, 4, 28
Lithuania, 205
Liturgical Congress, First International (1930), 15
Liturgical movement, in Germany, 134-135
Loisy, 86
Louvain, American College, 40
Louvain, University of, 4, 27, 28
Lublin, Catholic University of, 207
Lunacharsky, 219
Luxemburg, Grand Duchy, 1

MacMahon, President, 71
Madden, Marie, Ph.D., *Catholic Church in Spain*, 293-351
Marxian Monism, 216
Materialism, 214
Mathew, Father Theobald, O. M. Cap., 163
Maurras, 96
Maynooth, 158
McNabb, Vincent O. P., 57
Mechlin, Fourth Provincial Council (1920), 15-16
Mercier, Cardinal, 7, 35
Milan, University of the Sacred Heart, 191
Missiology, 114
Missionaries, Irish, 160
Missionaries, Protestant (Belgian), 40
Mixed marriages (Germany), 127
Modernism, 86-87
Monism, 215
Mussolini, 175-180
Mussulmans, in Russia, 251

Napoleon III, 71

National Basilica of the Sacred Heart (Brussels), 7
Newman, Cardinal, 48

Orthodox Church (Russia), 221
O'Rahilly, Alfred, 164
Orangeism, 151
Organizations, of Catholic Germany, 115-124
Our Lady of the Pilar, 294
Oxford, University of, 61-62

Parsons, Wilfrid, S.J., *Catholic Church in Italy*, 167-192
Parties, political, in Belgium, 5
Partito Popolare (Italy), 175
Patronato (Spain), 300
Persecution, in Russia, 262-265
Persecution, of Russian priests, 290-292
Philip V, 298
Pilgrimages, 135
Pius IX, 199
Pius X, 78, 89, 97, 329
Pius XI, 55, 171, 174, 183-187, 258-260, 268
Poland, Catholic Church in, 193-211
Poland, Catholic Hierarchy in, 203
Poland, Reformation in, 195
Polish Independence (1916), 199
Political parties (Belgium), 5
Pope Martin V, 27
Prayer-Book (Anglican), 53
Press, Belgian Catholic, 38
Protestant hostility (England), 67
Protestant Reformation, 47
Protestants (Belgium), 10

Quadragesimo Anno (1931), 187
Question, The Roman, 171-173

Real Patronato, 296
Redemptorists, 14
Reformation, Protestant, 47
Reformation Protestant, in Poland, 195
Regalia (Spanish), 297
Reig y Casanova, Cardinal, 330
Religious associations, in Russia, 237
Religious education, in Belgium, 28-29
Religious instruction, in Russia, 237
Religious liberty (Ireland), 145
Religious orders, in Spain, 306
Religious orders of men and women (Ireland), 160
Republic, Soviet, 214
Rerum Novarum, 17, 27
Roman Question, 171-173
Root, Elihu, 36
Russia and Turkey, 252-253
Russia, Catholic Church in, 212-292
Russia, Church Property Laws, 239-240
Russia, communism in, 233
Russia, Jews in, 250
Russia, Mussulmans in, 251

Date Due